LOWER-TRACK CLASSROOMS

A Curricular and Cultural Perspective

REBA NEUKOM PAGE

Teachers College, Columbia University
New York and London

Published by Teachers College Press, 1234 Amsterdam Avenue
New York, NY 10027

Library of Congress Cataloging-in-Publication Data

Page, Reba Neukom.
    Lower-track classrooms : a curricular and cultural perspective /
Reba Neukom Page.
        p.   cm.
    Includes bibliographical references (p.   ) and index.
    ISBN 0-8077-3092-0 (alk. paper). — ISBN 0-8077-3093-9 (pbk.:
alk. paper)
    1. Track system (Education)—Case studies.   2. Education,
Secondary—United States—Curricula.   I. Title.
LB3061.8.P34   1991   91-3141
373.12'54—dc20   CIP

Printed on acid-free paper

Manufactured in the United States of America

97 96 95 94 93 92 91   8 7 6 5 4 3 2 1

For my parents—
Marjorie Rosamond Love
George Burton Neukom

Contents

Preface

This book is about two high schools, their curricula, and their inhabitants. More particularly, it is about curriculum differentiation as it is manifested in tracking. In it, I portray what happens when the two schools provide different courses of study to different groups of students and what that differentiation of school knowledge signifies.

These issues concern all citizens and educators in other U.S. secondary schools, especially now, as the century turns and anxiety escalates about whether schools in a pluralistic society can contribute to both excellent and equitable education. Yet if knowledge and its distribution in schools generate public and pedagogical concern, they are also treated with a disregard born of familiarity.

Because curriculum differentiation is treated commonsensically, its discussion is typically simplistic, partisan, and redundant. Yes/no questions predominate: Does tracking work? Is differentiation fair? Should schools track? Such questions represent tracking as though it is a onetime choice between clear-cut alternatives: either a beneficent endeavor in which an individual's skills are matched with appropriate scholastic materials or, alternatively, an inherently inequitable placement of lower-class students in lower-track classes, which automatically deliver lower-status knowledge. In fact, an easy, stable choice has proved elusive, its promise belied by persistent contradictions in practitioner concerns, research findings, and policy directives.

Moreover, all-too-familiar school lessons play a complicated rather than a straightforward role in relation to these educational and social contradictions. Beyond the high ideals designated in curricula-on-paper lie the closely etched, daily negotiations of teachers and students that constitute the curriculum-in-use. Although seemingly mundane, people struggle there not only to teach and learn a given content but to define self, other, and the worth of knowledge and schooling as well. Viewed closely, then, school lessons bear surely if subtly on teachers' and students' lives. In them, individual talents and aspirations are fulfilled (or foiled), and lessons contribute thereby to the incorporation (or alienation) of thoughtful participants in schools and society.

To portray the processes of curriculum differentiation and the contexts that shape them, I specify knowledge that the two comprehensive high schools provided in eight lower-track Additional Needs classes and in the same teachers' regular-track classes. My focus throughout is the perspectives of the teachers and students, the people who encountered tracking most directly. More tellingly than abstract test scores or codified survey responses, their words and actions illumine the entanglements of curricular and social differentiation.

Such a focus points to the complexity of tracking and, even more startling, to its fundamental ambiguity. The practice is fraught with irreducible tensions, which make it a problem to ponder more than a puzzle to solve. Its ambiguity is perhaps nowhere more concretely visible than in documentation that, despite recurrent mandates to mainstream throughout the 20th century, almost all U.S. secondary schools track, yet almost all do so with considerable ambivalence.

The ambiguity at the heart of curriculum differentiation arises as schools translate a paradoxical culture. Although American culture typically is cast as either pure or polluted, its history and character elaborate an enduring pattern of counterpoint. The culture oscillates, oriented around fundamental but contradictory symbols of individualism and the common good. Because members, cherishing both, are unable to forsake either, the culture undergirds (and is re-created in) contradictory institutions, equivocal rhetoric, and pendulumlike policies.

The cultural pattern comes to life in curriculum. Understandably, then, U.S. schools individualize. They would risk violating public trust if they did not assert the importance of providing lessons for each student's educational abilities, interests, and aspirations. However, in a culture oriented as well around egalitarianism, schools must also mainstream to assure all students equal educational opportunities. The resulting conundrum is expressed in tracking: The high school curriculum must be differentiated, yet it must not discriminate.

Distinguishing differentiation and discrimination is difficult. Teachers know this who strive to balance a personal interest in each child *and* professional neutrality. The problem is known as well to researchers and policymakers who confront the varied, locally sensible amalgamations of individualism and community that America's diverse schools construct. Because in the main researchers seek in tracking a univocal measure and means, they have interpreted the mixed rather than robust data as weakness, attributable to educators' muddleheadedness, inadequate educational research methods, or the inefficiencies or inequities of the system of schooling.

However valid in particular cases, the criticisms misconstrue the significance as well as the pattern of the ambiguity. The ambiguity of tracking is structured: It elaborates institutional improvisations on an antiphonal culture, not passing aberrations that can be set straight with one-day teacher in-services in positive thinking, refined research strategies, or adamant, bully-pulpit pronouncements to track (or de-track). Moreover, ambiguity is precisely a source of tracking's power: However paradoxically, the practice (like American culture) endures, even though it perplexes, because it confounds confident assessment and certain resolution.

Like other research—perhaps particularly like other educational ethnographies—*Lower-Track Classrooms* is a highly personal volume. It originated in my own perplexity when, as a high school teacher, I encountered the deep contradictions in curriculum differentiation. Like the teachers about whom I write, I oscillated between treating all students equally and differentiating lessons to meet individual students' needs. Thus, during the heady days of President Johnson's War on Poverty, I agreed that teachers and schools could transform an inequitable social order into a Great Society. Believing that even academically unsuccessful adolescents are intellectually curious, I viewed the traditional curriculum as stifling and saw tracking as an unnecessary, if not invidious, ranking procedure that could be abolished with imaginatively designed lessons. In the 1970s, as optimism faded and curriculum bumped up against a changed economy and polity, I found myself struggling with somewhat different concerns: to design history and English lessons that matched the interests and talents of individuals, particularly those in special education classes. My alternation was characteristically American: I was in tune with the times as earlier communitarian reforms gave way to a rhetoric of individualized instruction and the high school population was perceived as increasingly—and problematically—diverse.

When I returned to graduate school in 1980, I carried the curious issue of curriculum differentiation with me, pursued it in my doctoral research, and watched it reemerge nationally as part of the critique of the high school. Continuing today, the critique reiterates the perverse agendas that many of us lived in the past. Clamorings to reinstitute a core curriculum and preserve the nation's cultural heritage alternate with injunctions for schools to attend more vigorously to each individual's needs, interests, and talents. The high school is enjoined both to abolish tracking *and* to shore up specialized curricula for the bilingual, gifted, handicapped, college-bound, work-oriented, average, or just uninterested.

At the same time, the recurrence of the debate demonstrates that curriculum differentiation is neither merely a personal matter nor a passing predilection of the decade. Nor is it a neutral or a strictly pedagogical matter of matching students' skills, texts, classes, and tests. Rather, curriculum differentiation marks the ebb and flow of long-standing institutional and cultural predicaments. It expresses insistent political questions about what and whom high school is for and, specifically, about the different forms of knowledge represented in the school curriculum and their distribution.

Hence, curriculum theorists, teachers and students, educational policymakers, and, ultimately, American citizens clash over what knowledge is most worthy and, therefore, should be enshrined in the school curriculum. A pluralistic society, replete with many forms of knowledge, argues about *whose* knowledge will be publicly sanctioned and required of all graduates. For example, should all or only some high schools distribute vocational training, trigonometry, or Advanced Placement English? Within each school, is it valuable for all students to engage in public debate over knowledge, or should instruction be individualized and streamlined? Most crucially, what are students' and teachers' places in relation to school knowledge and to each other in a school community, and what consequences accompany those places for present learning and future positions in the wider social order? Do the high school and the curriculum make a difference?

Questions like these remain largely unanswered by research. Indeed, as I suggested above, they are only infrequently posed, even though tracking has been the subject of literally hundreds of studies as well as of decades of debate. The research, like the rhetoric, founders on deep-seated, enduring, dualisms. If a host of studies pronounce curriculum differentiation to be an efficient, equitable means of meeting individuals' educational needs, an equivalent corpus denounces it as a pernicious discrimination that advantages the children of the elite and further disadvantages the already socially disadvantaged. The net research result: a seemingly ineluctable stalemate.

The research I report here takes a different tack from traditional survey and experimental studies. I ask the significance of curriculum differentiation and the recurrent contradictions surrounding it. Thus, I eschew either/or questions and a rigorously controlled study designed, once again, to prove the superiority of homogeneous or heterogeneous grouping for achieving some presumptive good, such as higher test scores. Instead, my task is interpretive. I detail how curriculum differentiation works in a small sample of classrooms at two schools and how teachers and students understand its significance. Furthermore, I analyze how their particular, local constructions of curriculum differentiation are linked with broader precepts of social and institutional differentiation and membership, such as academic ability, age, race, class, or gender.

I use the metaphor *translation* to capture the close yet contingent relationship between curricular and sociocultural differentiation. Much as a translator of literature must move beyond an original text yet adhere to its themes in creating its translation (Benjamin, 1969), so teachers and students construct the meaning of tracking from both stable and idiosyncratic cultural knowledge. Thus, U.S. culture furnishes no template and school knowledge is not deterministically *transmitted* by people acting mechanically, as "cultural dopes" (Garfinkel, 1967). Neither, however, is school knowledge culture-free, with teachers and students able to *transform* it or their relationships in any imaginable configuration. Rather, people in schools *use* culture: In school lessons, often tacitly, they refract its paradoxical tensions according to their perceptions of particular circumstances.

The organization of *Lower-Track Classrooms* reflects the conceptualization of curriculum differentiation as a scholastic, sociocultural, and political process of translation. The book traces the symbolic processes in which teachers and students negotiate definitions of their roles, relationships, and knowledge in the interconnected contexts of classroom, school, and community.

Hence, five chapters take a microlevel, classroom perspective. The teacher's greater power to shape classroom life is indicated in chapters focused on how the teacher defines the lower-track student's role (Chapters 2 and 3), the classroom climate and teacher's role (Chapters 4 and 6), and the lower-track curriculum (Chapter 8). The adolescent student's power to shape classroom life, manifested in responses to the teacher's lesson, also appears in the definition of the classroom's informal aspects, or underlife (Chapter 9). Two chapters furnish a broader, macrolevel perspective: Differences between the two school-communities and the mechanisms by which institutions inform, and are informed by, life in individual classrooms and their surrounding communities are the subject of Chapters 5 and 7.

As this outline suggests, the focus of the book shifts in the various chapters to trace the patterns and particularities of tracking. Opening with a wide-angle scope, the book explores the general impact of curriculum differentiation on the teacher's view of the lower-track student. It narrows in the middle chapters to pinpoint variations in tracking's enactment at the two high schools. Finally, the scope broadens again in the final chapters to consider steady patterns in the lower-track curriculum and the student's view of that curriculum.

The shifts in focus highlight the importance of comparison and context in understanding curriculum differentiation. *Lower-track* is not an unequivocal sign. It does not designate a uniform phenomenon: Lower-track classes differ not only in comparison with regular classes but in

comparison with each other. Nor does *lower-track* designate a discrete
phenomenon because, as schoolrooms, lower-track classes share many of
the features of regular-track classes. Instead, *lower-track* is a relational
term: Its significance arises in complex, often oblique *interactions* of
differences between schools and differentiation within a school.

Overall, this account of eight lower-track classes in two comprehensive American high schools offers a case study about the meaning of the
school curriculum, the dynamics of lower-track classrooms, and the contexts that shape regularity and variation in relationships between differentiated lessons, institutional membership, and social mores. The findings
are specific to its settings: They are not predictive nor are they directly
generalizable to other schools. However, the educational ethnography
provides detailed descriptions, attention to context, and an analytic model.
Therefore, readers can use this particular case as an analog to recognize,
compare, and interpret instances of curriculum differentiation in other
schools and studies they know.

ACKNOWLEDGMENTS

Many people have made the writing of this book not only possible but
exciting and rewarding. I am deeply grateful to them all.

The Maplehurst School District permitted the research to take place
in its schools. Teachers, administrators, and students at Southmoor and
Marshall high schools generously shared their time and ideas, thereby
providing me with the chance to understand schools better. If I still have
not got it right, it is certainly not through their inhospitality.

Teachers and colleagues were attentive readers, incisive critics, and
wise advisors. Herbert M. Kliebard, professor of education at the University of Wisconsin-Madison, first planted and then steadfastly nurtured the
idea that the story of Maplehurst's schools could be a book. Mary Haywood
Metz, George and Louise Spindler, Michael Apple, Gary Wehlage, Nancy
Lesko, Sue Jungck, and Linda Valli were also unflaggingly supportive in
their willingness to comment on various drafts of the manuscript. Although I bear full responsibility for the analysis of curriculum differentiation presented here, the compelling perspectives of these teachers are
pervasive.

Secretaries Sally Lanz, Susan Howard, Joyce Gracie, and Margie Bau-
man performed the tedious but crucial task of transcribing many interviews
and typing many drafts of the manuscript. Elizabeth King, an undergradu-
ate at Bowdoin College, and Cynthia Naranjo, Victoria Brookhart, and

Elizabeth Luke, graduate students at the University of California-Riverside, provided research assistance.

The generous financial assistance of The Spencer Foundation, under the direction of Lawrence Cremin, provided time in 1985-86 to analyze the perspective of adolescent students. A Spencer Fellowship from the National Academy of Education in 1986-87 (with additional support from Deans Al Fuchs and Craig McEwen at Bowdoin College) and a 1988 Summer Faculty Development Grant from the University of California-Riverside furnished the resources to complete a manuscript.

Parts of this book have appeared in other publications. An earlier version of Chapter 3, with portions of Chapter 2, appeared in Reba Page and Linda Valli, Eds., *Curriculum Differentiation: Interpretive Studies in U.S. Secondary Schools* (Albany: State University of New York Press, 1990), pp. 17-44 (Reba Page, "A Relevant Lesson: Defining the Lower-Track Student"). Portions of Chapters 1 and 10 were also drawn from the same volume, pp. 231-242 (Reba Page and Linda Valli, "Curriculum Differentiation: An Introduction" and "Curriculum Differentiation: A Conclusion"). An earlier version of Chapter 4, with a segment of Chapter 5, appeared in George and Louise Spindler, Eds., *Interpretive Ethnography of Education: At Home and Abroad* (Hillsdale, NJ: Erlbaum, 1987), pp. 445-472 (Reba Page, "Lower-Track Classes in a College-Preparatory High School: A Caricature of Educational Encounters"). Chapter 9 reworks materials that appeared originally in *Curriculum Inquiry* (1990) and *Journal of Curriculum Studies* (1989). A short segment of Chapter 7 appeared in *Anthropology and Education Quarterly* (1987). I thank the publishers of these books and journals for permission to use this material.

Lastly, my family has been unremittingly patient, proud, and encouraging. During the course of the study, my father and sisters provided sustained intellectual and emotional support. My children, Katie and Elliot, recounted anecdotes from their own classroom experiences, keeping me alternately sober or in stitches and, thus, providing the important reminder that schools are, above all, places where life goes on. So, too, my husband, Philip, also a teacher, has shared the work and pleasure of the interpretive process. Sometimes the project has made sense because of his insights, always because of his love.

Part I
INTRODUCTION

CHAPTER 1

Regarding
School Lessons

Educational ethnography entails the collection and the recollection of stories about school. The "Trivia Listening Quiz"* is one such story, cast into my net when I was a participant and observer in tracked classes in two of the city of Maplehurst's comprehensive high schools. Upon reflection, it recast my understanding of the construction, distribution, and significance of school knowledge. I retell it here because it exemplifies the ambiguity that both enriches and impairs curriculum in U.S. high schools.

I observed the quiz on a Monday morning in October 1982, in a lower-track, ninth-grade English class at a public, college-preparatory institution of excellent academic repute. The lesson began as Ms. Mitchell, a well-qualified, veteran teacher, entered the classroom clutching a sheaf of papers. Briskly, she announced the activity to the eight boys and two girls, all of whom, for a variety of reasons, had experienced difficulties in regular-track English classes but who, in general, were not extraordinarily socially or intellectually disadvantaged: "Clear everything off your desks— Now!—I've found this exercise, it's going to be kinda fun." As she passed out computerized test forms, Ms. Mitchell continued:

> Today, we are going to take a Trivia - - - Listening - - Quiz. (2.0-second pause). Many of you - - you have problems with listening. Lots of times you make mistakes on work, 'er, assignments, because you don't *hear* what's said. So we are going to work on that. Now, this test, this will improve your listening skills - - very important.

Ms. Mitchell explained that she would read 20 test items, repeating each item once. She admonished students to "listen carefully," then to mark the answers on the test sheets.

---

*The system for representing quoted matter is explained on p. 25.

Now, you are not expected to *know* these answers – – – yet! But listen carefully and make a good guess. Then, on Thursday, we'll do the same test again. And if you are careful listeners, your score will go up.

Ms. Mitchell carefully and slowly read the first item of the test from a "low-ability/high-interest" reading periodical, enunciating each word laboriously:

"HAM – burg – ers – – are – – from – GER – many." (2.0)
Mark your sheets now, true or false. (2.0) "HAM – burgers are –
   from – Germany." Remember, *listen* carefully. (3.0) Okay, number
two. "Lima BEANS – – are – from – – – Peru." (2.0) Ooh, that's
a hard one. "LIIIma beans are from – Perooo."

In similar fashion, Ms. Mitchell led the class through the remaining 18 items: "Brussels sprouts are from Belgium; tangerines are from Tangiers."
   After the quiz, students marked their own answer sheets as Ms. Mitchell reread all items, giving the correct answers and adding a bit of mnemonic explanation for some items. Most students sat quietly as Ms. Mitchell reviewed the items. None appeared particularly intrigued by the trivia and none asked a question, offered a comment, or smiled at the puns. They made few elaborative side comments, although they occasionally exchanged sardonic looks. As Ms. Mitchell collected the papers, she reminded students that "*this* quiz won't count." The class then spent the remaining 20 minutes of the period on an unrelated activity.
   The following Thursday, Ms. Mitchell repeated the quiz, this time commenting somewhat bitingly before beginning the quiz:

If you listened carefully the first time, your score will be better this
time. And judging from your first papers, some of you have no
place to go but up! Remember, *these* are the grades that *count*.

Then, as lugubriously as before, Ms. Mitchell enunciated the 20 items, and students marked the Scantron sheets, true or false. Some appeared to take the quiz seriously, attending to Ms. Mitchell as she read the items, shading in the "true" or "false" bubble after each and, on occasion, even copying anxiously from classmates. In contrast, other students simply marked answers randomly, completing the entire quiz by the time Ms. Mitchell finished reading the first item. Instead of "improv[ing their] listening skills," they put their heads down or looked around the room for the remaining 15 minutes. Ms. Mitchell concentrated her attention on reading the quiz and remarked on neither the copying, head resting, nor gazing.

The Trivia Listening Quiz is remarkable—and powerful—in its ambiguity. Neither of the traditional explanations of tracking explains Ms. Mitchell's and the students' half-hearted engagement. The lesson's explicitly "trivial" content and lackadaisical ways of knowing do not present a fair context that rewards individual merit or "effort" (Turner, 1960). Nor, however, is the lesson patently prejudicial to disadvantaged students who, as in a tournament, "lose forever" when they fail and are placed in a lower-track class (Rosenbaum, 1976, p. 40). Rather, the Trivia Listening Quiz is a game of chance in which school success is a matter of luck.

Accordingly, Ms. Mitchell's lesson reverberates with anxiety-producing dissonance: While it commands students' attention, it simultaneously prompts and legitimates their careless disregard of school knowledge. By adding luck as a principle of school success to traditional mores of talent and effort, the lesson invites students who are officially labeled deficient in English to relax about schooling. The Trivia Listening Quiz is a bagatelle, so one plays offhandedly, scoring with lucky shots. Yet the entertainment has an edge: No matter how much a game in which success depends greatly on luck, the quiz *will* eventually "count."

Moreover, the content of the Trivia Listening Quiz is self-avowedly "trivia." Ms. Mitchell offers no justification for the school knowledge. It has neither practical nor intellectual referents. Knowing the origins of foods—or, on other quizzes, tidbits about sports, music, or celebrities—is unconnected to students' mastery of English. It is not brought to bear on the topic that follows it (personal pronouns) or on other topics pursued in the class (e.g., *To Kill a Mockingbird*). Instead, the knowledge is recommended as "kinda fun." In a later interview, Ms. Mitchell elaborated the differentiated content's "relevance. . . . (It is) motivating. *These* students *like* the quizzes—They're interested in trivia."

Students are required to learn the quiz's trivial content, but the expected knowing is not "hard" and no instruction is provided. In contrast to Ms. Mitchell's regular-track classes, the quiz does not require students to use logic, rational argumentation, creative intuition, or thoughtful reflection. Even memory is unnoted. Instead, as Ms. Mitchell explains to students, they are "not expected to *know* these answers" (teacher's emphasis) but are to "listen carefully and *make a good guess*" (my emphasis). How one guesses or what constitutes a "good" guess remains mysterious. Ms. Mitchell provides no instruction in strategic guessing by explaining the trick, or pun, on which the food quiz items rely, nor does she furnish a rationale for intuitive or playfully spontaneous thinking (Bruner, 1977;

Lightfoot, 1983). The lesson implies that students should "know," but the teacher does not teach students how: Rather, as in bingo, success is virtually random and beyond the students' control.

The teacher's and students' interactions during the Trivia Listening Quiz make ambiguous even the lesson's explicitly formulated, cognitive goal: to improve students' listening skills. For example, although Ms. Mitchell suggests that quiz listening will transfer directly to other English assignments, she notes no such transfer opportunities. Moreover, as students' behavior during the quiz makes plain, listening is not simply a skill but, like other curricular activities, a negotiated choice: One listens when listening makes sense. Thus, several boys simply refuse to listen, whereas other students overlisten to the point of cheating. Furthermore, whether or not one listens or cheats does not matter, and the promised reward of "grades going up" is unfulfilled. Almost all of the students, the more obliging along with the recalcitrant, fail the second quiz.

Thus, like the individually meaningless digits on lottery tickets, the Trivia Listening Quiz reduces knowledge to disconnected bits of trivial information. Knowing is a matter of undirected guessing or free association, not a matter of gaining control over a body of knowledge. Yet, because school success is a matter of luck, both prior failure and present success are not students'—or anyone's—fault. If such a curriculum diminishes students' engagement with and control over school knowledge, the diminution is assuaged because lessons are, in any case, only a game: What student could object to skills improvement that is "kinda fun" or quarrel with a teacher over the Peruvian origins of lima beans?

However, for academically unsuccessful students much rides on the school game, just as much rides on lotteries for the disproportionate numbers of economically disadvantaged players they attract. The Trivia Listening Quiz displaces about one fifth of the week's time allotted for direct English instruction for students who are behind in school skills. Moreover, Ms. Mitchell admonished students to play because, no matter how trivial, the re-test is a "grade that will count." Thus, for lower-track students, the quiz *is* school knowledge by virtue of the teacher's designation, even though it confounds them with a catch-22 in which both learning the lesson and rejecting it as mindless produce mixed results.

The Trivia Listening Quiz is no one-time, one-teacher fluke. Ms. Mitchell is neither incompetent nor uncaring, nor is she the only teacher giving trivia quizzes in lower-track classes. Furthermore, the ambiguous principles of the Trivia Listening Quiz undergird other lower-track lessons in Maplehurst: All simplify school subjects as they make them "relevant," randomize knowing as they make standards "realistic," and prompt and legitimate lower-track students' passivity, even as they are

designed to remediate it. Ms. Mitchell echoes teachers' ambivalent perceptions as she explains the lower-track format's differentiated suitability:

> (Regular-track students) grow up during the ninth grade. . . . I see a
> big difference in the way they can think and the way they can rep-
> resent written material. . . . (With lower-track ninth graders,) I
> never see a similar shift. . . . I've seen a difference in a kid just as
> far as his own personality is concerned and therefore that is one of
> the progress. . . . A (lower-track) student will probably never be any
> great reader or writer but at least he's sitting there smiling and he's
> trying to get an answer and stuff like this, once in a while.

Finally, in its subtle amalgamation of differentiated yet traditional
academic and social relationships, the Trivia Listening Quiz translates
precepts of social as well as scholastic differentiation. The differentiated
curriculum arises as people in a school bend to local purposes the wider
culture's perplexing mixture of assumptions about academically unsuccessful students, the knowledge such students deserve, and the significance of
success in the game of school for success in the game of life. Embedded in
lessons, the ambiguous assumptions come to life in mixed messages, which
undermine confident participation in and assessment of the educational
enterprise.

FORMULATING CURRICULUM DIFFERENTIATION

Curriculum differentiation, its processes exhibited in the Trivia Listening Quiz, lies at the heart of perennially unsettled, unsettling debates
about schooling. It prompts perplexing technical questions, because we
know in only the most rudimentary way when to determine core requirements in curriculum or how to individualize lessons. The practice also stirs
deep-seated prior questions about the personal and public consequences of
schooling. Commonly manifested in U.S. secondary schools in tracking,
curriculum differentiation evokes an enduring cultural dilemma: the proper
relationship between individualism and the common good.

This cultural dilemma is typically expressed as a juxtaposition. Translated curricularly, schools should provide either an individualized education
for each student or an equal educational opportunity for all. Moreover, the
form of juxtaposition shapes the specific questions practitioners and
policymakers raise about curriculum differentiation. For example, should
high school students who are "gifted" or "slow," like Ms. Mitchell's, be
collected in classes in which they can "work at their own speed"? Should

college-bound students be provided college-preparatory classes and work-bound students a vocational curriculum? Should students from cultures other than the white, middle-class mainstream be offered classes in their native languages and cultures? Or should adolescents of all talents, needs, and aspirations be "mainstreamed" to study a common curriculum in preparation for participation in a democratic society?

The either/or alternation also underlies the queries of curriculum theorists: Is curriculum differentiation fair or discriminatory? Whose knowledge is distributed and to which groups? Can tracking in school transform racial or social-class differences, so that social mobility is realized? Or does tracking transmit such precepts, reproducing in the scholastic order the existing divisions of the social order?

Although compelling and frequently examined, curriculum differentiation remains an unresolved quandary. Since the early part of the 20th century, when tracking developed along with the American high school, debate and research about it have yielded mixed results. If educators and the public became convinced during that time that all citizens would benefit from high school, they remained uncertain about whether each deserved the traditional academic curriculum (Cohen, 1985; Kliebard, 1986; Krug, 1960; Oakes, Gamoran, & Page, in press). The nervous irresolution about curriculum differentiation continues today. It is reflected concretely in the widespread but ambivalent, often camouflaged, practice of tracking in U.S. secondary schools; a voluminous yet notably contradictory research corpus; and regularly recurrent but invariably deadlocked policy debates. To paraphrase Nell Keddie (1971), if there is little agreement about whether to "stream" students, there is nevertheless widespread agreement that the issue is arguable.

Contributing to the durability of curriculum differentiation as a topic of debate is its either/or formulation. It is discussed as though its manifestation in schools is uniform, its effects self-evidently good or bad, and, therefore, its practice merely a straightforward choice. For instance, reports, such as the National Commission on Excellence in Education (1983), advocate curriculum differentiation as a neutral, necessary accommodation of diverse students' individual educational needs. In this view, tracking is a realistic, efficient response to an increasingly diverse student population. However, critics (e.g., Goodlad, 1984; Oakes, 1985; Tye, 1985) are equally certain that tracking invidiously discriminates and should be abolished. Noting that poor, minority students are often overrepresented in low, special, or vocational tracks, whereas middle-class, white students are overrepresented in high, mainstream, or academic tracks, they argue that curriculum differentiation in schools reproduces the unjust socioeconomic differentiation in the wider society.

The fervor, certainty, and diametrical opposition of proponents and critics affirm curriculum differentiation as a simple choice: clearly beneficent or patently unfair. Moreover, the form of the discourse contributes to the polarization of the issue. Partisans from one side merely dismiss or discredit as wrong-headed the compelling arguments of the opposition. Portraying tracking as a puzzle whose answer can be ascertained once and for all, the discourse masks a historical pattern of ambivalence and ambiguity. It oversimplifies curriculum differentiation, minimizing its complexity and rendering it opaque—and, therefore, perennially debatable.

Traditional Studies of Curriculum Differentiation

An either/or contour also characterizes the questions researchers ask about tracking. In the main, studies are undertaken with the promise of an unequivocal answer as to whether or not tracking "works." Although by no means limited to the traditional or quantitative research paradigm (Bellack, 1978), an either/or formulation jibes with the presumptions of positivism. Traditional studies mount controlled experiments or large-scale surveys to measure presumably uniform inputs (e.g., track level) against self-evidently important outputs (e.g., achievement test scores). The research findings promise decisive generalizations demonstrating the utility of tracking (or lack thereof).

Despite the promises, however, traditional studies are distinguished for their persistently contradictory findings (see reviews by Gamoran & Berends, 1987; Goldberg, Passow, & Justman, 1966; Oakes et al., in press; Passow, 1988; Slavin, 1989). Even for academic achievement, the dependent variable most often considered, the impact of tracking is inconclusive. Depending on the study consulted, its effects may be positive (Alexander & McDill, 1976; Gamoran, 1989), negative (Oakes, 1990), insignificant (Coleman, 1966; Jencks & Brown, 1975; Slavin, 1989), or mixed (Goldberg et al., 1966; Kulik & Kulik, 1982; Slavin, 1987). The effects of tracking on other outcome variables, such as self-esteem or life chances, are equally contradictory (Goldberg et al., 1966; Gamoran & Berends, 1987).

In response to these divergent results, some scholars turn to process-product studies to maintain their hopes for a causal model of tracking. Looking inside classrooms and schools to measure the curricular and instructional processes that mediate between inputs and outputs and that are ignored or controlled in psychological experiments and sociological surveys, they assume that factoring them into equations will refine the measurement of tracking and clarify contradictory correlations.

Thus, for example, Oakes (1985) draws on both survey and observational data from hundreds of upper-, middle-, and lower-track classes in 25

U.S. secondary schools to show that when schools track, they also differentially allocate school knowledge. To lower-track classes, schools provide an alienating, trivial curriculum of passive drill and practice, whereas the upper-track curriculum encompasses more imaginative assignments with "high-status knowledge" such as Shakespeare or calculus. Oakes argues that the lower- and upper-track differences are "systematic" and are "institutionally created and perpetuated" (p. 94) through tracking, that they prompt a widening gap in achievement levels between upper- and lower-track students, and, because students who are poor or who are racial minorities are disproportionately represented in lower-track classes, that the scholastic inequities transmit rather than transform social inequities.

As with earlier traditional studies, however, contradictory data and interpretations also plague process-product research. For example, Oakes (also Goodlad, 1984; Tye, 1985) describes a negative, "flat" tone that permeates American secondary classrooms, whether they are upper-, regular-, or lower-track. However, the significance of this crucial *similarity* is not explained: How can tracking be deemed good or bad if regular-, upper-, and lower-track classes are indistinguishable on important dimensions? In like fashion, traditional studies of tracking often do not reconcile conflicting evidence of positive as well as negative enactments of tracking (for positive remediation efforts, see Barr & Dreeben, 1983; Heath, 1982; Heath & Branscombe, 1985; Metz, 1978; Valli, 1990; Wehlage, Stone, & Kliebard, 1980). Rather, because researchers presume clear-cut, measurable differences between tracks, within-study and between-study anomalies are added and averaged, so that their divergent impact is washed out. However, discrepant cases suggest the inadequacy of the very units of analysis in process-product studies: High-, regular-, and lower-track classes may not be so unequivocally distinguished as school labels suggest or as statistical manipulations require. Fundamentally at issue is an adequate theory of curriculum differentiation rather than apposite methods: The problem—as Ms. Mitchell and her ninth graders experienced—is figuring out *what* counts, not *how* to count.

Interpretive Studies of Curriculum Differentiation

In contrast to research in the traditional paradigm, a small but growing body of interpretive studies asks different questions about curriculum differentiation, probing its multifaceted meaning for the teachers and students who experience it directly; its complex, often contradictory processes; and the entangled contexts of school and society whose kaleidoscopic configurations it translates (Ball, 1981; Hargreaves, 1967; Keddie, 1971; Metz, 1978; Page & Valli, 1990; Rosenbaum, 1976; Schwartz, 1981).

Incorporating rather than averaging out untidy data, interpretive studies suggest the inadequacy of formulaic notions about tracking. Moreover, a few (Cohen, 1985; Kliebard, 1986; Labaree, 1987; Passow, 1988; Varenne, 1974) note the persistent inconclusiveness in debates about curriculum differentiation and analyze the significance of the oscillations. Exploring such issues, interpretive studies reformulate curriculum differentiation: Neither a solely academic procedure performed in a neutral ivory tower nor a foreordained correspondence to the social order, curriculum differentiation is a contextualized social construction.

My research is located within this smaller group of interpretive studies. Accordingly, I ask: What does it mean to be a student or a teacher in a lower-track classroom and what knowledge characterizes the curriculum? How do roles and knowledge acquire differentiated meanings, such that regular track is distinguished from lower track? And how are the particular meanings that individuals in classrooms generate—often, like Ms. Mitchell, with the very best of intentions—related to stable, socially consequential precepts of difference, based on academic ability, age, race, or social class, which democratic schools are supposed to ameliorate?

I studied these questions beginning in the 1982–83 school year when I was a participant-observer in lower- and regular-track classes at two high schools in a midwestern, middle-class, medium-sized city I call Maplehurst. Throughout, my purpose was to understand tracking, not to evaluate whether it was good or bad. Consequently, I asked how people in Maplehurst constructed school knowledge and how the constructions made sense to them, given their contexts. The cultural and curricular analysis of differentiation that these questions imply emerged during fieldwork and has evolved further over the course of several years. I summarize its main dimensions here to provide the reader an introductory framework. Specifically, I describe the general orientation of the interpretive research paradigm, the cultural and curricular theory that informs my analysis, and the place of this research in relation to other interpretations of tracking.

AN INTERPRETIVE ORIENTATION

The fundamental interpretive assumption is that the social world is distinctively different from the natural world because human behavior is mediated by the meanings people give to situations (Schutz, 1962; Waller, 1932). Hence, interpretivists distinguish between *facts* of social and educational difference and their *meaning*. Certainly, real differences abound: Ms. Mitchell's students differ in IQ, track placement, race, levels of self-esteem, and countless other traits. However, the meaning of any difference emerges only as she and the students interpret and act on it. Thus, none of the traits is automatically or inherently significant. They become important as people in classrooms *make* (or do not make) them important in particular ways. Consequently, teachers' and students' specific understanding of differences is not extraneous to or a mere mediation between differential stimuli and responses, as traditional or process-product studies assume. Instead, meanings *are* the inputs and outcomes (Erickson, 1986), and teachers' and students' understandings of differences are intrinsic to differentiation.

From this emphasis on human meaning-making flow several related ideas. Meaning is both patterned and idiosyncratic: Individuals express the world creatively, but their creativity is shaped by durable social precepts, such as those concerning social class or academic differences. Accordingly, rather than assuming that humans are either radically free or that they follow uniform, predictive, social scripts, interpretive studies acknowledge and seek to explicate a structured sociocultural world within which variation, choice, and human agency are predominant features (Spindler, 1982; Erickson, 1986).

With this perspective, the meaning of tracking is a *social construction*. It cannot be attributed to individuals, whether a caring (or prejudiced) teacher or a stigmatized (or unskilled) student, because individuals designate meaning in response to other people with whom they interact; to a grand social order, because its reach is neither absolute nor unmediated; or to a senseless randomness, because human practices pattern events.

"Social" in the phrase, social construction, has two connotations. First, meaning is a *joint* production. Even though meaning is taken as something each person designates, individuals' perspectives are shaped, moment to moment, by the perspectives of others. Working face-to-face to negotiate their different perspectives, people construct a definition of the situation (Schutz, 1962; Waller, 1932). For example, Ms. Mitchell is formally designated the sole authority in her classroom, but she modifies her behavior, often tacitly, in response to her students and to the informal standards of faculty peers. Moreover, such social modifications are also political: Formally, Ms. Mitchell, as a teacher, has more power than students to insist on her point of view.

"Social" also connotes the impingement of wider contexts on the meanings individuals construct face-to-face. Ms. Mitchell and her ninth-graders are not free to relate together in simply any fashion they choose. They do not create anew such categories as "school," "the 1990s," or "remedial." Rather, they act with those categories. Into their local classroom negotiations, they bring conventional, historical, and institutionalized precepts of membership and differences from their families, their pasts, the larger school, and a wider community. Broad, multivocal social structures and symbols figure as indeterminate constraints and resources. People use them for particular purposes and, as they use them, they reflect and re-create them (Fish, 1980; Mehan, 1979; Wehlage, 1981). Without cultural knowledge, Ms. Mitchell and the ninth graders would not know how to interact and their interactions could not constitute "school" or "remedial."

A CULTURAL AND CURRICULAR ANALYSIS

This study shares with other interpretive accounts of curriculum differentiation the general theoretical emphasis on meaning, process, and context, but it adds an explicitly cultural and curricular analysis. Accordingly, it attempts a "thick description" (Geertz, 1973, p. 6) of the strangely familiar lower-track world in the two comprehensive high schools, an account both particular and analytic, which conveys the delicate yet durable processes by which school participants learn their places as they learn their lessons.

Reasoning that familiar, at-home practices, such as tracking, are difficult to scrutinize because they are so commonsensical, I cast curriculum differentiation as no less "strange" than the exotic customs anthropologists chronicle in foreign cultures. Hence, I treat school inhabitants as complex meaning-makers rather than self-evident functionaries; their words as evocative rather than ordinary texts; schooling and tracking as arbitrary rather than necessary social inventions; and school knowledge not as a neutral tradition but as a potent resource that participants use in establishing fateful social and scholastic relationships.

At the same time, I also recast curriculum differentiation to make it "again familiar" (Spindler & Spindler, 1982) or understandable. Thus, I detail lower-track events and dynamics, compare inhabitants' perspectives with those of participants in regular classes, and explicate the explicit and tacit principles that pattern relationships in lower-track classes and that connect them to the patterns of wider school-communities. Through detailed analyses of daily school lessons such as the Trivia Listening Quiz, I try to render particular enactments of tracking sensible (if not necessarily just), given the processes and contexts of the participants' performances. My foci throughout are the coiled relationships among culture, politics, schools, and curriculum.

Culture

In this account, I regard culture as the "webs of significance [in which] man is suspended [and which] he himself has spun" (Geertz, 1973, p. 5). A

cultural analysis of schooling seeks "cultural knowledge": what people
know, both explicitly and implicitly, that makes what they do sensible
(Spindler, 1982). Both definitions emphasize culture as a symbolic, social
process (Varenne, 1983). People make or "spin" signs, which constitute,
and are constituted by, a culture's particular order or "webs." Moreover,
people live "suspended" within the webs, so that culture is neither a
subjective abstraction in someone's head nor an objective structure that
dictates behavior. Rather, culture provides the resources with which people
bring themselves and their worlds into being while, at the same time, it
constrains the selves and worlds that can be made.

Thus, like language, culture simultaneously differentiates and integrates: It is a process of carving the inchoate world into distinctive domains
while also integrating the domains in a system of relationships. Cultural
integration through differentiation is especially heightened in the United
States, a pluralistic New World of immigrants. More than traditional
cultures, America is expressed precisely around categories of membership
and difference (Perin, 1977; Varenne, 1986).

Moreover, as artists and scholars in diverse disciplines note, American
culture is distinctively paradoxical. Its orienting symbols—the common
good and individual freedom—are not only cherished but contradictory
(Bellah, Madsen, Sullivan, Swidler, & Tipton, 1985; Brann, 1979; Edelman,
1977; Kammen, 1974; Merelman, 1984; Riesman, 1950; Varenne, 1977).
Hence, the nation's vision of itself is anxiously schizoid: Does the United
States correspond to the traditionalist's myth of an unerringly just society
or to the revisionist's myth of entrenched inequality? Social institutions
(and research about them) also embody the endemic counterpoint. Americans are intoxicated with legalism but love lawlessness (McClosky, 1971);
rampant individualism, idealism, and breaks with the past are matched by
conformity, materialism, and orthodox faddism (Kammen, 1974). The
mythic double-speak poses everyday problems for the culture's members as
well: What centers a nation of free individuals or, to use David Riesman's
(1950) poignant antiphony, "the lonely crowd"?

Furthermore, although individualism and community are expressed
and experienced as oppositional, paradoxically they form two aspects of a
single, defining, internal pattern of alternation (Varenne, 1981). They
represent a conflict *within* Americans. On the one hand, Americans value
individualism. Choice is an important symbol of individuals' freedom to
define themselves. In contrast to traditional societies, Americans exercise
considerable freedom in designating their associates (Varenne, 1977), their
loyalties and beliefs (Bellah et al., 1985), and even their kinship relations
(Schneider, 1968). Symbolically, Americans are free to name a godmother
"Aunt Rosie," even though no objective blood lines make her an aunt.

On the other hand, freedom simultaneously—and ironically—constrains. It pushes citizens *to* choose even when, in the face of a pervasive loneliness and insecurity, they might prefer the certainty of invariant, enduring social relationships. For example, parents expect and help their adolescents to separate from them, even though separation is painful and they long for children to remain within the family.

With a cultural analysis, then, individualism and community exist in relation to each other. The whole-hearted pursuit of either is impossible because each symbol transforms into its opposite:

> The centrifugal movement produced by individualism is . . . balanced by the centripetal movement produced by the special anxiety that is the by-product of individualism. This persisting bi-modal tension leads to the yearning for consensual, covenantal communities; environments where a person voluntarily and freely gives up his selfhood for the greater good of his friends. . . . Both these themes of individualism and community are quintessential American values. (Varenne, 1981, p. 3)

In short, American culture exists in the ongoing play between individualism and community. Selection of one symbol over the other is not possible since both are cherished. Because the symbols are also contradictory, the culture, like the practices and institutions that embody it, is neither fundamentally fair nor irredeemably inequitable but paradoxical.

Cultural Politics

Cultural ambivalence pervades American politics (Edelman, 1977; Douglas & Wildavsky, 1982; Merelman, 1984). As Edelman (1977) explains, Americans learn to use two contradictory cognitive structures to explain complex social problems. Both structures are fluid constellations of loosely related, emotionally laden ideas, the evocation of any one of which may jangle the entire frame. One structure centers on individualistic explanations and the other on "the system." For example, faced with a crisis such as falling test scores, Americans may blame school failure on uninterested or untalented individuals (whether teachers or students) and insist on tougher standards or longer training. Alternatively, and even in the next breath, they may also blame school failure on an inefficient, impersonal bureaucracy or an unfair social order and insist on reforms to make schools efficiently "accountable" for instructing everyone.

According to Edelman, the contradictory structures allow citizens to oscillate within simplistic dualisms. Yet ambivalent responses do not resolve difficult social problems. Indeed, they may perpetuate the problems by forestalling "self-consciously tentative" interpretations of complex problems and competitive interest groups (p. 20). Thus, Ms. Mitchell confounds her own and her lower-track students' understanding of education when she differentiates the curriculum to make it "relevant" to their particular deficiencies, even as she also seeks to incorporate students by "making them feel a little bit better about themselves." At the same time, if the distinctive, internal tension between individualism and communitarianism prompts inconsistent accommodations, it has also fueled imaginative social inventions: a bicameral legislature built on juxtaposed principles of majority rule and minority rights (Kammen, 1974) ; a federalist formulation of states rights and national purpose (Douglas & Wildavsky, 1982); and a pragmatic appreciation of the flux of democratic, pluralistic processes (McClosky, 1971).

School: A Cultural Institution

Whether generative or paralyzing, the paradoxes of the polity lie at the heart of American schools. Thus, even as different interest groups, struggling over schooling, may give greater or lesser emphasis to egalitarian or individualistic programs, all experience internal tension between the two: The conflict *within* Americans over schooling deserves attention as well as the conflict among them. *Both* equality and individualism shape institutional structures; school participants, like Ms. Mitchell and her students, perform both in ambiguous lessons.

Thus, the public expects virtually all American youth to attend school where they will learn a shared intellectual heritage, democratic processes, and the prerogatives and responsibilities of adult society. Embodying the common good, high school is presumed to be an equivalent, standardized, egalitarian setting, such that a student in Ms. Mitchell's lower-track English class in Maplehurst progresses toward graduation and citizenship as much as an upper-track student in the same school or another student in an urban school on the Atlantic coast. Invoking a competing set of individualistic norms, however, the public also expects the high school to respond to local and regional values and to each student's abilities, needs, and aspirations. This individualistic mandate charges the institution to alter efficiently the common rite of passage, accommodating local predilections, changing environmental conditions, and private choices.

In short, curriculum differentiation is undergirded by both individualism and community (Varenne, 1974) rather than by one or the other. In tracking, the high school attempts to meet each student's "individual educational needs" while, at the same time, it attempts to provide all students with "equal educational opportunities." The enduring curricular dilemma is that differentiated environments, such as special education, women's literature, or lower-track classes, risk charges of discrimination even as students in each may establish a common ground, but a universalistic course of study risks charges of standardization and constraint because it fails to individuate. Paradoxically, in regard to the secondary curriculum, "we want it all" (Boyer, 1983; Goodlad, 1984).

As a result, teachers, students, and schools cannot choose between egalitarian and individualistic purposes because both are prized. Instead of clear-cut options, they face uncertain conundrums: When and on what basis should teachers, like Ms. Mitchell, differentiate knowledge? How much differentiation is enough? At what point does a differentiated lesson, such as the Trivia Listening Quiz, become discriminatory? When is tracking stigmatizing and when is it genuinely remediating? Because the demarcation between discrimination and differentiation is indeterminate and contingent, school participants find confident performances and assessments of tracking difficult. Accordingly, they may persist in practices whose effects they may not intend. Exacerbating the confusion are the diverse modes that tracking assumes, as particular schools draw from and improvise on the mixed cultural tradition according to local perceptions of the differences that should (or should not) count in school.

From a cultural perspective, then, the well-documented contradictions in tracking are not inconsistencies that can be resolved with better logic or more rationality. They are signs neither of a single-minded "system's" unerring fairness (or inequity) nor of individual teachers' or students' undisciplined thinking. Rather, the contradictions are local educational renditions of enduring sociocultural and political dilemmas. Culture and politics intertwine with schooling and curriculum as teachers and students negotiate definitions of self, each other, and knowledge (Keddie, 1971) in particular institutional contexts.

The concepts, ambiguity and paradox, give access to these negotiations and contexts. Rather than simply explaining away as hopelessly muddled the struggles over schooling that occur among groups, they are lenses that capture both the complicated local circumstances that influence the various micro-constructions of curricular and social differences and the larger macro-framework within which the many variable translations of differences make sense.

The metaphor, *translation*, captures this intimate yet indeterminate relationship between curricular and sociocultural differentiation. On the one hand, it portrays curriculum differentiation less statically than does the social scientist's description of schooling as cultural *transmission* or socialization. That is, people in schools are not "cultural dopes" (as Garfinkel, 1967, noted), acting out inexorable social scripts or driven by deterministic social facts. Instead, they act *on* the facts, interpreting and bending them to fit their particular circumstances and purposes. On the other hand, translation connotes a less revolutionary institution than does the image of schooling as *transformation*, which, with an eloquent rhetoric and long history, is favored by many educationists, policymakers, and citizens. But the transformation model implies that the behavior of school participants is free and that all meanings are possible. Rather, school practices and participants' ideas make sense only in light of the acknowledged norms and the structures of particular classrooms, schools, and communities.

Therefore, as a third metaphor, translation emphasizes an interchange, or bridging, between meaning systems, which credits both the limitations and the power of the high school curriculum. Accordingly, in schools, as in linguistic translations, exchanges are never a simple problem of matching synonyms from different languages or spheres but are instead creative acts of interpretation. The translator of *Madame Bovary* must select words that denote the explicit meaning of the original novel, that connote its style and tone, yet that simultaneously produce a text that is sensible according to the grammar of the second language. Just so, teachers and students make creative choices as they consciously and unconsciously convey particular social and educational information to and about each other from the broad social manuscripts of particular schools and the wider society. They are bound by the standard order of the classroom and culture in their selections, else they would compose incomprehensible fictions of educational and social relationships. Yet, within those limits, room abounds for choice and improvisation. The ability of school participants to select from rich, multivocal symbols is a chief source of the power of schooling to influence society as well as to be influenced by it.

Curriculum Studies

The formal rationale of public schooling is curricular: to provide all youth with access to society's valued knowledge as embodied in the school curriculum. However, the process is reciprocal: If culture shapes curriculum, curriculum also affects culture. Hence, local high schools vary in the publicly sanctioned, institutionalized rites they provide, through which uninitiated generations encounter, are taught, assess, and are inducted into particular versions of the wider, paradoxical, adult culture. Understanding the multiple translations of curriculum differentiation requires a curricular as well as a cultural analysis.

I study aspects of curriculum that have been largely ignored in other accounts: (1) the manifest as well as the hidden curriculum, (2) mundane as well as extraordinary classroom talk, and (3) informal as well as formal school structures.

The Formal Curriculum. Few studies of tracking examine what schools teach explicitly or how the curriculum influences the meaning of tracking. Instead, they ignore school knowledge to focus on the presumably more important "hidden" curriculum, they concentrate solely on grouping effects, or they infer rather than demonstrate the importance of the manifest curriculum. For example, Rosenbaum (1976) documents that students' IQ scores drop after a year of lower-track placement, but he does not detail the curricular activities that might have effected the decline. Metz (1978) describes the greater time teachers spend on control rather than educative concerns in lower-track classes, but she does not examine how control of course content contributes to control of student behavior. Oakes (1985) characterizes lower-track lessons as trivial, but she hypothesizes rather than describes how lower-track knowledge may alienate students.

This account moves beyond the hidden curriculum, grouping, and inferences about curricular effects to detail the give-and-take of the curriculum-in-use. It describes the differences in teachers' and students' opinions about what knowledge is important. Examining their negotiation in daily lessons, it specifies the topics teachers select, the purposes to which they are turned, and the reactions they prompt in students. In particular, it explores the entwined sociocultural and scholastic rationales that ground the distribution of knowledge, as curriculum is used to discipline both behavior and intellect.

Curricular Language. My principal data are the words of school participants. I consider how teachers and students use them to construct explicit and implicit meaning and to perform different academic and social roles and relationships. From this perspective, the significance of track placement is public and emergent, not buried in participants' heads and expectations or established decisively in a one-time labelling event: Teachers and students make it visible and consequential in their daily talk.

In studying classroom discourse and its tracked variations, I combine research about the distinctive, three-part form of classroom language (Bellack, Kliebard, Hyman, & Smith, 1966; Cazden, 1988; Edwards & Furlong, 1978; Mehan, 1979) with research about the contribution of linguistic differences to classroom misunderstandings and conflict (Au, 1980; Erickson, 1984; Heath, 1982; Jacobs & Jordan, 1987; Labov, 1970; Philips, 1983). Thus, this analysis probes how teachers, like Ms. Mitchell, communicate different instructional norms in their regular- and lower-track classes by using subtly different language forms. They differentially allocate topics, speaking prerogatives and obligations, and, therefore, types of roles and relationships, all of which may or may not match students' expectations.

Curriculum Contexts. Finally, because schools mediate between individuals and society, this account examines the institutional as well as the classroom and the cultural dimensions of tracking. It posits a complex *interaction* between differentiation within a school (by tracking) and differences across schools (by school culture). Thus, its institutional focus contrasts with two other lines of research on school effects: (1) comparisons of tracked classes within a single school, which assume that the differences schools make lie in internal differentiation (e.g., Rosenbaum, 1976, following Jencks, 1973); and (2) comparisons of schools of varying socioeconomic status, which assume that the differences schools make reflect a straightforward correspondence between curricula and objective differences in communities (e.g., Bowles & Gintis, 1976; Coleman, 1966).

Although ephemeral, a school's distinctive culture—its "we-feeling" (Waller, 1932, p. 13)—reflects and re-creates its participants' interpretations and negotiations of the community it serves and, therefore, of the school knowledge it appropriately offers. The result is that enactments of tracking vary across schools. Furthermore, the meaning of tracking also varies within a school, because schools are a "curious melange" of three subcultures: faculty members, community, and students (Waller, 1932, p. 107). Thus, although many studies ignore student reactions to lessons, treating them as the extraneous, off-task misbehavior of the unskilled, or as evidence of adolescents' inherent disdain for scholastic endeavors (Coleman, 1961; Cusick, 1973; Willis, 1977), this study explores the perspective of the academically unsuccessful adolescent as it is shaped by and shapes classroom and school events.

Thus contextualized, curriculum differentiation is the province neither of individuals (whether teachers or students) nor of "the system"; instead, informally and formally, tracking influences and is influenced by particular schools and by students as well as by adults. To explore the influence requires ethnographic methods.

RESEARCH DESIGN

Ethnographic methods of investigation parallel the theoretical orientation to curriculum differentiation as a constructed, contextualized translation of scholastic, sociocultural, and political meaning. Because educational meaning is seen as a joint, ongoing accomplishment of classroom participants rather than as an unequivocal given produced by grouping or the social order, I study it as it is produced in naturalistic, face-to-face interactions. Because communication is a matter of cultural style and contextual constraints (Hymes, 1982) as well as of grammar (Chomsky, 1965), I also study the connections between the meanings individuals construct in classrooms and those from institutional and community contexts.

Sample

I conducted the research in the school district of Maplehurst, gaining permission to study in two of the district's five large comprehensive high schools after a semester-long pilot study of curriculum differentiation in all of them. Beginning on the opening day of the 1982–83 school year, I became as unobtrusive a participant-observer as possible in four lower-track Additional Needs classes in English and social studies at Marshall High School. Two weeks later I added the same role in four Additional Needs classes at Southmoor High (just across town).* Alternating between the two schools, I attended classes daily through February 1983, returned for occasional visits through June 1983, and revisited the schools and teachers informally during the 1983–84 school year. I also observed systematically although less regularly in the teachers' regular-track classes.

I selected Maplehurst because, in many respects, its public schools are so unspectacular. With mostly white, middle-class students, Southmoor and Marshall can be considered average institutions. They do not face the massive poverty and perils of many urban schools, where issues of class and race may compound or overshadow school effects (yet where tracking is most often studied). At the same time, Maplehurst's schools are not so homogeneous as suburban schools that confront fewer problems of comprehensiveness. Therefore, the Maplehurst setting afforded a chance to study the differentiating power of the school at its most mundane, in schools where one might expect a relatively modest need for tracking. In

---

*I also observed regularly in a fifth class at Southmoor, Ms. Chadwick's Adolescent Literature class. Although officially a regular-track English course, during 1982–83, more than half the students were Additional Needs students who had no place to go when the school principal determined at the last minute that there would be fewer lower-track classes. The class would offer interesting data about the impact of labeling on teacher and student behaviors if I had a comparative class and could then distinguish teacher and track effects. However, because it is a one-of-a-kind class, I omit it from this account.

addition, because even Maplehurst's lower-track students are relatively advantaged, the impact of curriculum on the distribution of social and educational roles could be clarified.

The eight Additional Needs classes that were the principal locus of study promised both common and variable elements of differentiation. On the one hand, all the classes shared a designation within the Maplehurst School District as Additional Needs classes. By virtue of that designation, they had several features in common that established them as a lower track of classes. First, all but one were funded between 1979 and 1982, in part or entirely, through special district monies that supplemented each school's regular budget. Second, all the classes operated within comprehensive high schools rather than as self-contained programs in separate buildings. Third, classes were considerably smaller than regular-track classes (about 15 instead of 25 to 35 students). Fourth, all served academically unsuccessful high school students who "fell between the cracks": Students referred by teachers for placement in Additional Needs classes had failed or were deemed unable to succeed in regular-track classes but were ineligible for placement in special education classes. Because placement procedures in Additional Needs classes were less formalized than in special education, teachers, counselors, and, indeed, students themselves could initiate placements. Although students could refuse placement and remain in regular classes, to my knowledge none did, nor did Additional Needs placement preclude enrollment in some regular-track classes. Finally, Additional Needs classes were distinguished by "adaptive" curricula, which teachers designed to meet students' "individual educational needs."

On the other hand, the eight Additional Needs classes were quite diverse and, thus, promised the possibility of variable means and meaning in tracking. They varied in subject matter, size, grade level, instructional modes, and materials. Individual teachers' styles, along with unique clusters of students, added to the diversity. In addition to class idiosyncrasies, the informality of Additional Needs, compared with the mandated differentiation of special, bilingual, or talented and gifted education, meant that each Maplehurst school designed its own array of Additional Needs classes. Thus, each school's classes offered an example of a particular faculty's view of academically unsuccessful students. Finally, Additional Needs classes were originally funded by the school district's central office in response to pleas for support from local schools rather than being imposed from above. In Additional Needs classes, teachers had virtually complete autonomy regarding the curriculum's appropriate "adaptation." Therefore, the classes offered sites in which to study empirically the effects of teacher engagement in bottom-up curricular design.

Design

To study curriculum differentiation in Maplehurst's Additional Needs classes, I used a double comparison research design: I compared regular- and lower-track classes within each high school and also across the two schools. With two sites, I could check processes observed in one school's lower-track classes for their occurrence in the second school's. This provided assurance that observed differences between regular- and lower-track classes were functions of tracking, not of a school's peculiarities.

Formal similarities between the two schools enhanced such comparisons. Southmoor and Marshall are equally large institutions, serving about 2,000 students in grades 9 through 12. Both are comprehensive high schools, offering advanced, regular, and remedial levels in academic, general, and technical classes to students who are, in the main, white and middle class. (In none of Maplehurst's high schools do minority students make up more than 12% of the student body.) Mean scores on district-wide intelligence and achievement tests differ only slightly across the district, and, generally, Maplehurst students score well above national averages. Although Marshall's building is newer than Southmoor's, both schools are well maintained, with impressive athletic facilities, industrial and fine arts shops, and well-stocked instructional media centers. Both school budgets reflect the district-wide formula. At both, the teaching staffs are highly trained, with over half the district's teachers having a bachelor's degree plus 24 hours. Faculty members are experienced and loyal as well: At the time of the study, the average Maplehurst teacher had almost 15 years of experience, 12 of them in the district.

Although similar on many counts, the two schools also differed, which allowed comparison of institutional enactments of tracking. I originally selected Southmoor and Marshall from among Maplehurst's five high schools on the basis of faculty members' reports of socioeconomic differences between the student bodies: working class at Marshall, middle and upper-middle class at Southmoor. From other studies of tracking and schooling, I knew the theoretical importance of social class for educational practice and effects. However, my understanding of the reported socioeconomic differences altered significantly during the study. I learned that schools define rather than merely divine students' characteristics: In Maplehurst, reported differences between the two schools turned out to be symbolic, not straightforwardly structural. This key element in Maplehurst's story—a direct outcome of the interpretive research process and time in the field—altered my understanding of the power of the high school curriculum and its limited independence from factors of social differentiation.

Strategies

To gather data, I combined three research strategies: intensive and extensive participant observation in the two schools; interviewing of teachers, students, and administrators throughout the schools and the school district; and audiotaping of lessons. Extended, naturalistic observations in classrooms and corridors provided categories of data that arose from the context and the school participants rather than strictly from the researcher. This was important for an inquiry into the bases for differentiation that people in schools actually use rather than those predicted by armchair social theorists. Interviews with participants, along with many less formal conversations, allowed for fuller articulation of participants' perspectives. Because I wanted to know not only what school inhabitants did but how they understood and were able to express what they did, interviews clarified observations of behavior and elicited information about each person's perspective of how other people viewed the situation. The third strategy, audiotaping classroom lessons, provided yet a finer level of communicative data. With transcripts, I was able to check whether the meaning attributed by one individual to another was indeed oriented to and seen as meaningful by the designated other (including my attributions from the back of the classroom). Combining these three strategies enhanced the overall validity of results in an interpretive framework.

The data I collected are the words of school participants. Whether used in interviews, informal conversations, written texts, or lessons, their words are neither exact markers of an objective, static reality that they selected automatically nor are they mere symbols they picked randomly, without constraint. Rather, just as all sentences are both unique yet exhibit a deep structure, so teachers' and students' talk about tracking is creative, yet echoes conventional school practices, cultural resources, and political power.

In short, participants' words reflect and constitute a vernacular, or language (Jackson, 1968), of education. It makes available to teachers, administrators, and students the opportunities and the limits within which they can talk about curricular and social differences. The vernacular is a cultural resource that faculty members and students use to comprise, signal, order, and negotiate their perspectives and places.

In presenting the data about curriculum differentiation in Maplehurst, I strive to convey both the particularities and the patterns with which people at Southmoor and Marshall high schools demonstrate educational and social differences. Consequently, I display abundant examples of extended quotations from interviews and long segments of classroom discourse. I also often mark (with quotation marks) short phrases of exceptional force as well as mundane words and phrases that participants nevertheless make noteworthy through sheer repetition. In the latter case, the quotation marks do not indicate that I question a speaker's veracity. Rather, they indicate the particular artifacts that people used to construct their situations.

I sift the words of people in Maplehurst in an effort to trace their multilayered strata of meaning, connect metaphors spoken in different contexts, and document shifts and stability in themes of differentiation that echo across levels of classroom, school, and community. In this endeavor, I cannot describe without interpreting or analyze without valuing (see discussions in Bernstein, 1985; Clifford & Marcus, 1986; Fish, 1980; Geertz, 1986; Miller, 1979). Hence, the story of Maplehurst's schools is as much mine as it is the participants': To paraphrase Agar (1986), the text is my interpretation, written for interpreting readers, of the interpretations of the people in Maplehurst's schools. On occasion, I call attention to the text as my construction by interjecting first-person pronouns. In the main, however, I have framed the manuscript to foreground participants and their accounts of tracking. Failure to explicate my explicating should not be taken as an indication that my rendition of Maplehurst's story is the privileged last word.

I indicate characteristics of talk using the following symbols:

- Overlapping utterances by an opening [bracket]
- Short, untimed pauses by - , slightly longer pauses by - - and - - - , and timed pauses by (seconds)
- Emphasis by *italics* and greater emphasis by CAPITAL LETTERS
- Elongated pronunciation by repetiiitions of letters
- Descriptions or explanations of the situation by (parentheses)
- Ellipsis by . . .
- Speakers by pseudonymous names or by S (student), Ss (students), T (teacher), and I (interviewer)
- Lines from long segments of talk may be numbered for reference purposes; numbers do not correspond to lines in raw transcriptions of lessons

I include numerous details about the people, talk, and events of Southmoor and Marshall. Teachers' and students' specific words and phrases, particular lessons, and concrete classroom jokes, materials, and routines, provide readers a "surrogate experience" (Wehlage, 1981, p. 214) of the lower-track world in the two Maplehurst schools. As with fiction, readers can get to know characters and events they have never encountered in fact. With details, they can compare the lower tracks of Southmoor and

Marshall meaningfully with classrooms they know directly through experience or indirectly from research reports.

At the same time, I frame the details of Maplehurst's lower-track worlds by using concepts, or what Dewey (1929) called "intellectual instrumentalities" (cited in Bellack, 1978, p. 31). Thus, for example, I explain the disengagement in Ms. Mitchell's lesson by looking at events through the lenses of the manifest curriculum in English and the hidden curriculum of social control; I use the metaphor of the lottery to capture the ambiguity and contingency that connect specific details of the lesson. Thus, theoretical concepts enhance the accumulation of data within the case of the Additional Needs class.

Concepts also furnish analogies with which to compare lower-track situations elsewhere. Institutional and cultural precepts such as tracking, luck, or social class structure teachers' and students' behavior in other locales. And, although apparently lawlike, such regularities are themselves cultural productions that are peculiar to a time and place. Therefore, the analysis of these regularities, as much as of local details, is necessary for understanding cultural and curricular knowledge.

THE COMMUNITY OF MAPLEHURST

Individuals talk about and thereby enact curriculum differentiation in face-to-face interactions that echo precepts of differentiation from wider contexts. Southmoor's and Marshall's Additional Needs classes reflect Maplehurst's particular translation of the defining contradictions of American culture. With sharp if subtle effect, teachers and students play out the alternation between individualism and the common good in an "All-American" city deep in the heartland of the country.

As its name perhaps implies, Maplehurst is a charming place to live. The city is replete with tree-filled parks, well-kept neighborhoods, and respected schools. The seat of a large county government, Maplehurst is also home to many large white-collar industries, several large blue-collar industries, and a branch of the prestigious state university system. These attractive features have mitigated flight to outlying small towns and rural suburbs, and Maplehurst real estate values remain high. Although only about a quarter of the city's population has children in the public schools, citizen pride in the public system is very great. Few private schools compete for students or the public's support.

Maplehurst's citizenry also prides itself on being attuned to political processes and on devising solutions that keep the city viable and humane. Predominantly white and middle class, it espouses the values of harmony and tolerance. People take civic life rather seriously. They express informed, self-interested, and civic opinions, and they debate these in the public arena. For example, Maplehurst has many small but active neighborhood associations. These receive recognition in the local media for their distinctiveness and their contribution to the quality of life in the city. The associations also battle for their parochial interests in the city council. Many assume responsibilities in neighborhood schools, enriching the curriculum through volunteer services or fighting school closings and budget cuts before the school board.

Although overwhelmingly white and moderately prosperous, Maplehurst's population is somewhat more diverse than that of other midwestern cities its size. City jobs attract people from the rural areas of the state. Traditionally liberal welfare and police policies support discharged persons from nursing homes and state institutions. Maplehurst's churches sponsor Latin American and Asian refugees. The state university adds an international student population to the melange.

Blacks form the largest minority group, comprising 3% of Maplehurst's population. Although small, its size has tripled in the last 20 years, with most recent arrivals coming from nearby metropolitan areas and from upper southern states to join Maplehurst's core of long-established black residents. The proportion of minority children in the schools has increased as well in these years. About 10% of Maplehurst's students are minorities, more than half blacks; the rate of increase is about 0.5% annually. The black community's spokespersons have the ear of local political and educational organizations, and there are strong conventions for racial tolerance. Both city and school administrators are quick to respond when racial issues come to the fore.

Maplehurst's diverse citizens are not rigidly segregated. Census data document the predominance of middle-class neighborhoods. Large, scattered, numerous parks and recreational areas encourage socioeconomically mixed neighborhoods rather than large homogeneous tracts. Still, it is more common to find professors living near the state university, recent rural arrivals in the southern sections of the city, and poor black newcomers on the west side. These housing patterns influence school populations at the elementary and middle school levels, as children attend neighborhood schools. The five comprehensive high schools, drawing from larger attendance areas, are less distinctive. Although each has a local identity, all student bodies are overwhelmingly white and middle class.

Many Maplehurst residents work at the university or in the county government. These industries offer the community some protection from the economic stress of recessions. Nonetheless, with recent property tax revolts, the general economic decline of the Rust Belt, and federal cutbacks,

Maplehurst has increasingly experienced the consequences of hard times. This, in turn, has produced difficult political choices, as various groups confront each other not only symbolically but over shares of the pie.

The shrinking of the economy, combined with declining enrollments, a rising proportion of minority students, and an increased number of identified academically unsuccessful students, has affected Maplehurst's school system and the community's attitudes toward it. Very high citizen interest in education continues: The election for school board members often attracts more attention than the mayoralty race. Financial support is also high, although more grudgingly maintained of late. The Maplehurst School District continues to win regional and national recognition for its excellent programs and above-average student achievement scores.

However, demographic and economic changes expose the power structure that underlies the political debates in the community. Several school closings, although justified by the school board and the district administration in terms of money and numbers, were highly political decisions. For example, several years ago a class action suit charged the district with closing schools to produce de facto racially segregated schools. The plaintiff's complaint was affirmed and the district has begun steps to rectify the imbalances.

Economic and political factors have also produced structural changes in the Maplehurst School District's administration. For example, for more than 10 years the district administration, under a horizontal organization, promoted local school autonomy. Each of the district's five comprehensive high schools was encouraged to emphasize the curriculum it deemed appropriate for its students. Hence, at some high schools the core of the curriculum was strongly academic, whereas at others, vocational courses received a heavier emphasis. With shrinking dollars and rising questions about educational quality, the district administration initiated a reorganization plan to increase consistency of policies and programs across the district. Moreover, by 1988, the district predicted its high schools would operate at 50% of capacity. The impact of this enrollment decline may necessitate further reductions of programs, discontinuation of a comprehensive educational program at each high school, or the closing of one of the high schools. Any of these decisions would prompt heated confrontations among Maplehurst's constituencies.

Economic and political factors have produced curricular debates, as well. One central question is whether programs for less-advantaged, handicapped, or academically unsuccessful students have received so much support that programs for average and talented students have been neglected. Although the district continues to state its commitment to an excellent instructional program for all, cuts have been necessary. (After a decade of strong expansion, special education staff was reduced.)

Maplehurst's Additional Needs classes have not escaped the cuts. Their checkered history reflects the contradictory cultural values and political contests exemplified in curriculum differentiation in general and its particular enactment in Maplehurst. As I learned during the pilot study, the classes developed during the liberal reforms of the late 1960s. At that time, the district abolished extensive formal tracking by ability levels. However, at the same time, it expanded special differentiated programs such as special education, talented and gifted, and advanced placement. Additional Needs classes also arose, initiated by faculty members who faced newly heterogeneous regular-track classes and who were frequently frustrated in securing placement in special education classes for students who experienced difficulties. Teachers proposed the less formal Additional Needs category, arguing that students needed individual attention and appealing to the central district office for supplementary funding for smaller, "adaptive" classes. Thus, even as the Maplehurst School District moved to abolish differentiated ability grouping, it simultaneously reinstituted differentiation in special programs.

The Additional Needs budget fluctuated with shifts in the district's and community's priorities. Allocations from the district office were first provided as an ad hoc supplement at Maplehurst's most troubled high school: The school received extra teacher positions in recognition of its more needy and demanding student population. Subsequently, the district's other four comprehensive high schools pleaded for extra teacher allocations to staff Additional Needs classes. The Additional Needs allocation process was formalized in 1979–80 and, in 1980–81, the budget exceeded $500,000.

Even with formal funding, however, the purposes of the classes remained uncertain. Formally, the extra district monies were provided to educate needy students; informally, they saved regular staff positions at a time of declining enrollments. For example, some lower-track classes at Marshall and Southmoor were funded out of each school's regular budget before they were placed under the Additional Needs rubric. Then, during a period of intense personnel cuts, teachers who were willing to teach an Additional Needs class were kept on the full-time payrolls of the two schools rather than being reduced to half-time or required to teach part of the day in a second school. In 1982–83, however, the Additional Needs budget was lost in contract negotiations with the teachers' union. At first, Maplehurst's high schools continued many of the classes in reduced form by again using regular staff allocations. As overall staff reductions con-

tinued, such decisions became more difficult, so that in 1983–84 at Southmoor High, half the additional Needs classes were deleted.

Disjunctive school policies translate the multiple, often contradictory
norms, politics, and economics of the Maplehurst community. The community swings ambivalently amid concerns for the common good, equity, and
justice and the values of individualism, efficiency, and competition. Concern for all the children oscillates with ensuring the advancement of one's
own. Such grand societal tensions are lived and learned in the particular
shifts in the fortunes and lessons of Maplehurst's Additional Needs classes.

Part II
DEFINING THE LOWER-TRACK STUDENT

CHAPTER 2

How Teachers Talk

What does it mean to be a lower-track student? Are lower-track students less academically able, or "slower," than regular-track students? Are they "behavior problems," disdainful of "bookish" endeavors, and susceptible to the allure of peers and the street? Or are lower-track students principally lower-class adolescents? Do ascriptions of academic or behavioral disabilities simply serve as proxies for institutional or social discrimination?

Teachers provide crucial elements of the definition of the lower-track student. In a variety of explicit and implicit ways, they signal the seriousness with which students should regard lessons or homework, the kinds of topics appropriate for students' attention, the degree to which students will engage with and contribute ideas, the respect they will accord peers, and a host of other activities. To define the student's role is one of the teacher's fundamental obligations and prerogatives. It manifests the teacher's greater authority and power in the classroom.

Central to the definition is the balance the teacher indicates between educative pursuits and social control. Because classrooms are crowded public places, teachers must ensure that groups of students behave if individuals are to learn (Cusick, 1973; Jackson, 1968; Metz, 1978). At the same time, unyielding control can dampen students' academic enthusiasm and effort. Teachers depend on students' civil engagement so that lessons can go forth. Thus, teachers' juxtaposition of educative and instrumental goals is delicate as well as critical.

The balance teachers establish varies with context and provides for differentiated student roles. Tracking is one important context. Some analyses explain that tracking provides for a fair assessment and neutral accommodation of students' interests and needs (see the review in Goldberg et al., 1966). Other analyses explain that tracking furnishes teachers with ready-made, hierarchical labels and expectations (Oakes, 1985; Rist, 1979; Rosenthal & Jacobsen, 1968). Accordingly, teachers expect "trouble" and therefore emphasize discipline with lower-track students, but they expect regular-track students to be "good" and, consequently, emphasize academic progress. Some data indicate that teachers' characterizations of students by track are veiled references to students' social-class characteristics (Bowles & Gintis, 1976; Oakes, 1985).

Despite important differences, these analyses assume a single correspondence between the teacher's definition of the student's role and tracking. However, for the most part, they do not specify how tracking shapes the teacher's definition of students or how students react. Rather, students appear as Pygmalions, fulfilling tracking's prophecies by taking on automatically the attributes that Higgins-like teachers expect of them.

Tracking influenced the balance that Maplehurst teachers establish between order and education and, as a result, the differentiated roles teachers define for students in their Additional Needs and regular-track classes. In many respects, labeling theory (Rist, 1977) predicts the Maplehurst definition: Teachers negatively differentiate lower- from regular-track students; they expect lower-track students to be "academically unskilled," intellectually uninterested, and behaviorally "immature"; and they imply that "keeping order" is their preeminent concern in lower-track classes.

However, even though teachers at Southmoor and Marshall emphasize the negative, their definition of lower-track students is considerably more complex than the simple correlation of low track/low expectations suggests. First, teachers express considerable ambivalence regarding Additional Needs students rather than characterizing them with a straightforwardly negative or strictly neutral stereotype. They lament the apathy and lack of engagement of Additional Needs students, even as they also emphasize "keeping order" as a principal concern. They worry aloud that lower-track students flatly disdain academic activities, are erratic in attendance, or have the potential to drop out. Apparently, if teachers have clear misgivings about lower-track students' "acting out," they have equally clear worries about their not acting at all.

Second, the complex definition of the lower-track student is compounded by students' reactions. Just as Pygmalion eventually acts, so Maplehurst's Additional Needs students are not abjectly docile. Nor, as a group, are they the severely handicapped or alienated youth who are described in other studies as inhabiting the lower echelons of imperiled, discipline-oriented, mostly urban institutions (Schwartz, 1981; Willis, 1977). Rather, the great majority of Maplehurst's lower-track students, like Maplehurst's regular-track students, are white and middle class. On average, lower-track students score in the third rather than the bottom quartile on standardized achievement tests. Thus, if they are not as advantaged or as skilled as some of their regular-track peers, neither are they traditional school resisters. Instead, most acknowledge education's importance and most state a commitment at least to survive the passage through Maplehurst's institutions. In other words, Maplehurst's lower-track students do not straightforwardly match, agree with, or assent unquestioningly to institutional definitions of their role.

Given teachers' ambivalence and students' reactions, therefore, the definition of the lower-track student's role is not a precise correlation of traits and tracks but a knotty dilemma. Its ambiguities challenge the conventional wisdom that the teacher's definition of the lower-track student is simple: either a fair estimation of students' individual, principally academic, needs or a prejudiced assessment based on behavioral, track, or sociocultural stereotypes.

More accurately, Maplehurst's lower-track teachers worry persistently about keeping control, yet control is of uncertain warrant. Hence, even as teachers predict students' failure, they expect students to "try." They anticipate students will devalue scholarship yet insist that they care about it. They expect lower-track students to be "out-of-control" yet also notably passive. If Maplehurst teachers regularly voice a stereotypical view of lower-track students as academically, socially, and behaviorally incompetent, they also regularly act on expectations that students will be engaged, will enjoy educational opportunities, and will achieve educational success.

The fluctuations in the definition resonate with Additional Needs students' own uncertainties about their ability to succeed in an academic institution that they nevertheless acknowledge is important. They also echo broader normative contradictions of public education in the United States: Although all children are required to attend school and are guaranteed an equal educational opportunity, differentiated course work must also be provided because it is assumed that many individuals will not value or cannot excel at scholastic pursuits (Powell, Farrar, & Cohen, 1985). In short, antiphonies, not a monochromatic melody, define tracking.

To convey the complexity of the Maplehurst teacher's definition of the role of Additional Needs students, I develop two analyses. First, I present data from interviews and informal conversations with teachers to document that individual teachers' perspectives, although each is unique, reflect and constitute a common, informally acknowledged body of pedagogical lore about lower-track students. Teachers draw on a freewheeling, complex constellation of academic, social, and behavioral competencies in their characterizations; they resolve its inevitable inconsistencies by falling back on a predominantly negative stereotype. Thus, individual teachers' definitions of the lower-track student's role are an unwieldy social construction rather than strictly personal predilections, rational assessments of objective facts, or a knee-jerk prejudice.

In Chapter 3, I present the second analysis. I examine one lower-track lesson to trace how a teacher communicates to students the ambiguous, tacit definition; the circumstances that prompt the stereotype's emergence; and students' responses. As I document, this Maplehurst teacher rarely states negative views to students directly. Nevertheless, they are apparent as he relies upon assumptions about lower-track students to define, interpret, direct, and negotiate the exigencies of classroom interactions. In turn, the teacher's choices provide for students' responses. Together, then, in the indeterminate but nonrandom talk of daily lessons, teacher and students bring the lower-track student's role to life.

STORIES IN COMMON

Formal descriptions of teaching prescribe that teachers instruct and assess students professionally and without prejudice, according to students' demonstrated academic achievement. The image of the teacher is that of impartial, technical expert dealing with unequivocal facts and neutral curricular materials. The teacher assesses students' skills, provides lessons matched to their levels, and monitors the students' progress.

However, when teaching is examined as it occurs in schools, it emerges as considerably more fluid than labor contracts, education textbooks, or professional ideologies suggest. Individual teachers acknowledge a complex, often tacit constellation of axioms, traditions, and lore in defining students (Sarason, 1971; Schwab, 1969). Thus, like lower-track teachers in other schools (Keddie, 1971; Leacock, 1969; Metz, 1978; Rist, 1973) and professionals in other fields (Schön, 1983), Maplehurst teachers define students in colloquial stories as well as in formal reports; their accounts mix social and behavioral information with scholastics; and teachers' implicit and explicit interpretations bend information about students in ways that are sensible at Southmoor and Marshall. Even though Maplehurst teachers have little time to engage in formal conferences or extended diagnostic exchanges, their individual stories exhibit a common pattern of differentiation.

The patterned complexity of the teachers' definition of the lower-track student role is evident both in what teachers say about students and in how they say it. Ms. Mitchell, an English teacher at Southmoor, reveals the way Maplehurst teachers compound academic with social and behavioral traits when she talks about differences between her regular- and lower-track ninth graders:

> I think the most fun with the (regular-track) ninth graders starts from the beginning of the second semester, when you can begin to see that they're growing up. I just *adore* that adulthood that I see. I

don't mean physically, but I mean the grasp of some of the more
abstract concepts that I've been trying to teach them. It's fun to see
that they stop fooling around with, teasing each other, you know,
and, uh, silly little things, like poking each other or hiding pencils.

Additional Needs students are, "unfortunately, less likely to make that
same kind of a shift," either in terms of maturity or academic achievement:

> They are *not* good readers. They're poor in composition, poor in
> writing skills. Their self-image is poor. I mean, one of the, um,
> things we're hoping for, some of the kids in this (Additional
> Needs) class, if we don't do anything else but make them feel a lit-
> tle bit better about themselves, that's all we're aiming for.

Nonetheless, Ms. Mitchell continued, not all students referred to Additional Needs classes appreciate the special placement, and this

> may reflect family problems. What happens, generally, parents, you
> know, they'll try getting them to a different (school) system, think-
> ing that possibly there's hope there. . . . Or they move a lot. They
> have been known in the past, you see, to be rather flighty from one
> school to another.

Ms. Mitchell characterizes her present Additional Needs class as "one of
the worst I've had in many years," not just because some students are
"hyper and never keep their mouths shut" but, additionally (and contrarily), because "it's like pulling teeth with that group to get them to discuss.
Ah, they're, they're *negative*, many of them, their attitude is not positive. I
think they're down on themselves in some respects. I think they have
problems."

The "problems" Ms. Mitchell enumerates are not so much intellectual
as social and behavioral:

> Now, Jim Rodriguez is too bright to be in here, but he's got to have
> other problems that are holding back his education - - Mike Put-
> ney is just shy. And Jules Massalio, I know that it's a broken home.
> Um, I know that he was in a private school last year. I know he's
> very, very into football. Who knows, it might even be his size,
> 'cause he is very small. Plus there's a feistiness about him. He just
> won't follow the rules; he's always late, he forgets his books . . . I've
> suspected drugs.

Ms. Mitchell's characterization of Additional Needs students is a personal, creative construction, not a script. Nevertheless, it resembles the characterizations voiced by other Maplehurst teachers. All unfold in story-like informality. All blend diverse student traits in a loose, multidimensional web in which any one feature may evoke another. Teachers occasionally cite research or media reports to confirm their characterizations, or they appeal to general sociocultural understandings about important human differences, such as differences in intelligence. But, in the main, the definition of the student is a kind of pedagogical lore, spoken in the school's vernacular. Teachers share it informally in lunch conversations, jokes, and gossip. It acknowledges and contributes to rarely analyzed assumptions about students, teachers, knowledge, and the differences that count in school and society.

Such a mixed student portrait has been interpreted as evidence of teachers' prejudice (Rist, 1973) or of their befuddlement (reported in Jackson, 1968): If bad teachers could just be weeded out or if all teachers could be trained to greater sensitivity and higher expectations then, according to a rationalistic perspective, all students would receive a good, equal education. However, the definition of the lower-track student is not a logical taxonomy. It is a fluid, contextualized, social construction, not unlike the often contradictory presuppositions all of us use every day to get through an inchoate world sanely.

Furthermore, the definition is skewed by the irreducibly contradictory norms that bespeak U.S. teachers' relations to students. On the one hand, teachers are to minister fairly to all students, particularly in regard to academic development. From this perspective, teachers are to be color-blind, gender-blind, and class-blind: As if standing above and outside a differentiated society and its institutions, they are to judge intellectual merit as a thing unto itself. On the other hand, equally potent traditions suggest that teachers *should* consider students' social and behavioral needs. To consider only students' intellectual talents is to ignore their "individual educational needs"; it is to disadvantage some by failing to offer compensatory, "relevant," or "special" education. As a result, in their definitions of students, teachers, like Ms. Mitchell, necessarily tangle students' sociocultural, behavioral, and academic features so that each is interwoven with and reinforces the others.

Crosscutting individual teachers' idiosyncratic renditions of this broad dilemma is a common structure that reflects tracking's particular translation in Maplehurst: Lower-track students' behavior and its control outweigh concerns about their intellect and its development.

One teacher explained grimly: "You've probably figured out that academics is not the reason for Additional Needs classes." Another, more therapeutically inclined, insisted, "There's not that much skills improvement, but Additional Needs classes let them get their feet on the ground and adjust to high school." A third identified the importance of efficiency and control in recounting his request to a principal to remove a student from an Additional Needs class:

> It's a waste of the taxpayer's money and the teacher's time (to keep the student in school). He had one-eleventh of the assignments in, an average of 0.414. He was suicidal and his mother doesn't know where he is half the time, and doesn't care. I suppose you could say I was cruel and inhuman but I don't need kids like that in this class. This class is easy enough to get off the track anyway.

Overall, students' potential disruptiveness and teachers' general concern for classes getting "off the track" justify curriculum differentiation.

Thus, in interview after interview, Maplehurst teachers cite students' deficiencies, beginning with the academic but always moving to the behavioral. Thus, lower-track students "lack basic skills," are "close to illiterate," or "are frustrated and can't make it academically." The litany then moves to social history: Additional Needs students have "families that don't value education," are "from single-parent homes," or "have nobody who gives a damn about them at home." Most adamantly, however, staff members insist that lower-track students are "behavior problems": They exhibit a pattern of truancy, "off-the-wall" actions in class, or discipline problems of vandalism, drugs, "immaturity," or fighting.

This pattern reflects acknowledged strategies by which teachers manage the conflicting institutional and cultural norms that they feel expected to consider in ministering to students: They resort to a largely negative stereotype of the lower-track students as "troublemakers." For the most part, the informal consensus across individual teachers' perspectives is not achieved through official exchanges of diagnoses, theories, or pedagogical strategies. Nor is it the outcome of clear, accountable, administrative policies. Rather, "everyone knows" that lower-track students at Southmoor and Marshall "need structure." The local pattern echoes and draws its potency from a more widely acknowledged stereotype of students who fail in school. The stereotype allows Maplehurst teachers to comprehend ambiguously specified social and educational phenomena. It is a professional and cultural resource, which teachers use and re-create as they define students in Additional Needs classes. To explicate its complexity and power, I turn to a closer examination of teachers' ambiguous assemblages of students' academic, social, and behavioral characteristics.

Characterizations of Academic Ability

As one might expect, teachers focus most readily and with greatest self-assurance on descriptions of students' academic abilities. Thus, in explaining recommendations for track placement or pedagogical practices in Additional Needs classes, Maplehurst teachers invariably begin by noting that students are "slow," or "behind," in the race up the ladder of schooling and American life. Usually, teachers mention students' "low skills," particularly their below-grade-level reading achievement scores. They also point to "poorly developed thinking skills." Students "can't make connections between things"; they are said to be less able to generalize or "think abstractly"; long-term projects, which might lead to in-depth study, are impossible because "these students don't remember things from day to day."

Because teachers are educational professionals, one might expect that their academic assessments are based on objective information, such as students' achievement test scores or intelligence quotients; that they are exchanged in formal, possibly multidisciplinary, diagnostic sessions (required by law in special education, for example); or that they are couched in terms of an explicit theory about academic deficiencies. Instead, although teachers describe students' academic characteristics with alacrity and confidence, portraits are anecdotal, informal, and shot through with contradictions. Although rarely explicit, disjunctions abound: between subjective and objective measures of ability, competing interpretations of performance, or the importance of academic criteria in comparison with social and behavioral criteria.

Instead of formal diagnoses, stories form the stuff of teacher talk, and Maplehurst teachers rely on anecdotes to communicate notions about students' academic ability, even as they acknowledge the achievement and aptitude tests that, as they say, "provide something objective." Fleetingly articulated in 5 minutes between classes or over a hurried half-hour lunch in the lounge or the departmental offices at Southmoor and Marshall, stories are convincing because of their specificity and their drama. They are virtually irrefutable, given their form. For example, a telling, inarguable point about the reading ability of a lower-track student is communicated in a touching story of an "illiterate":

T: Miller came in from Detroit, or somewhere, and is totally – *totally* – illiterate.

I: Illiterate?

T: That's the word, illiterate. Period. Not an – – opinion. That's a fact. You know, sometimes you say a kid's illiterate and people say,

"What do you mean?" But I think *anybody* - - no matter what rationality they'd use, would call him illiterate.

I: Why do you say that?

T: 'Cause he couldn't read - - one word.

I: He couldn't read *anything*?

T: He didn't know *the*.

I: Really?

T: That's real - - I, I asked him, I found that out, 'cause the one day he showed up in class, I pointed to *the*, he couldn't read it.

Such a narrative lends itself poorly to consideration of other "rationalities": that Miller might not have been trying to read; that literacy is not an absolute state but a continuum; that reasonable diagnoses of learning difficulties require more than "one day" of evidence; or that another student in the lower-track class scored above the 90th percentile on a local reading test. Discussion is not invited nor could it counter the symbolic impact of the teacher's story.

A similar story involved a usually laconic freshman. One day he "surprised" his teacher by accurately and vividly recounting a biography of Jim Thorpe he had read recently. His teacher interpreted the detailed account not as fluency but as possible evidence of "perseveration," a learning disability in which attention is fixated. Thereafter, the mention of the student's name almost always provoked a repetition by the teacher of the Thorpe incident, with a negative interpretation of it. Retold around the faculty lounge, the story spread the lower-track student's character as "learning disabled."

Teachers use stories to typify individual students like Miller and the Jim Thorpe fan. They "type" a student when they infer a person's character from the evidence of a few actions (Hargreaves, Hester, & Mellor, 1975, chap. 6). If "Miller can't read *the* on the one day he showed up in class," the teacher infers and implies that "Miller is an illiterate," despite Miller's other attributes. Spread casually throughout a faculty, such typifications develop lives of their own beyond the events and personalities in which they originate. Some become departmental and institutional sagas (Clark, 1972). Legends, caricatures, and exemplary fables grow out of historical events and particular people, but they also spread across settings to shape perceptions of subsequent actions and different actors. They furnish a resource that encodes and influences teachers' fundamental assumptions about a school's members, outsiders, and social system.

Colloquial forms of information exchange prompt and perpetuate the contradictions and negative stereotype in teachers' characterizations of lower-track students. For example, teachers' informal assessments of students' academic ability do not match the students' "objective" scores on achievement tests. Mr. Bradley was sure that Dick, "one of the smartest boys in the (Additional Needs English) class, had a reading score near the top of the class." Actually, although Dick did indeed exhibit bright behavior in class, his reading score was the lowest in the class. However, the teacher's assessment was correct, if for reasons different from those he could uncover: Dick's score was not only low but invalid. He took the exam by speeding through it, randomly penciling in the multiple-choice "bubbles." Student ability is not as easily ascertainable as pedagogical theory or lore may imply.

Moreover, after typing begins, even disconfirming evidence may be reinterpreted to fit and confirm the type. For example, a Marshall teacher emphasizes that students in his ninth-grade Additional Needs class have very low reading scores, even though the test scores indicate a wide range (5% to 78%) of measured academic skills, with most scores falling in the third quartile. At Southmoor, the specific goal in some Additional Needs classes is to improve students' reading scores on locally normed reading tests to the point that students answer at least 50% of the questions correctly, but over half the students placed in Additional Needs classes answer more than 50% correctly *at the time of placement.*

When faculty members do acknowledge the diversity of academic ability in Additional Needs classes, they nevertheless resolve the problems of diversity by highlighting the negative extreme:

> Most of the kids, I shouldn't say most, but – it's not unusual to
> have a kid in the 20th percentile in reading in that class. So – and
> below. Some of them are in the first and second percentile. . . . And
> it's very difficult sometimes to teach those kids because some of
> them are in the 30th percentile and some of them are between one
> and five – – It's not like you have a homogeneous group.

Echoing the teacher's complaint, a school social worker proposed the solution to diversity that is commonsensical in Maplehurst and in many other American schools (Powell et al., 1985; Sarason, 1971), even though the solution reduces only a fraction of student heterogeneity (Goodlad, 1984): A new *"low* low-track" should be established for students of "low intelligence who just don't fit into Additional Needs classes."

Students' performances in classrooms, as well as their scores on formal tests, suggest the range and the variability of Additional Needs students' intellectual competence but also the power of images, which provide shortcuts in dealing with vexing phenomena. For example, teachers note correctly that a few students are barely able to read simple sentences aloud. However, they mention less emphatically the other students in the same class who can finish a short novel in a night. Students' grades in Additional Needs classes certainly cover the spectrum from A to F, but most are satisfactory B's and C's, not D's or F's. Further, academically unsuccessful students who may be reticent in answering the teacher's substantive questions are nevertheless quick to understand and produce hilarious, sarcastic repartee. When a student stuttered that he had "a test in, uh, in, uh, art, and uh," a peer interrupted in mock-adult patronage: "C'mon, Tim. Spit it out." Another promptly rejoined, "*Don't SPIT!*" and the class broke up in laughter. Similarly, when students arrived in class with a story about being locked in the local hangout because a bag of quarters was stolen, the teacher commented: "A bag of quarters? That's a lot of money!" However, a student corrected her with a quick quip: "If it's a *big* bag!" Maplehurst teachers' puns and jokes, interspersed in lectures and worksheets, are complex in their allusions, yet they provoke knowing laughter (and reciprocal puns) from lower-track students. These observational data suggest that lower-track students in Maplehurst are not as uniformly deficient in intellectual skills as teachers usually picture them or as cultural images suggest.

However, typifying stories reduce the data to a convenient corpus that confirms a negative image of Additional Needs student as a group. Teachers draw on it when they read differently the behavior of lower- and regular-track classes. Thus, teachers say Additional Needs students have less command of general information relative to their regular-track counterparts. They do not imagine students' ignorance; students indicate lack of knowledge regularly. For example, in a lower-track history class when the teacher asked students how many branches of government the United States had, sophomores guessed two, then four, then asked how many. In another lower-track, tenth-grade history class, when asked when World War I took place, students guessed 1814 and 1819.

Even though similar lacunae occur in the teachers' regular-track classrooms, teachers interpret them differently. For instance, in a regular-track, ninth-grade history discussion of the Democratic convention of 1968, the mention of "looters" prompted a student to ask what a "looter" was. In grammar exercises, regular-track students appear to guess at whether clauses are subordinate or coordinate as frequently (and inaccurately) as lower-track students guess whether a word is an adjective or adverb. With regular-track students, teachers regard these lapses as momentary aberrations that instruction can correct, but in lower-track classes, such lapses often are cited as stigma that inhere in persons and the group (Hargreaves et al., 1975).

Overall, stories told by Maplehurst teachers about lower-track students are framed to deny virtually all academic competence. Like many teachers, Ms. Mitchell simply ignores students' academic progress, instead stressing "improving students' self-image (through) a lot of tender loving care." Other teachers discount grades: "He gets a B from us. It doesn't mean he could function in a regular class. If a kid shows a real desire to move up and out, and is doing real well in our class, *then* we won't stop him." Those teachers who do focus on students' intellectual development insist unremittingly on Additional Needs students' intellectual disabilities and compare them invidiously to regular-track students. After directing a lively discussion in his Additional Needs class, Mr. Reed insisted:

> Oh, they may be able to think *out loud* abstractly, but they could not put it down in writing. They cannot *read* things and recognize
> those kinds of things happening either. They can't continue the discussion the next day. Sure, once they start talking about it, for one day, and especially like, like Arthur, is really sharp.

Here, Mr. Reed both acknowledges and derogates Additional Needs students' skills. In fact, when lower-track students perform well, he and other teachers may react as though something is wrong: "At the beginning of the test, they were so still you could hear a pin drop. It'll never happen again! I don't know why. I thought maybe they had the flu (laughs). Be thankful for small favors, I guess."

In sum, "no matter what rationality they'd use" to make sense of profuse, often contradictory data about students' academic ability, Maplehurst teachers' commonsensical understanding of Additional Needs students is that they are almost irremediably academically deficient. The negative stereotype furnishes teachers a means of managing necessary ambiguous information about individuals and groups of students.

Yet, even though teachers mention lower-track students' academic ability explicitly and frequently, intellect is not the most salient factor in teachers' stories. Rather, "discipline" competes with—and frequently outweighs—academic ability as a factor in placement and instructional decisions. Hence, at Marshall, all ninth graders are given the Stanford Reading Diagnostic Test, Form A, during the first week of school. Any Additional Needs student who scores above the 50th percentile is replaced in a regular-track class (even though the student's eighth-grade teachers have recommended lower-track placement). However, students in regular-track classes who score below the 50th percentile are not necessarily removed to lower-track classes. One teacher explained explicitly the limits of academic ability as a measure of a student's track: "We try to keep them in regular classes if we can. The student's *attitude* is 90% of the ball game."

Social Motifs

Maplehurst teachers cite "family background" as a factor in students' placement and performance in lower-track classes almost as readily and self-assuredly as they cite academic ability. As with their view of students' academic capacities, however, they are ambivalent about its significance. When they must resolve the complexity posed by students' social characteristics, they rely on a negative stereotype.

Expressing their ambivalence regarding students' social backgrounds, teachers say both that a student "would be better off if her parents would let her alone" and that students would perform better "if only their parents cared." Thus, one teacher noted the lower-track parents' lack of involvement with their children's education as the reason for Additional Needs students' school failure:

Now, this school has a pretty good relationship with parents in the community. Parents show an active interest in their children's education. I had full classes on Parents Visitation Night. Of course, those were the college-bound classes. In the Additional Needs classes, only one mother came. Parenting is reflective of the child: With low-level kids, the basic problem is poor parenting. The parents don't care, so the kids don't care.

Teachers expand the family's influence to students' psychological states:

He is really sharp. But he is, ah, so off-the-wall socially, and behaviorally, and so on. And he just can't relate to people – – He comes to school looking like he slept in the back of a truck and his parents let him do it.

Yet in contrast to recommendations like these, which would seem to favor parental involvement, Maplehurst teachers, like all teachers (Joffe, 1977), simultaneously distrust parental influence. For instance, a student who is frequently absent from school is described as having a "mother who will write her an excuse for anything. If she stubs her toenail, she doesn't come. But the next day she appears in class with a blue (excused absence) card." Still another teacher argues that lower-track students' parents care only about "whether the kid gets the piece of paper after 4 years, not whether he learns anything."

In anecdotes similar to those they tell about students' academic disabilities, Maplehurst teachers simplify their characterizations of students' family backgrounds. For Additional Needs students as a group, families are "disadvantaged," "single parent," "not in the picture," or "do not care about education." Again, teachers do not make up the facts: Some students do live with a single parent, a disproportionate number are poor, and disadvantaged minorities are overrepresented in Maplehurst's Additional Needs classes. Nevertheless, the stereotype shapes teachers' perceptions as much as it represents students' situations. Maplehurst's Additional Needs students come from a broad range of socioeconomic backgrounds rather than a single stratum. In contrast to the familiar stereotype, the lower-track ranks include the children of doctors, truck drivers, skilled and unskilled factory workers, managers, welfare recipients, retail clerks, and city officials. No students dress raggedly or describe themselves as "disadvantaged." The majority of students have the socioeconomic and academic advantages of the middle class.

Consequently, the stereotype—that lower-track students suffer deprived backgrounds that render them uninterested and unskilled in school—represents a particular interpretation of multifaceted facts, diverse experiences, and competing values. Teachers simplify the complex character of students' family background and its impact on school success in a way that mirrors their and society's ambivalence about connections between curriculum differentiation and precepts of social differentiation, such as race, class, or gender.

The relationship between curricular and social differentiation may be particularly salient in Maplehurst, given the city's history and politics. For example, more than teachers in less liberally oriented communities (see Metz, 1986, for a contrasting example), Maplehurst teachers readily remark the influence of social class on students' school success, even though they do not specify an explicit theory of class conflict or have regular contact with students' families. One spoke without hesitation about the different values of lower-track, presumably lower-class, families:

> Parents of lower-track students are blue collar. They're that type that doesn't value education - - - There's no home emphasis on learning - - on scholarship. They say, "Let the kid take all these courses now so when he's a junior or senior, he can be off in the afternoon at work, making money to get the material things that will make him happy."

Although this teacher's different values are evident, so is the recognition that schools are expected to accommodate differences. Accordingly, teachers often explain the overrepresentation of working-class or poor students in Additional Needs classes as a matter of students' choice, based on social-class values over which teachers expect to have little influence.

Teachers' reactions to the overrepresentation of male students in seven of the eight lower-track classes parallel their reactions to the overrepresentation of poor students and clarify the similar "rationalities" with which teachers discuss distributions of students in tracks. When I broached the topic, teachers' first reaction was that the preponderance of boys in lower-track classes was an unremarkable "scheduling fluke." They reasoned that "the computer did it," or that "the master schedule may have misfired." Upon further consideration, however, teachers stated they were "unsurprised" by the larger male population after all. Some then cited "research" about boys' generally poorer reading skills as the reason for their predominance in lower-track classes. More frequently, teachers drew on cultural assumptions, suggesting that boys are "less well-behaved than girls, and behavior is a basis for placement in Additional Needs classes." In this same vein, a few stated that they hesitated to recommend girls to lower-track classes even when their skills were very low, so long as girls' behavior in regular-track classes was acceptable: They reasoned that lower-track classes were "full of troublemakers and loudmouths . . . and the girls are under pressure because of all the fellas."

Thus, teachers' estimations of students' social characteristics and of their influence on placement and curricular decisions blend pedagogical and sociocultural factors in ways comparable to the pattern undergirding their stories about students' academic competence. Again, a negative stereotype provides a way to manage the contradictory norms and complex data about students' backgrounds.

At the same time, social characterizations are often softened and rendered more pedagogically confusing by teachers' genuine concern for students' welfare. Maplehurst teachers often express their greatest sympathy when describing students' sociopsychological circumstances. Much more than their sometimes shrill accounts of students' academic deficiencies, the stories of students' hardships are touchingly, even eloquently, related. Concern for students' psychological well-being is genuine, and many teachers consider the development of students' self-esteem the prime goal of Additional Needs classes.

Despite concerns, however, teachers have little leverage to affect the social and familial factors that they see limiting the school performance of lower-track students. Moreover, they rarely connect curricular development, over which they do have some control, with improved intellect and self-esteem. As a result, despite the concern teachers evince, the emphasis on sociopsychological factors often functions as an excuse. As with teachers' attributions of academic incompetence, the negative stereotype into which social characterizations typically resolve makes students appear inherently ineducable. In a sense, teachers suggest that the *best* they can do is maintain control of students who are academically deficient and socially disadvantaged.

Themes About Behavior

When asked to clarify the factors that influence students' performance or their referral to lower-track classes, teachers at Southmoor and Marshall invariably add negative behavior to the litany of academic and social factors. In fact, almost all teachers occasionally characterize Additional Needs classes as "holding tanks" or "dumping grounds" for students with behavior problems rather than as educational settings. All teachers identify one student, and usually several, who was placed in Additional Needs classes "despite his brains but because of his behavior." Conversely, teachers mention their efforts to maintain students with low skills in regular-track classes "if their attitude is okay."

Thus, the stereotype of lower-track students in Maplehurst, as in many other schools (Metz, 1978; Schwartz, 1981), is that lower-track students are "discipline problems" first and foremost. To a few teachers, this means that lower-track students, or at least one or two, are untrustworthy, even to the point of being dangerous: "I can't turn my back on the class"; "I wouldn't want to be in a room alone with *him*." More often in middle-class, midwestern Maplehurst, the "discipline problems" Additional Needs students present are "irritating" behaviors that threaten teachers' professional self-esteem and patience. The specific problems teachers enumerate include tardiness, being unprepared for class, truancy, not following directions, or impoliteness.

Teachers explain "discipline problems" with as much ambiguity as they explain lower-track students' academic and social competence. For example, they characterize students as acting both too young for their age ("like naughty fourth graders") and too old ("13, going on 30"). Thus, like young children with "short attention spans" or, alternatively, like hostile adults, students get restless in a 45-minute class period: They talk out, put their heads down, or turn to chat with friends. Almost all teachers lament as well that they were "not hired to be baby-sitters" or "social workers," yet they concentrate on admonishing students to bring pencils, to stop talking, or to "grow up and act your age." Equally contrarily, they are dismayed by students' evident "apathy," yet they regard students' engagement in lessons warily, worrying that classes will "explode" if students take matters too seriously.

Unpredictability in behavior seems to worry teachers most:

In general, lower-level kids are distracted. In class, there are callouts. They're up walking around the room when they shouldn't be.

They haven't been socialized to the middle-class Marshall classroom. They're really uncivilized, I guess you could say. Their attitude varies daily; they're not consistent. They can be good one day and bad the next. You can't count on them. Any one thing can set them off.

Because teachers perceive Additional Needs students as "not consistent," their preponderant concern becomes "keeping order." They "keep order" by taking measures to forestall its dissolution.

As with students' academic skills and family backgrounds, teachers use a negative stereotype to demarcate lower-track students' behavior from that of regular-track students, even though the differences can also be seen as a difference of degree, not of kind. Thus, when regular-track students arrive late, come unprepared for class, or are too boisterous, teachers do not infer fundamentally negative characters from such evidence. Indeed, obstreperousness in a regular class is sometimes labeled creativity. Furthermore, not all lower-track students behave as teachers claim, by talking too much or too hostilely, or by forgetting a pencil. Nevertheless, like academic competence, the behavioral competence of Additional Needs students receives less recognition in teachers' characterizations than students' potential for misbehavior. In teachers' commonsensical stories, Additional Needs students are "out-of-control."

In sum, Maplehurst teachers construct elaborate, dramatic, highly contradictory yet symbolically resonant stories to describe their understanding of and experiences with lower-track classes. The portrait blends multifarious intellectual, social, and behavioral traits. It informs teachers' perceptions and maintains a negative stereotype of the lower-track student, which appears commonsensical. Derived from snippets of educational research, media accounts of youth, local events, contexts of tracking, and broader sociocultural precepts of differentiation, the stereotype is visible in the order and emphasis undergirding the ambiguous, idiosyncratic anecdotes teachers tell. In Maplehurst, teachers manage the complexity lower-track students present by delineating their academic deficiencies, social and psychological disadvantages but, most emphatically, their "off-the-track" behaviors. Accordingly, although teachers are confused or pessimistic about students' ability or willingness to learn, they are less confused about students' need for control.

CHAPTER 3

What Teachers Do

If the teacher's definition of the lower-track student's role emerges in informally shared, ambiguous stories, like those recounted in Chapter 2, it is nevertheless not "merely" a story: an inconsequential, symbolic fiction recounted in interviews with an ethnographer or circulated privately within the realms of faculty lounges. Nor, however, does the teacher's reliance on a negative stereotype preordain self-evident outcomes by virtue of being a one-time label (Rist, 1979), an omnipotent teacher expectation (Rosenthal & Jacobsen, 1968), or a correspondence to objective or structural reality, whether intellectual, racial, or socioeconomic (Bowles & Gintis, 1976). Instead, the definition of the student's role matters when it becomes consequential in classroom lessons: Teachers design differentiated lower-track lessons, which translate their mixed expectations for students; students experience and react to the definition. In this chapter, I focus on the negotiations of the definition in a single lower-track lesson by analyzing that most common and mundane of classroom activities: talk.

DISCOURSE AND DISAGREEMENT IN TRACKED CLASSES

Classroom talk both exhibits and effectively maintains the school's "perilous despotism" (Waller, 1932) and the unequal social and intellectual roles of classroom participants. For example, its characteristic structure—a reciprocal, recitative exchange of teacher-question, student-answer, and teacher-reaction, followed by a next question (Bellack et al., 1966; Cazden, 1988; Dillon, 1988; Edwards & Furlong, 1978; Mehan, 1979)—provides for the orderly coverage of curriculum by 25 to 35 participants under one person's direction. In addition, teachers sometimes plan alternatives to the recitation: Discussion, debate, and disagreement may be instituted to "liven up the lesson" or because such forms are thought to better facilitate democratic, intellectual engagement (Battistoni, 1985).

Yet, the processes and effects of teachers' lessons are often unintentional and paradoxical. Their ambiguity can be specified by comparing the evolution and management of the usual structure of classroom discourse and an alternate form, disagreements, as they occur in Maplehurst's regular- and lower-track lessons. Talk provides a medium through which to track the production of lower-track "trouble" (even though conditions in Maplehurst's lower track auger for academic achievement), the emergence of the negative stereotype (even with reasonably competent lower-track students and experienced teachers), and the ironic, if subtle, impact of curricular ambiguity on students (even though lessons appear engaging and imaginative).

Discourse in Regular-Track Classes

Maplehurst's schools enjoy excellent reputations. Regular classes at Southmoor and Marshall are not the bland, privatized educational settings described in other high schools, where teachers and students negotiate "treaties" of low academic requirements in exchange for compliant behavior (McNeil, 1986; Powell et al., 1985; Sedlak, Wheeler, Pullin, & Cusick, 1986). Instead, regular classes are academically purposive, competently managed, and occasionally inspired. With considerable regularity, they are distinguished by lively public exchanges between and among students and teachers over the academic substance of the curriculum. Therefore, as evidenced in classroom talk, the regular-track student's role in Maplehurst's high schools is one of relaxed intellectual endeavor.

Teachers structure regular-track lessons to promote students' engagement with academic subject matter and skills. Without relinquishing their prerogatives and obligations to direct the sequence, topic, and meaning of classroom talk, teachers curb their dominance in classroom discourse and authority over knowledge to provide for student contributions. Because teachers expect diverse opinions to arise in the course of lessons, they plan lessons that allow for debate. Several emphasize the teaching of "critical thinking skills: I want them to get the facts and become aware that authorities like the press or governmental officials don't always tell all the facts, or slant the facts." Moreover, rather than perceiving disagreements as primarily disquieting events, teachers acknowledge them as the epitome of intellectual and democratic exercises and as signals of student involvement. Indeed, for many, the teacher's authority itself is not immune from criticism. Students may confront a teacher with the question, "Well, how do you know that?" and the query will not be regarded as impertinent. Teachers also allow the development of discordant exchanges between students. In short, teachers define the role of Maplehurst's regular students as recruits to the storehouse of knowledge, not as impassive imbibers.

Consequently, when Maplehurst teachers shift a structure of usual classroom discourse, it reflects the parallel shift in role definitions. The regular student's role is public as well as participatory, with the result that Maplehurst's regular classes are noticeable for the variety of voices. Recitations and lectures, punctuated by occasional seminarlike discussions and small-group work, are common modes of instruction. Individualized, silent, worksheet activities are rare. Teachers promote the public expression of students' opinions through explicit allocation of the floor to students. Two history teachers require regular-track students to begin class with presentations of extended, oral "editorials" to which peers respond directly. The teachers often validate the "editorials," not just with a perfunctory acknowledgment or a check in the grade book but by incorporating them into the development of the official lesson. In a regular English class, after students read their short stories aloud to the class, the teacher referred questions about themes or characters to "the author: Is that what *you* intended?" and thereby called attention to the student's authority over knowledge.

Discourse in Lower-Track Classes

In contrast to Maplehurst's regular classes, lower-track classes are notable for the absence of talk. All kinds—recitation, disagreement, debate—are less frequent than in regular classes. Instead, individualized work—worksheets, films, and silent reading—on noncontroversial topics is the most common activity. In several lower-track classrooms, worksheets constitute a near-invariant daily routine.

Thus, anticipating "trouble" from students whom they regard as uninterested in academics and as "lacking the critical thinking skills to participate in a discussion," teachers structure lower-track lessons for control. Yet, at the same time, Maplehurst teachers also provide for whole-class activities, in some of which students are expected to "discuss" or to "formulate disagreements." As teachers explain, classroom pragmatics require breaks in what can otherwise become deadening routines: They accede that instruction in the "basics" must also be "relevant" if students are to be motivated. Fundamentally, however, such lessons confuse: Reflecting teachers' mixed expectations, they both legitimate and circumscribe students' engagement with knowledge.

A LOWER-TRACK LESSON ABOUT GROUP COMMUNICATION

The lesson I analyze occurred in October 1982, in Mr. Bradley's ninth-grade, lower-track English class. Its "relevant" content (how people, including students, communicate in groups) and engaging form (discussion and disagreement) capture the ambiguity with which teachers define students in "adaptive" lessons.* On many counts, the lesson can be considered good: less trivial and controlling than many I observed in Maplehurst or than those summarized in research about tracking (see, e.g., Oakes, 1985). However, despite its commendable features, including the positive lower-track student role it implies, the lesson fulfills the teacher's prophecy that lower-track students will present "trouble" and that, because of their unpredictability, teachers cannot overemphasize "keeping order." Thus, the lesson exemplifies the troublesome anomaly posed by Maplehurst's lower track: A thoughtful, competently taught lesson that "hooks" scholastically uncertain students degenerates nevertheless to a "shouting match," reinforcing the negative stereotype and confirming the need for individualized instruction. The lesson poses the lower-track conundrum: How *does* a "circus" arise, especially when, as teachers acknowledge in both their talk and their lesson plans, Maplehurst's students are not wholly unskilled, uninterested, or antagonistic?

In Mr. Bradley's lower-track English class, there are just 18 ninth graders, rather than the 25 to 35 students he has in his regular-track classes. Sitting in alphabetical order in six rows of desks, all but three students are male; one is black; all are neatly, stylishly dressed; and all attended Maplehurst's public middle schools, except for two transfers from a local Catholic school. Students' scores on a standardized reading achievement test are below the 50th percentile, but most fall above the 25th percentile.

Although they are not high achievers, Mr. Bradley's ninth graders are good-natured and always ready to talk. Students come into the class chattering about boyfriends, sports, cycles, or the dissection of frogs, and they continue with conversations even after the bell rings. In interviews, they express eagerness to do well in high school and to earn a diploma. Almost all attend Mr. Bradley's class regularly, make some show of completing homework, and participate obediently in the daily lesson.

Mr. Bradley, a veteran of 14 years of teaching at Marshall, makes a conscious effort to encourage this informality and loquacity. Somewhat less traditional in his relations with students than other Marshall teachers, although not unlike many in the Maplehurst district in his informality, he expresses a rather hip style in his predilection for jeans, flannel shirts, and a moustache. Also, his ear for the adolescent vernacular, flair for the dramatic, and occasional use of small groups make Mr. Bradley's lessons more spontaneous, noisy, and at times rambunctious than other lower-

---

*For the "relevant" lower-track curriculum, see also Chapter 8.

track classes. For example, Mr. Bradley gives a quiz at the end of the first week that requires students to reproduce a class seating chart. As he explains, the activity helps the ninth graders learn each other's names and therefore to participate more comfortably in whole-class activities. And, more than other lower-track teachers at Marshall, Mr. Bradley engages the class by presenting or reconstructing topics so that they are "relevant" to students. Thus, although still distinguished from regular classes by a predominance of worksheets, films, and silent reading periods, Mr. Bradley's lower-track class includes occasional extended recitations.

Planning a Lesson: Considering "Relevance"

The lower-track recitation I analyze occurred as part of a 2-day lesson about the "communicative power" of a group of six fictional characters. Legitimating public discourse about a controversial topic, the lesson was the culminating activity of a 3-week unit on group communication. The communication unit followed a 4-week stint reading *Romeo and Juliet* and preceded a 4-week unit on the mechanics of composition.

Early in the communications unit, Mr. Bradley taught students that various factors influence group communication: group size, the importance to discussants of the topic, whether discussants know one another, and whether the group is "cohesive—are they like the other members in the group?" Furthermore, Mr. Bradley gave the lesson a political cast. He taught that people wield "power" when they communicate in groups. Some participants "come to a group with more power," depending on their education, age, looks, or wealth. Others "earn power" in the group, because they are experts on the topics to be discussed. Basing these general notions about communication on a chapter in a college speech text, Mr. Bradley presented them in a variety of modes during the 3-week unit: brief lectures, films, recitations, short stories, and written worksheets.

On many counts, the lesson and the unit project the teacher's positive assessment of Additional Needs students and a positive student role. The curriculum offers substantive, academic content; it requires higher-order and divergent thinking skills; and it prompts students' active, public contributions to school knowledge. However, the unit's final lesson also fulfills the prophecy of lower-track "trouble": As it unfolds, students exhibit the very academic deficiencies, obstreperous behaviors, and educational indifference that Mr. Bradley predicts in interviews and then uses to justify the more common routine of individualized seatwork.

Thus, Mr. Bradley voices considerable ambivalence about the unit and its final lesson. Because of his interest and training in speech, Mr. Bradley is certain that "all freshmen need a unit on group communication." However, he is "less certain that Additional Needs students get anything out of the unit." And, even though students are actively involved in the final lesson, Mr. Bradley expresses concern afterwards about both their orderliness and their understanding:

> I never know quite how far to let things go. I want them to talk about these things, but they can get out of hand so easily. Then I have to stop it - - - I think one of the things that I feel with them is that a lot of times you can't really get into the things that you'd like to get into, that you can teach to regular classes. Or you can't get the depth. It's kinda fun to make a connection with something that is a little bit more than just the basics in teaching, you know. And it's not often possible to do that with Additional Needs kids because they're so limited. And so you can't really dig in very deeply - - - What we were doing today (in the lesson to be examined here), maybe that was a mistake, I think generally, overall, those kids didn't know what they were doing.

Setting the Stage: A Commonsensical "Story" About Social Relationships

The perennial classroom dilemma, coupled with expectations that skew its enactment in Maplehurst's lower track toward an overemphasis on control and a deemphasis on education, is visible in the explicit *content* of Mr. Bradley's last lesson in the communication unit. That is, Mr. Bradley signals his expectations for students in the subject matter he presents. Indeed, he expects to motivate students by casting school knowledge in terms they will find "relevant."

Mr. Bradley sets the stage for the following day's final recitation by telling a "story of six hypothetical characters: We're going to put (them) together in a group and see how they will communicate." In a lively but unrushed mode, with fluorescent lights dimmed, and making occasional notes on the softly humming overhead projector, Mr. Bradley describes the fictional characters. While he tells the "story," students take notes, occasionally interrupt to ask questions, or interject comments and quips of their own.

The first character, *Mike*, appears:

> Mike is 14 years old, a ninth grader at the high school. . . . His father makes $90,000 a year - - so he's pretty well off. . . . Mike gets along with the parking lot crowd at the high school but is not a part of it (doubting noises from some students). . . . He letters in

three – THREE! – sports: football, basketball, baseball. This is very unusual, but he was able to do it. . . . Is he smart? He is an honor student, straight A's. . . . And he's very good-looking. . . . He's also the student body president. . . . You might think he'd be a snob, but he's not. Kids like him. All the girls would like to have a date with him. . . . Oh, yes, and he races a dirt bike in the summertime (appreciative murmurs from the boys in the class, many of whom carry cycle magazines to class).

A foil to Mike, the second fictional character, *Ray*, is a stereotype of the lower-track student:

Ray is handsome – 15 years old. A high school dropout, but he is smart. He didn't drop out because he couldn't do the work . . . he comes from a different economic background than Mike: He has eight brothers and sisters, his dad has left home, and his mother works as a waitress, making $8,000 per year. . . . Because of his family, to help out his mother, Ray has had to work part-time jobs for quite some time. . . . He's been in a little trouble, here and there, suspended for this and that: drinking, or drugs, or cutting classes. . . . He's having kind of a tough time of it, not because he's a *bad* kid, but because of family problems. . . . He is the oldest of eight kids. . . . Ray has a pretty tough life, needless to say.

Mr. Bradley describes the other four characters in the fictional group in a similar fashion. *Mr. Smith* is the 58-year-old principal, well-educated and well-off. He has grown children and grandchildren and spends time working with youth groups in the community. He is a "good fellow, most of the kids like him at school, everybody thinks he's pretty fair." *Officer Bill* is a 27-year-old policeman who works in the Drug and Alcohol Program at the high school of which Mr. Smith is principal. He "busted" Ray on at least one occasion. "But he's not like the usual policeman who rides around in a patrol car and tells you to get out of the local Stop 'n Go - - He's more like a counselor." *Leroy Johnson* is a 32-year-old black teacher at Smith's high school. He has a reputation for being a "tough teacher: You have him and you work in class. It's not like this class." Both Ray and Mike are students in Mr. Johnson's class.

The last character Mr. Bradley introduces is *Mary*. A male student wisecracks, "Virgin Mary," and the Additional Needs class dissolves in laughter. Dramatically, Mr. Bradley walks across the room, puts his hand on the student's shoulder, and quietly, but firmly, says: "Will! you! please!

be! quiet! You *know* you tend to irritate me." The laughter subsides easily and the teacher continues with the "story":

> Mary is 24. . . . She is a secretary, makes about $12,000 a year. . . . She graduated from high school, but not from Smith's high school. . . . She's very good looking - - this (pointing to his cartoon drawing on the overhead) is just a bad photo of her (laughter, catcalls from the students about the teacher's artistic ability and Mary's hair style). . . . She's single. . . . She was an average student in high school. . . . She does have two younger brothers who attend Smith's high school. . . . Mary is the only person of the six in the group who doesn't know anyone else in the group before its first meeting.

After the description of Mary, Mr. Bradley explains that the group of six characters is convened to "discuss the problem of drugs and drinking going on around the high school and how to solve it." He closes his introduction of the fictional group by assigning homework: On the basis of his descriptions, students are to apply their knowledge about group communication by ranking the six characters in terms of their communicative power. Students are given 20 minutes to "get started on working individually on the homework," and most finish before the bell.

This "story" of six characters, the recitation that follows it the next day, and the 3-week unit of which both are the culmination present students with classroom exercises in which the explicit goal is higher-order thinking skills: Students are to apply the abstract principles of group communications in the analysis of the dynamics of a particular fictional group.

Furthermore, Mr. Bradley's description of the communicative behavior of the fictional group of six characters has added personal meaning for students by virtue of its "relevance." Following common prescriptions for remedial lessons, Mr. Bradley's "story" parallels the particular realities of Additional Needs students in Maplehurst. Several students in Mr. Bradley's class are like Ray: They are 14 or 15, have been "busted" for drugs, and have contemplated leaving school. Some belong to the "parking lot crowd" that Mr. Bradley mentions, the label by which Marshall's delinquent students are known. Indeed, Mr. Bradley explicitly directs students to "put yourself in the group" to determine how characters will influence one another. He admonishes them: "*Romeo and Juliet* may have seemed like it was 'out there.' This stuff is not out there; it's right here and now."

Nevertheless, if Mr. Bradley's presentation of communicative principles is designed to motivate students to "*think*" about social and communicative differences, it also maps the social world in a particular way. For example, in the teacher's account, the straight-A student, Mike, will be expected to influence the principal more than Ray, the dropout. By contrast, Ray will evoke sympathy: "He's had a tough life." Mr. Bradley does not discuss why group communication works this way. As a result, although the teacher constructs the group's characters so that stereotypical differences between them will provoke students "to bring all the things (communicative principles) into play," the academic material and the significance of its latent sociocultural assumptions are also presented as self-evident and realistic.

Students react to the lesson with interest. They accept many of the links between the lesson's formal content, their knowledge of the way the world works, and their personal school situations. For example, they extend the descriptions of the characters by adding their own common-sense knowledge. One student suggests (with the hesitancy appropriate to broaching sexuality in schools) that Mike and Ray may be competitive in the group "'cause Mary's there, and she's kinda young, and you said she's good-looking, and they're kinda - - you know - - they'll show off."

As the lesson intertwines theoretical precepts about group communication with students' experiences, it forges a particularly tight relationship between curricular, cultural, and personal knowledge. Its content furnishes students an analogy: The educational and social principles that govern communication in the fictional group will govern discourse in Mr. Bradley's lower-track classroom. Thus, the content of the "here and now" lesson presents real students with information not just about abstract communication but about *their* communicative role.

Framing the Lesson for Differences of Opinion: "More Than One Right Answer"

The teacher's definition of the lower-track student's role is also translated and made visible to students through the *form* of classroom talk. That is, students learn about group communication, theoretically and personally, through how they are allowed to talk, as well as through what they are allowed to talk about. Specifically, in this case, students encounter disagreements as the height of intellectual discourse, but their engagement in it is limited.

Mr. Bradley, in his introduction to the communication lesson, explicitly states that students will participate publicly in a group discussion that will include disagreements about the relative communicative power of the fictional group members. He sets down the ground rules for an activity in which "several right answers" are legitimated:

1 T: *Drinking* and *drugs* in the high school, awright? That's the
2   topic that's going to be discussed (by the fictional group).
3   What I want to do - - is *find out* how you ranked them
4   positionally - - how you ranked them according to earned
5   power. . . . Awright! And this is important - - I *don't*
6   *think* - - that there is *onnne* right answer here. As long as
7   you can tell me *why you feel* that so-and-so might have more
8   positional power than so-and-so, you, there may be *several*
9   right answers, as long as you can back up your answer. I
10   think in *sommme* cases - - some answers are better than others,
11   some are *morrrre* right than others, but there are a lot of
12   them that could be about the same. So. Let's take a look
13   (1.0) and start with Mr. Green. Let's just run through your
14   ranking. Who did you rank one, two, three, four, fiiive,
15   six?

Although Mr. Bradley legitimates diverse opinions and open-ended discussion in this framing move, he also interjects elements of ambiguity. On the one hand, the teacher indicates that he wants "to find out" how students rank the fictitious characters. To encourage participation in the recitation as it gets under way as well as for content objectives, he emphasizes that there is no "*one* right answer." This comment forecasts the possibility of controversy and differing opinions. Instead of univocal answers, Mr. Bradley insists twice that the correctness of an answer will be determined by whether participants can give reasons for their opinions on the issues and "back up" their ideas. Hence, his position as teacher will ostensibly not be the traditional one of determining right and wrong answers according to an answer sheet but, instead, will involve judging students' skills of argumentation. On the other hand, Mr. Bradley also states that some answers are "more right than others." Because he does not specify how the "better answers" will be identified, he retains authority in the discussion, but he defines it so that its scope is uncertain.

As it turns out, the ambiguity of the frame sets up the lesson's. One might predict that Mr. Bradley's lesson will have considerable debate about the relative power of the six characters: It is possible to imagine one student's proposing Mr. Smith as first in positional power because of his age and job and another's proposing, in disagreement, Officer Bill, because of his job and expertise with the drug problem.

Instead of debate, however, usual classroom discourse prevails. Constructing the ritualized ping-pong that distinguishes classroom talk, the class spends the first 25 minutes in orderly, uneventful coverage of the controversial topics. They agree that Mr. Smith, Mike, and Officer Bill come to the group with the most power; Ray is deemed a particularly good candidate for earning power once the group begins meeting because he has had experience with drugs; no one nominates Mary, the secretary, or the black teacher, Mr. Johnson, for powerful group membership or, indeed, even mentions them. Overall, direct disagreements in a lesson that begs for them are remarkable by their *absence.*

Establishing the Recitation: The Achievement of an Absence of Disagreements

The absence of direct disagreements in the first half of Mr. Bradley's lesson is an *achievement.* The absence is achieved primarily through participants' collaboration in establishing the usual tripartite recitation structure of teacher-question/student-response/teacher-reaction. This three-part discourse form allows teachers and students to accomplish the two major classroom goals: They "cover" the controversial material that Mr. Bradley designed, and they do so in an orderly fashion. In the collaboration, teachers control the topics and the turns of talk, because they occupy the third, or reacting, position. However, recitations remain joint constructions: If students do not participate, a recitation will flounder, and the teacher will not be able to teach. In short, if Mr. Bradley is too harsh in his evaluations, students may withdraw, but if he does not evaluate at all, the lesson's meaning will deteriorate.

Following the initial framing of the lesson, Mr. Bradley and students set in motion the ritualized structure of the recitation. The teacher calls on Steve to "run through" his ranking of the six characters in terms of the power with which they enter the group. Orienting to Mr. Bradley's question, Steve reads from his homework and responds:

```
16   STEVE:  Mr. Smith, Officer⌈Bill,
17      T:                     ⌊Mr. Smith came first. Officer Bill,
18           second. Look at your own list right now.
19   STEVE:  Leroy Johnson, Mary⌈-
20      T:                       ⌊Leroy Johnson, Mary
21   STEVE:  Mike 'n Ray.
22      T:   Mike (1.0) and Ray - - last. Okay! (snaps fingers)
```

The opening lines of discourse illustrate the reflexive, social, three-part structure of usual classroom discourse. Like an intricate, coordinated dance, participants in the structure reflect and re-create the crucial, yet delicate, balance between educative and instrumental goals. Mr. Bradley opens with a question. Working reflexively, Steve matches his response to the teacher's elicitation. Promptly, he provides the appropriate content (name of characters) in the correct form (a list) at the appropriate juncture (after the question). In reaction, Mr. Bradley validates Steve's answer (lines 17–18). He interrupts him to repeat and broadcast the two names. Simultaneously, he clarifies that Steve's list of names is appropriately ranked: "Mr. Smith came *first*" (my emphasis).

Mr. Bradley concludes his interruption of Steve with a multipurpose directive to the rest of the class that illustrates the economy of classroom talk: "Look at your *own* list right now." With only these few words, Mr. Bradley confirms that the list being offered is not the only list possible and that there may be different lists: Each person in the room has her or his "*own* list." The directive also anticipates the future contributions of the rest of the class when Steve's list is completed, thus reminding students that this is a *class* activity. Further, it reminds students that at present they are only to "look" at their lists, not shout out where they differ with Steve. Economically but powerfully, the opening exchange establishes the ritualized form of talk that children learn in school (Mehan, 1979), secures orderly exchanges, and accomplishes topical coherence by echoing the teacher's frame and foreshadowing future issues.

When the teacher completes his first interruption (line 18), Steve resumes his list: "Leroy Johnson, Mary –." In this second turn, Steve hesitates after naming the next two characters. The pause recognizes Mr. Bradley's previous interruption and provides the opportunity for the teacher to comment again. Hearing the pause, Mr. Bradley fulfills the expectation by again repeating Steve's answer, in both cadence and content (line 20). Then Steve completes his list by naming the last two characters (line 21), and Mr. Bradley's repetition again confirms Steve's answer as an acceptable ranking: ". . . and Ray – – *last*" (my emphasis). Together, reciprocally, teacher and students develop the lesson.

Although collaborative, the familiar rhythm of classroom discourse concentrates control of the lesson in teachers' hands. Because possession of the floor returns to them in the third, reacting, move, teachers can shape meaning, guide topic development, and direct turns at talk. Furthermore, from the third position, teachers can also manage the emergence and evolution of disagreements. In particular, by occupying the third position, teachers can stand between, or buffer, the response of one student from the different response of another.

The processes by which Mr. Bradley controls the occurrence of disagreements yet retains students' active and necessary participation so that a recitation proceeds are well illustrated in the talk following Steve's list:

22	T:	Mike (1.0) and Ray - - last. Okay! (snaps fingers)
23		Let's run around and get a couple more here. Yeah, some,
24		anybody, have - - something *different* from that one?
25		Butler, yeah.
26	BUTCH:	Mr. Smith, Leroy Johnson, Officer Bill - - MaryMike'nRay.
27		(4.0)
28	T:	That's almost the same, wasn't it?
29	BUTCH:	Yeah, but Leroy Johnson and Officer Bill are
30		(undecipherable).
31	S:	I put Leroy Johnson
32	S:	- Ray, you know -
33	T:	Okay - - Here - - Number one (writing on the overhead
34		projector). Let's do it *this* way.
35		Smith - - (2.5)
36	BUTCH:	(yawn-groan)
37	S.	Let me write that down.
38	DICK:	I got something.
39	T:	Okay! Hang on. Did anybody else put - - a *different* person
40		(snaps fingers) in the number one spot? (snaps fingers)
41	DICK:	I put the cop.
42	T:	Okay, that's Officer Bill. (4.0). Awright.

Here, from the third position in usual classroom discourse, Mr. Bradley
controls disagreements in a variety of ways. For example, he adheres to the
lesson's design for more than "one right answer" by explicitly asking for a
list of characters that is "different from" Steve's (lines 23–24). Butch
(Butler) responds. He reads the names of his three most powerful characters slowly, pauses, then adds the last three characters in a rush: "Mr. Smith,
Leroy Johnson, Officer Bill - - MaryMike'nRay." The phrasing of the
answer signals that the difference between Butch's list of six characters and
Steve's lies in the first three positions and not in the last three rushed items.
However, a long, 4-second, silence (line 27) follows Butch's response rather
than an expected "Okay" from Mr. Bradley. The teacher, perhaps intuiting
the confusion that surrounds a complex comparison of 18 different lists of
six characters each, abruptly changes the topic to one of naming the single
most powerful character: "Here. Number one. Let's do it *this* way" (lines
33–34). This strategy makes differences easier to manage because it does
away with students' having to compare long lists, as they had to do with
Steve's and Butch's lists of six. At the same time, it limits the number of
potential disagreements that can reach the floor at any one time.

Furthermore, Mr. Bradley's reaction to Butch's list also reflects the
care with which differences of opinion must be handled. The 4-second

silence, followed by a correction put in question form—"That's about the same, isn't it?"—allows Butch the time and turn to repair his answer himself (Schegloff, Jefferson, & Sacks, 1977). Use of this mode, preferred in naturally occurring conversations, contributes in classrooms to the student's motivation to continue in the recitation and, hence, to the accomplishment of Mr. Bradley's overall goals. Had Mr. Bradley declared, rather than asked, "That's about the same as the first list we heard," his evaluation of Butch's list would have been harsher. Although teachers in the reacting position have the prerogative to make such an evaluation, they must always balance ensuring students' active participation and the recitation's continuation against evaluating students' responses and possibly discouraging ongoing participation.

Most importantly, from the third, reacting position in usual classroom discourse, Mr. Bradley can buffer students' differences with each other and prevent direct disagreements. When Butch proposes a ranked list of the six characters that is different from Steve's, he speaks to Mr. Bradley, not to Steve. Moreover, it is Mr. Bradley, not Steve, who reacts to Butch's list. Therefore, the usual classroom discourse structure allows for a variety of "right answers" to a question to be *arrayed*. Contradictory ideas can be set side by side, without calling attention to the fact of their opposition as would happen in any direct conversation between the students. This meets the ambiguous requirements of Mr. Bradley's curious lesson in which differences of opinion are explicitly solicited but are not constructed as direct, potentially uncontrollable disagreements: Students are encouraged to express a variety of "right answers" about a controversial topic (the lesson's educative goal), while simultaneously their disagreements and any anger are neutralized by the teacher (the lesson's instrumental goal).

Achieving a Classroom Disagreement: Conflict Between the Forms of Usual Classroom Discourse and Disagreements

Remarkably, Mr. Bradley designs a lesson that legitimates disagreements, yet he implements the lesson so that disagreements are absent. This inconsistency is understandable, given teachers' profound ambivalence regarding disagreements, which itself resonates with the wider culture's ambivalence toward conflict.

For example, Maplehurst teachers claim to welcome and provide for disagreements because they "liven up the lesson," indicate student involvement, and are the epitome of intellectual and democratic exercises. However, the implicit rules of classroom talk do not allow students to express the evaluation on which disagreements depend (Bellack et al., 1966). Furthermore, teachers portray children and adolescents—particularly academically unsuccessful adolescents—as less sophisticated than adults in skills of argumentation and as uninterested in or uninformed about the academic topics of school lessons. Therefore, any discussion that "takes off," as disagreements do, also threatens the orderliness of the classroom. Although a good argument may provide intellectual energy, it also contravenes teachers' control of noise levels, topics, meanings, and, ultimately, the teachers' authority.

Nevertheless, disagreements do arise in high school lessons and they differentiate regular- and lower-track classes in Maplehurst. Disagreements are not unusual in regular lessons in Maplehurst because teachers plan for them. Indeed, they may account for the élan of Maplehurst's regular classes and the regular students' active, public role.

Surprisingly, given teachers' feeling that conflict is much greater in lower-track classes, disagreements there are quite uncommon. Nevertheless, their significance is considerable: In their evolution, they make visible the. ambiguity of the students' prerogatives, students' struggles to act competently in the face of mixed messages, and the cross-purposes with which teachers and students may interpret school knowledge.

The first and the major disagreement in Mr. Bradley's lesson concerns Mary, the secretary. Voiced only after 25 minutes of ritualized recitation have elapsed, during which time Mary is not even mentioned, the disagreement begins with four students but eventuates in a long string of confrontations that draws in almost all other students and Mr. Bradley. It echoes through the remainder of the lesson, prompting continuing argument whenever Mary's power to influence the fictional group is broached. Indeed, it becomes part of the history of Mr. Bradley's lower-track class: When students reviewed for the final examination 2 months later, Mary revived all the passions of the original encounter.

The meaning of the lengthy disagreement about Mary is carried in both its substance and the way Mr. Bradley manages it. Through the disagreement, lower-track students learn that neither their perspectives nor the teacher's perspectives are entirely commonsensical. In addition, the students experience that their prerogatives are decidedly ambiguous: In disagreements about school knowledge, even in a lesson that calls explicitly for their participation, their participation is very limited.

The disagreement about Mary begins as Mr. Bradley turns the class to a consideration of the secretary's ability to earn communicative power:

101   T: Um. (3.0) Who haven't we talked about in terms of earned
102   power? (1.0) How about Ma⌈ry?
103   PATTY: ⌊Mary.

104	T:	How about Mary?
105	DICK:	She ain't ⌐ – (softly)
106	T:	⌊ Where's Mary going to fit into the picture?
107	BUTCH:	At the end (softly).
108	T:	Where's Mary going to fit into the picture? Yeah! Butch!
109	BUTCH:	At the ennnd.
110	T:	Why at the end? I agree with you. Tell me why.
111	BUTCH:	She's only ⌐ a secretary –
112	DICK:	⌊ She's just a secretary.
113	BUTCH:	– What's she know about this problem?
114	PATTY:	Yeah, but she, ⌐ she's got – younger brothers ⌐ and –
115	TIFFANY:	⌊ She's got – ⌊ – younger
116	PATTY:	– sisters that ar ⌐ e in school.
117	TIFFANY:	⌊ – involved in school.
118	T:	She's got two younger brothers – –
119	BUTCH:	Well, she talks to them every day about it (sarcastically,
120		facing Patty and Tiffany).
121	T:	She's got two younger brothers – ⌐ –
122	PATTY:	⌊ She might have given
123		them (advice?)
124	T:	Okay! Okay. Hang on. (1.0) Go ahead, Louis.

The emergence of disagreements is difficult to predict, but their form is as recognizable as that of usual classroom discourse. An assertion by one speaker prompts another's counterassertion (e.g., "no"; "yes, but"), which is then followed by moves to resolve the disagreement and, eventually, by a final exiting move (whether or not the disagreement is resolved). In Mr. Bradley's lesson, an assertion by one class member (line 109) provokes a counterassertion by another (line 114). Butch, supported by Dick, sarcastically responds to the teacher's question about Mary's role in the group. Emphatically, Mary is powerless: "She's only a secretary – – What's she know about this problem?" (lines 111-113). The boys' assertion prompts a counterassertion by two girls, Patty and Tiffany (lines 114-117). Contradicting Butch's and Dick's opinion (and Mr. Bradley's, line 110), Patty asserts that Mary may be able to earn power in the group, rather than occupy a position "at the end" of the ranking. The initial confrontation then spawns a train of heated resolution moves and additional disagreements about Mary.

The noteworthy feature of direct disagreements is that the counterassertion is a *reacting* move. That is, a student, rather than the teacher, performs the evaluation. Patty's reaction follows the event that precipitates it—Butch's extreme answer—with no buffering move by the teacher.

Consequently, the teacher's position of control over the direction and content of classroom talk is preempted as Patty and Tiffany take the reacting position. Structurally, direct disagreements (teacher question/ student response/ *student* evaluation) contrast with usual classroom discourse and the merely implicit expression of disagreement through arraying (teacher question/ student response/ *teacher* evaluation).

The course of a disagreement, once voiced, is mutually charted by participants in the classroom as they work to resolve it. In their negotiations, participants are at cross-purposes on substantive issues; that is, they disagree about some topic. In addition, they may act at cross-purposes within contradictory discourse structures that specify different rules for one's talk and role (Pomerantz, 1978). That is, classroom participants may also differ about whether having a disagreement is their appropriate agenda.

For example, from the teacher's vantage point, students may appear "out of order" when they operate within the disagreement structure and therefore occupy the third, reacting position. Indeed, in the third position, students *are* out-of-the-order of conventional classroom discourse and the respondent's role. Thus, when teachers say that arguments give unequal amounts of floor time to a few students, lead to "free-for-alls" and "crushed feelings," or sidetrack coverage of the lesson, their perceptions are neither uptight, knee-jerk prejudices nor authoritarian personality defects. Their perceptions have a real, if largely unconscious, basis in the structure of classroom talk.

Contrarily, in the view of students who operate within a disagreement structure, they are legitimately engaging with the lesson's content because, in a disagreement, one *must* occupy the third position to make the counterassertion. Thus, students may discount as illegitimate teachers' attempts to stop disagreements, regain control, and reestablish regular classroom discourse. From that perspective, "Teachers just don't listen to what we have to say."

The contradiction between the discourse structures resonates with teachers' differentiated expectations for regular- and lower-track students. Whereas in regular classes Maplehurst teachers promote and sustain students' public disagreement, they read similar behaviors differently in the lower track: Disagreements there are "shout-outs," "childish arguing," "trouble," or a "circus." Within such a context, and even though he has planned for disagreements in the lesson, Mr. Bradley's immediate impulse is to *stop* the disagreement between Patty/Tiffany and Butch/Dick to regain control of the situation. He interjects a reaction (line 118), possibly a correction, to Patty's counterassertion, noting that Mary has "got two younger brothers" and therefore may know something about the drug problem at the high school. However, even when repeated a second time (line 121), Mr. Bradley's interjection fails to stop the direct disagreement between the absorbed students. Finally, Mr. Bradley loudly suggests that the disagreement be set aside momentarily: "Hang on" (line 124). He then calls on Louis, a student who heretofore has not been a party to the disagreement, perhaps hoping that a new discussant will divert attention from the argument about Mary.

Despite the teacher's efforts to stop the disagreement about Mary and thereby regain control of the lesson, students, with Louis leading off in the second round, persist in their interest in the formal topic of Mary's power. They are engaged by Mr. Bradley's lesson:

```
125    LOUIS: She isn't even in that school and she doesn't have nothing
126           to do with it and that - ⌈-
127    BUTCH:                        ⌊(She's got (indecipherable)
128    LOUIS: - and she ain't going ⌈to be talking to her
129    PATTY:                        ⌊(undecipherable)
130    LOUIS: little brothers and stuff ⌈when, you know, every time
131    BUTCH:                            ⌊(undecipherab⌈le)
132       T:                                          ⌊(snaps fingers)
133    LOUIS: when they ⌈come home from school.
134    PATTY:          ⌊(giggles)⌈
135       T:                     ⌊(snaps fingers)
136       T: Did you hear that?
137    PATTY: (giggles)
138    BUTCH: Yeah.
139     DICK: Yep.
140       T: What's her only link? Probably her little brothers.
141          Is that a strong link?
142    CLASS: (in unison) NOOOOOO.
143       T: Probably not.
144     MIKE: They probably wouldn't tell her anything anyway.
145       T: Probably wouldn't tell her too much anyway.
146    PATTY:          ⌊They're *not* going to tell her *nothing*!
147       T: She's 10 years, what's she, 24?
148       S: Yeah.
149       T: So she's probably, uh, 7, 8, 9 years older than
150          they are anyway. She is *not* in the high school. (1.0)
151          She, she's got a couple of things going for her, but none
152          of them are strong. She, I doubt, I agree with you, I
153          don't think she's going to earn a lot of power. How many
154          people had Mary *last* on their list? How many people had
```

155   Mary last on their list? Hands! (only three students raise
156   hands) Now that surprises me.

Here, Patty and Butch continue their interchange about Mary in illicit whispers (lines 127–134), even though the teacher has given the floor to Louis. Mr. Bradley implicitly recognizes the operation of both the disagreement and official structures when he snaps his fingers at Butch and Patty as they continue their disagreement sotto voce (lines 132; 135): He reprimands the two disputants for continuing to talk, but he does not interrupt the usual classroom discourse structure that he has just reestablished and under which Louis has the floor.

Furthermore, as their discourse illustrates, the lower-track students are not only "hooked" by Mary but they pursue their disagreement with considerable skill and perseverance, notwithstanding Maplehurst lore that disparages their ability to debate. Patty, Butch, and other students spiritedly, not mindlessly, offer reasons for their positions and rebuttals to those they oppose. For example, Patty and Tiffany assert that Mary will indeed know something about the drug and alcohol problem through her younger brothers. Butch counters that he doubts that Mary talks to her much younger siblings about such topics (lines 119–120). But Patty responds that an older sister might give some occasional advice (line 122). Thus, students follow Mr. Bradley's directions in the original framing of the lesson: Using argumentation and justification of opinions, they "back up" their answers by telling him "*why* (they) *feel* that so-and-so might have more power." At the same time, they persevere with the disagreement. Indeed, Mr. Bradley has some trouble getting students to shift their attention to the next character, Mr. Johnson, even when he adds the weight of his personal opinion: "Still, though, Mary would be on the bottom of my list. I think Mike would be in front of her, *I* think so."

Double Differentiation

Teachers' intuition that they lose control during disagreements is prompted as well by a second feature of direct disagreements in classrooms: siding. In this phenomenon, students take sides with one or the other of the original disputants in a disagreement so that volume and numbers, rather than argumentation, often take precedence. Siding may appear especially problematic to lower-track teachers because it corresponds to their perceptions of the classes as "dumping grounds for behavior problems," or as classes "without positive role models." If several students join together, teachers may feel themselves outnumbered by a "negative peer group."

In the disagreement about Mary, siding occurs in the opening salvo, when Dick collaborates with Butch in his assessment of Mary's rank, even to the extent of echoing Butch's derogation of Mary: "She's only a secretary"/"She's just a secretary" (lines 111-112). In parallel fashion, Tiffany joins Patty in the counterassertion: "She's got younger brothers and - - sisters that are in school"/"She's got - - younger - [?] - involved in school" (lines 114-117).

Concern about "shouting matches" and the emergence of unified groups of students is reflected in Mr. Bradley's response to the disagreement between Butch/Dick and Patty/Tiffany. Rather than legitimating their difference of opinion by directing one party to state its case and the other party to listen and respond, he gives the floor to Louis, a student who was not a part of the original disagreement. Louis, however, does not deflect but extends the disagreement as he sides with the other males. He offers a new reason for Mary's uninfluential position in the fictional group: Mary won't know about the drug problem at the high school because she is not in the high school. This part of Louis's statement functions not just as another reason in an array of reasons for Mary's lack of power but also as a disparagement of Patty's reasoning (in line 122). It implicitly denies Patty's argument that Mary can learn about the drug problem at the high school through her siblings. In addition, Louis goes on to make his siding with Butch explicit. He repeats Butch's earlier statement about Mary: " - and she ain't going to be talking to her little brothers and stuff when, you know, every time when they come home from school" (lines 128-133). Thus, although Louis is new to the discussion and may have been called on by the teacher to divert the argument between Patty and Butch, this is not what happens. Instead, students align themselves with each other in disputes, and the teacher's ability to direct classroom talk and maintain order is potentially diminished.

Siding also has important ramifications for processes of differentiation *among* students in a lower-track class. In Maplehurst, male students outnumber females by a large margin in seven of the eight lower-track classrooms I regularly observed. In Mr. Bradley's class, there were 15 boys and 3 girls. Because of the operation of siding, lower-track female students may find themselves simply outnumbered rather than outargued. Thus, when girls (or others of minority status) argue, they may appear strident and may therefore be dismissed as cranks, simply because they are so few. This is precisely what happens in Mr. Bradley's lesson. As the subject of Mary continues in renewed debates, Patty consistently but unsuccessfully carries the defense. Only once does a male student contribute an argument in favor of Mary's having power in the group. Such an imbalanced outcome is less likely in regular-track classrooms where the sexes are generally more evenly distributed.

Furthermore, the judgment about Mary's position may intensify the role of the three girls in Mr. Bradley's classroom because of the way Mr. Bradley structures "relevance." In his "story," Mary is the only woman and she is a secretary: "She didn't fit real well (in the group) and you had to think about why she didn't." Yet the fictional group could have been equally "relevant" and illustrative of communicative dynamics had it included several women, such as a female student or administrator. Instead, Mr. Bradley's narrative reproduces a negatively stereotypical image of women's place in the world and provides for its continued viability in his lower-track class.

Are Patty and Tiffany, like fictional Mary, to accept a powerless position in the classroom because, as Patty eventually notes in explaining Mary's lack of power, "She's the only female"? In the fictional group, gender sets Mary apart from the other group members. She has many status-enhancing characteristics, according to the commonsensical factors enumerated in Mr. Bradley's introductory description: money, education, age, and appearance. On at least three of these, she outranks both Ray and Mike, the teenage students. Nonetheless, Mr. Bradley's predominantly male class argues that the male adolescents have more power than a female adult. Analogously, do Butch and Dick have more power in Mr. Bradley's classroom than Patty and Tiffany because they are in the male majority?

Here, the complexity of curriculum differentiation and its translational relationship to broader precepts of social differentiation is particularly salient. The overrepresentation of boys in lower-track classrooms, the discourse phenomenon of siding, and the "relevant" content conjoin to produce important differentiated meaning for the lower-track student's role in general and added impact for a particular subgroup. Although gender is not supposed to be a factor in one's role as a student, in this lesson it is both visible and troubling. The oblique operation of these processes suggests how other minorities—blacks, mainstreamed special education students, poor students, English-as-a-second-language students—may experience a doubly differentiated lower-track student role (see also Goldstein, 1990; Lesko, 1990).

Resolving Classroom Disagreements

Siding and the contradictory discourse structures of disagreement and usual classroom talk stimulate negative aspects of teachers' ambivalent expectations regarding lower-track students. They prompt teachers to stop direct disagreements quickly so as to regain control. Even in lower-track classrooms, however, teachers' strategies for managing disagreements cannot be too heavy-handed. Concern for order is balanced by educational concern to keep the lesson moving and the recitation viable. If teachers impose their opinions or terminate disagreements too autocratically, students' willingness to participate as respondents in recitations may be squelched. Furthermore, imposing one's will in regard to an issue of meaning or content uses up authority that teachers in lower-track classrooms may want to conserve for more critical control issues (Metz, 1978). Finally, as in Mr. Bradley's case, the nature of open-ended lessons with "several right answers" makes the teacher's authority to pronounce *the* "right answer" less certain.

Teachers' resolution strategies reflect these constraints. As a result, disagreements in lower-track classrooms are closed subtly, so that conflict between teacher and students is concealed but the teacher's point of view prevails. Students are rarely encouraged or allowed to resolve disagreements among themselves.

Teachers' resolution strategies include taking a vote, amalgamating divergent opinions, imposing teacher categories, and simply going on. Taking a vote is a strategy in which the teacher avoids imposing his or her own opinion and appeals instead to majority rule. Mr. Bradley takes a vote when he asks whether Mary's link to the drug issue at the high school is a strong one, and the class choruses a unanimous "NOOOOOO" (lines 140–142). In a vote, it is not Mr. Bradley's authority, or argumentation, that decides the issue of Mary's influence but the perspective with the most adherents. If, however, teachers disagree with the outcome of a class vote, they may then try to discount it. When the question of Mary's power erupts a second time, Mr. Bradley explicitly asks for a show of hands regarding Mary's position (lines 153–156). Expecting validation of his own low rating of Mary's influence, he is "surprised" instead (line 156) when only three students share his idea that Mary is "last." Therefore, Mr. Bradley redirects the "surprise" (in a discussion not included here) in an attempt to reverse the effect of the vote. In both these instances, taking a vote is used to settle a disagreement without the teacher having to appeal overtly to his own authority. It is a particularly apt way to maintain the design of an open-ended lesson like Mr. Bradley's, where there is "no one right answer" and no criteria are given for choosing between conflicting opinions. The strategy is more common in lower-track than regular-track classrooms in Maplehurst, reflecting in part teachers' concern about making demands on students that they cannot enforce. Votes on substantive matters are rare in regular-track classes, although they are used to resolve procedural matters, such as whether a test will be given on Friday or Monday.

A second resolution strategy amalgamates the divergent opinions. In the amalgamation, teachers repeat the positions of disputants and array them side by side. Neither is clearly deemed incorrect, nor are any contradictions explicitly noted. Both are validated to some extent just by being repeated. For example, Mr. Bradley, trying to resolve the initial disagreement about Mary, asks how Mary is linked to the topic of drugs at the high school. Rhetorically, he answers his own question and repeats the position of Patty and Tiffany: ". . . her little brothers [are the link]" (lines 140–141). Mr. Bradley then immediately invokes the argument of Butch, Dick, and Louis: "Is that a strong link?" "NOOOOOO" (lines 141; 142). Thus, the amalgamation resolves the disagreement, because by implication Mary's position is shown to be "at the end." However, in contrast to a vote, this form of resolution credits all disputants' opinions in the disagreement. The disagreement is closed and the lesson can go on; discussants stay involved, but conflict among them is veiled; the teacher settles the disagreement but without overtly imposing his own judgment. The amalgamation is like the array of divergent opinions created through usual classroom discourse sequences. It recognizes divergent opinions and joins them without emphasizing contradistinctions between them.

A curious feature of amalgamations is that they are not as neutral as their form implies. Even in open-ended discussions, teachers have core ideas they want to convey and answers they are waiting for students to discover (Edwards & Furlong, 1978; Frankel, 1982; Sharp & Green, 1975). As Mr. Bradley says in the framing of the lesson, "Some answers are more right than others." However, the designation of the "more right answer" is very subtle. In the case of Mary, who is linked to the topic of drugs through her brothers, the teacher's point of view is that Mary belongs "at the end" of the power ranking (line 110). When Mr. Bradley asks what Mary's link to drugs is, he asks for her "*only*" link" (line 140, my emphasis) and he provides a single answer: "Probably her little brothers." However, as students point out in later recurrences of the debate about Mary, other links are possible. For example, one student hypothesizes that Mary might know about the drug problem because of having used drugs herself. Thus, the phrasing of the teacher's question, by implying that there is only one link, diverts attention from the possibility that other factors could contribute to Mary's power in the group. Furthermore, when Mr. Bradley asks if Mary's siblings furnish a "strong link," there is no discussion of why they do not. The elicitation points toward a simple yes or no response. Although the teacher seemingly credits the arguments of both sides in an amalgamation, he also phrases the comparison so that one position is more correct than another and thereby manipulates a resolution of the disagreement.

Third, teachers occasionally resolve disagreements by asserting their authority openly. Mr. Bradley states his position on Mary as soon as Butch offers his original disparagement of her power: "Why at the end? I agree with you. Tell me why" (line 110). Teachers also interject technical terms to control a disagreement. In the midst of a subsequent argument about Mary (which is too long to repeat here), when Dick asserts that Ray, the dropout, will have more power than straight-A Mike, Mr. Bradley interrupts to ask what Dick means by "power." Dick cannot recall the term *earned power*: "Oh, uh, uh, that, uh, what - - ." Even when the teacher provides the technical phrase, Dick is so disconcerted by the interruption that he loses his train of thought, forgets Mary, and changes the topic.

Finally, teachers end ongoing disagreements by appealing to time constraints. They glance at the clock and suggest that the class will never "cover" the lesson's material unless they move on. This is how Mr. Bradley finally exits the long disagreement about Mary in this segment of the lesson: "Okay. Let's go on here before we, and if we're done . . ." Although all teachers share concerns about getting through lessons, Mr. Bradley's appeal to time constraints at *this* juncture closes a disagreement he was unable to resolve in any other fashion.

Recurrent Disagreements

Teachers' attempts to quell disagreements often backfire. Even going on to new topics may work only temporarily, because disagreements resurface within lessons and across lessons.

In Mr. Bradley's lesson on group communication, Mary persists as the topic of dispute. Thus, after the initial disagreement between Butch and Patty, the class ratifies Mary's low position, seemingly to everyone's chorused satisfaction (line 142). However, the argument breaks out anew almost immediately. In a parting shot, Mike suggests a new reason for Mary's being last on the list: "They (the brothers) probably wouldn't tell her anything anyway" (line 144). This statement is extreme in its disparagement of Mary's influence: It is not just that Mary will not talk to her brothers after school, as Butch argued earlier (lines 119–120), but that the younger siblings will not deign to talk to Mary about "anything." Immediately, Patty offers a counterassertion, stressing her disagreement through use of the double negative: "They're *not* going to tell her *nothing*" (line 146). Thus, the initial disagreement about Mary that Mr. Bradley had closed begins again with renewed heat.

In the remainder of Mr. Bradley's lesson, the question of Mary's position in the fictional group provokes four additional disagreement sequences. Each time, only the three girls in the class defend Mary's power. Their isolation is particularly visible in the last few minutes of the lesson. The dynamics of this final altercation especially reveal how teachers' ambivalence surfaces in confused lessons that control students by leaving them bewildered about their responsibilities and prerogatives.

The teacher asks whether the topic of drugs in the high school is important to the fictional characters:

201	T:	Mary! (Is drug use an important topic to Mary?)
202	SEAN:	Minus.
203	T:	Could be, very likely could be. Not involved in the
204		problem; out of high school. Might not be important to
205		her *at all*.
206	PATTY:	(softly) Yeah, but she has her brothers.
207	T:	What?
208	PATTY:	Nothing.
209	T:	She has to - (2.5) - What?
210	PATTY:	(shrugs)
211	T:	Okay. I, could be a topic, excuse me, it could be
212		interesting -⌈-
213	TIFFANY:	⌊She could have a ⌈*friend* like that.
214	T:	⌊- - could be important. She
215		could have what?
216	PATTY:	A friend.
217	T:	More than friends.
218	TIFFANY:	Brothers.
219	T:	Her brothers, who would be involved, and that might be a
220		plus.
221	DICK:	I'll bet (softly, sarcastically).
222	LOUIS:	Well, why would they, uh, where do you get Mary from? Why
223		would you put her life in, in there?
224	T:	Why'd I put Mary in this group? Good question. Why would
225		I put Mary in this group?
226	MIKE:	I guess she's not involved with the school or
227		nothing or she having, no, no reason,
228		her brothers⌈-
229	PATTY:	⌊She's the *only* female.
230	T:	What did I want to do with Mary? Why did I pick Mary - -
231		and make her who she was when I made this up? So that,
232		what was my purpose for that?
233		(1.5)
234	LOUIS:	To get all the things.
235	T:	To show (3.0) both si - (sides?). What if I took
236		everybody - like Smith and Officer, Officer Bill -
237		and - - Johnson and three other faculty members - - What

238   would that show you? I don't think you'd have to, I don't
239   think you'd have to *think*, you wouldn't bring as many of
240   the things into play. And so, I threw Mary in there
241   because - she *didn't* fit real well and you had to think
242   about *why* she didn't and Ray, I think - - he's a tough one
243   to figure, I think he's probably the hardest to figure.
244   It's difficult to - speculate where he would be, he could
245   be *anywhere*. (2.0) Okay, I want you to take the last
246   3 minutes, right now - - -

Here, "at the end," as in the initial disagreement, the delicate balance that classroom participants produce between educational coverage and "keeping order" is evident. Having presented her point of view regarding Mary in four earlier disagreement sequences, Patty again disagrees with a negative assessment of Mary's status. However, this time, her counter-assertion is qualified and spoken very softly: "Yeah, but she has her brothers" (line 206). In contrast to her earlier spirit, Patty, doing battle one last time, appears finally to have learned her lesson. When Mr. Bradley asks her to repeat what she says, Patty refuses to participate further in the discussion (lines 208; 210). She expresses her disagreement only nonverbally, by shrugging, twisting in her seat, and looking disgruntled.

In turn, Patty's refusal to discuss Mary upsets Mr. Bradley's ability to go on with the lesson. He stammers and excuses himself (lines 211-212). He allows Tiffany to interrupt with a reason why the topic of drugs could be important to Mary: "She could have a *friend* like that (who uses drugs)" (line 213). Patty then reenters the discussion (line 216), joining with Tiffany in a last defense of Mary. Possibly to secure Patty's reengagement, Mr. Bradley then reverses the position he has held throughout the lesson in regard to Mary. He prompts Patty and Tiffany to suggest that Mary's relation with her brothers *is* significant (line 217), even stating the importance of this relationship himself: "Her brothers, who would be involved, and that might be a plus" (lines 219-220).

This closing interchange exemplifies the delicate balance that classroom participants produce between educational coverage and order and its significance for lower-track students' scholastic uncertainty. Having repeatedly presented her point of view regarding Mary only to have it overridden by the teacher and the majority of the class, Patty makes one last, half-hearted defense and then quits. She refuses to disagree further. At that point, the teacher finds himself losing the participation of an active student and, simultaneously, the recitation. To allay the loss, the teacher not only invites Patty to participate but reverses his position relative to the disagreement's topic. That is, to keep the recitation alive—to teach the lesson he has planned—he encourages a perspective on Mary that previously led to direct disagreement and loss of control (and that even here, "at the end," threatens to erupt again with Dick's disdainful reaction, "I'll bet" [line 221]).

Other Additional Needs students also participate in ambiguous interchanges. These are provided for in contradictory lessons that translate teachers' mixed expectations. As in Mr. Bradley's lesson about group communication, students may experience rewards when they behave passively, as much or more than when they engage actively with the lesson's subject matter. By refusing to disagree verbally at the end of the lesson, Patty wins encouragement to participate as a disputant. She also wins long-sought recognition by the teacher of her substantive position on Mary's—and women's—communicative power. Other students—majority or minority—may experience similar feelings of power when they withdraw from active participation in class activities. By making teachers "'pull teeth" to secure their involvement in recitations (as one Maplehurst teacher put it), lower-track students reassert their significance as classroom actors. Furthermore, although these processes also occur in regular classes, the dynamic is particularly charged in lower-track classes where teachers' ambiguous role definition for students promotes conditions in which participants can find themselves at cross-purposes.

This "thick description" (Geertz, 1973, p. 6) of a lesson also unveils some of the taken-for-granted principles that govern remedial lessons. "Relevance"—in the lesson's content and form—produces some unintended consequences for lower-track students, in some cases a double impact. Thus, Patty is an exemplar of the lower-track student in disagreement with teacher and peers over an issue that is not distantly academic but that is definitive of self. Patty hears that Mary has no power because she is "only a secretary" who knows little about anything. Yet secretarial work is precisely Patty's career choice, as it is the "modal choice" of many other lower-track women (Rosenbaum, 1976; Valli, 1986). Often singlehandedly, because of the overrepresentation of boys in the Additional Needs class and the discouragement from Mr. Bradley, Patty protests Mary's dismissal by citing sources of her strength. But Patty is also shown that she herself has little power. Like Mary in the fictional group, she is outnumbered in the real-life group. Her series of disagreements with the teacher and most of her classmates is managed so that thoughtful argumentation appears futile. Eventually, Patty withdraws from the discussion and her exclusion is achieved. Yet, in an ironic twist, it is precisely her passivity that produces salutary recognition of her ideas: Patty's passive stance as a student and as a female, as much or more than her active, direct disagreement, is reinforced at the lesson's end. Male students' experiences are hardly more promising.

They also can be arbitrarily closed out of serious public discourse. And the view of social relationships that at least some boys brought to this classroom, if confirmed, hardly augers well for their civility.

Finally, this "thick description" of the anomalous student role, which is defined in Mr. Bradley's lesson, sketches the interactive variables, aperiodic processes, and multilayered contexts of curriculum differentiation. It demonstrates that many processes influence the definition of the lower-track student's role: instructional practices, such as public recitations or individualized seatwork; material constraints, such as the overrepresentation of males in lower-track classrooms; students' and teachers' ambiguous expectations of each other and self, expectations that are shaped by the school's tracking order and the wider social order; and the unconscious but crucial contradictions between the usual classroom discourse structure and the discourse structure of disagreements.

Accordingly, curriculum differentiation is much more complicated than is implied in psychological theories of labelling or expectation, political theories of teacher power and student resistance, organizational theories concerning the structure of tracking, or curriculum theories that promise that innovations, such as "relevant" lessons, can ameliorate student deficiencies or disdain. Nor will processes of curriculum differentiation vanish simply because policies abolish tracking.

In sum, the power of Mr. Bradley's lower-track lesson lies in its ambiguity, not in its heavy-handed control or straightforwardly educative purposes. In other lower-track classrooms in Maplehurst as well, the content, form, and management of discourse combine to produce as well as to reflect a situation in which students experience public engagement and disagreement ambivalently. That is, in a lesson with many good features, students nevertheless alternate between active participation and passive withdrawal. Therefore, lower-track students *are* "out-of-control," "not consistent," and, in teachers' definitions, annoyingly "unpredictable."

Yet students' unpredictable behavior is in part a response to teachers' anomalous lessons. In design and execution, Mr. Bradley calls for "more than one right answer" yet squelches all but his own. He stresses "giving reasons for opinions" but relies on his formal authority to resolve differences of opinion. He effectively and imaginatively engages students in important topics but punishes the engagement. Indeed, ironically, *both* students' engagement in *and* their withdrawal from classroom activities confirm pedagogical lore about lower-track students: If students argue, they are "like little kids . . . in shouting matches"; if they withdraw, they "don't care about ideas." In short, lower-track lessons present students a very powerful catch-22.

"At the end," we may well recall that Mr. Bradley is not insensitive to classroom dynamics, following by rote a textbook on tracking, incompetent in subject expertise, or aggrandizing his own power. And Maplehurst's lower-track students are neither boorish louts nor uninterested or incompetent in dealing with academics. Further, as the oblique processes that differentiate the roles of regular- and lower-track students suggest, tracking itself is not an omnipotent structure that renders lessons either inequitable or excellent. In contrast, this close-up analysis suggests the value of examining presumed categorical descriptions, such as "relevance," "remedial," or "resistance," and the scholastic and social lore in which they are embedded. The exercise illustrates that the entanglements of curriculum differentiation are more extensive and less rationally grounded than pedagogical lore suggests. Indeed, as I consider in the next chapter, the effects of the practice extend to lower-track teachers' definitions of their own role, a subject that has received considerably less attention than curricular differentiation's effects on students.

Part III
DEFINING THE CLASSROOM CLIMATE AND LOWER-TRACK TEACHING

CHAPTER 4

Chaos and Conflict
in Lower-Track Classrooms

What is the climate, or atmosphere, in lower-track classrooms? Are classes purposive and engaging because teachers set lessons at appropriate levels so that students can work successfully, as advocates of tracking suggest? Or are classes "dumping grounds," fostering a "negative peer group" and resistance among the disadvantaged, as critics proclaim? Does classroom climate vary across tracks? What influences classroom climate and its concomitant, the teacher's role?

Traditionally, analyses of classroom climate have focused on teachers' personal styles, students' characteristics, or the hierarchy of tracking. Accordingly, a negative tenor is attributed to the lower-track teacher's authoritarian style, incompetent management, inexperience, or disdain for a low-status assignment (Rosenthal & Jacobsen, 1968; White & Lippett, 1960). Or climate is deemed a function of student characteristics: Because students are academically unskilled, have anti-educational upbringings, or are immature and delinquent, lower-track classrooms may be "circuses" (see review in Hargreaves et al., 1975). Grouping theory suggests that when teachers and students are placed at the bottom of the school hierarchy, they develop antischool attitudes; even students who are socially advantaged and who should be educationally committed may be alienated by placement in the lower track (Finley, 1984; Hargreaves, 1967; Lacey, 1970; Stinchcombe, 1964).

However, explanations centered on individuals or the mechanism of tracking account inadequately for the relationship between classroom climate and curriculum differentiation. Descriptions of the climate in lower-track classrooms, for example, are decidedly mixed. In some studies, extreme disorderliness is noted as their distinguishing feature (Furlong, 1977; Metz, 1978; Schwartz, 1981). In others, a pervasive "flatness" is deemed characteristic (Goodlad, 1984; Oakes, 1985). Still other studies document lower-track classes that are purposive and academically engaging (Barr & Dreeben, 1983; Valli, 1990; Wehlage et al., 1980). Moreover, the

81

inconsistent descriptions are matched by contradictory explanations: Sometimes, but not always, "democratic" styles produce a positive climate, but highly directive teachers can be effective (and ineffective).

In this and the next three chapters I examine the relation between the climate and its concomitant, teaching, in regular- and lower-track classes at the two Maplehurst high schools. Although classroom climate is often charged to individual teachers with low (or high) expectations or training, such attributions are too linear and simplified. Rather, just as the teacher's definition is a complex if subtle determinant of the student's role, as I discussed in Chapters 2 and 3, so it is of classroom climate. Accordingly, teachers have the responsibility and the prerogative to stipulate whether classrooms are businesslike or boisterous, enlightening or merely entertaining. In defining an atmosphere, teachers simultaneously signal an attitude toward their own role: Both explicitly and implicitly, they indicate the nature of their relationship with students and with subject matter. Their classroom definitions translate broader institutional and social precepts of differentiation and membership as well. As a result, the teacher's role is bound up reciprocally with the definition of the student's: In Maplehurst's lower-track classes, teachers' expectations for themselves are as contradictory as their expectations for students.

In this first of the four chapters I develop two themes. First, I look in Additional Needs classrooms at college-preparatory Southmoor High School to describe the chaos that prevails in them, in contrast to the relaxed, academic, orderly climate that teachers define in their regular classes. Then I analyze how the differentiated, lower-track climate is generated. Scrutinizing 3 minutes of talk from an Additional Needs lesson, I specify that the chaos is a necessary outcome of neither the teacher's incompetence nor the students' indifference. Rather, teachers and students produce the chaos together.

SOUTHMOOR HIGH SCHOOL

One would not expect any teachers at Southmoor High School to have low expectations for students or for themselves. They teach in a well-equipped school that is nestled amid expansive, turn-of-the-century houses in Maplehurst's "Hill" district and within easy reach of the state university campus. Their colleagues are experienced, support services are generous, and the curriculum is comprehensive. Their students, most of whom are white and middle class, may choose from an array of more than 200 officially undifferentiated courses, ranging from civilization to music theory to welding. And, students succeed with their choices: Over half of the seniors plan to attend 4-year colleges or universities, and a large coterie regularly wins top honors in state and national competitions. In short, Southmoor perceives itself to be and operates as a preeminently academic, college-preparatory high school.

Teachers take pride in students' academic accomplishments, and they are credited with contributing to students' success. Thus, teaching at Southmoor is an important and prestigious occupation, perhaps the most important role in the school. The powerful faculty takes seriously its responsibility to run the daily life of the school and preserve thereby a sound tradition of academic excellence. Teachers' enthusiasm for their work translates into a seniority system in which "being a teacher at Southmoor for 15 years is still to be a newcomer." Teachers stay because, as one remarked, "Coming to teach at Southmoor was like arriving in heaven." Students are typified as coming "from upper-middle-class, professional families." They make Southmoor "heavenly" because they are "motivated."

> They are *easy* to teach, *easy* to relate to. You don't have to *work* to relate to them. . . . Usually, I give them an assignment and they take it from there: I do hardly anything and they're off and running."

Most staff members also feel they, themselves, are "treated like professionals. Nobody's running around checking up on you, seeing if you've done your job. Oh, there are a few that are not professionals, even here. But, I mean, no place is *perfect*."

Regular-Track Classes at Southmoor

Relying on a definition of the student body as high-achieving and on organizational features that allow "professionals" to teach as they deem best, regular teachers as Southmoor express their right and obligation to be academic experts. They guide "easy-to-teach" students to think critically, broadly, and with enthusiasm about traditional academic subjects, which they present as important to students' present and future educational success. As a consequence of teachers' serious and enthuasiastic role enactment, the classroom climate in regular-track courses at Southmoor is orderly but informal, purposive and academically demanding, but also exploratory and spontaneous.

A ninth-grade American history lesson is representative of the intellectual purpose and camaraderie. The lesson began with a student "editorial," each student being required to present his or her opinion on an issue in the news during the semester. On this day, a boy spoke eloquently for several minutes, decrying the acceptability of publicly slandering homosexuals. When the boy finished, another student turned in her desk to ask him directly for clarification of a point. Other students also offered comments. After several minutes, the teacher intervened with his reaction, simultaneously turning the class to the day's lesson: an examination of the Haymarket Riot. In the shift, however, the teacher wove together the thesis of the student's "editorial" and the lesson's. For example, he pointed out that the labels in the 1890's riot, "anarchists" and "commies," functioned as political slurs, "just like what John told us is happening today with Reagan saying the nuclear protest movement is being infiltrated by 'homosexuals'." Near the end of the lesson, he tied the events of the war protests of the 1960s and 1970s and the trial of the Chicago Seven back to the Haymarket Riot and forward to the current nuclear freeze movement, again citing the contribution of John's editorial.

The discussion of the Haymarket Riot was based on a homework assignment. Students were to have read a chapter from a text that, according to its preface, presented case studies to encourage students "to inquire, to investigate, to develop their own points of view using skills of critical thinking and analyses." In the discussion of the Haymarket Riot, students first presented the facts of the event. Then, under the teacher's skillful questioning, they began to enumerate the inconsistencies of the official report of the riot. Although the teacher directed the ensuing recitation, much of his work was simply indicating which student had the floor. Students themselves were ready to counter or support arguments from peers without a directive question from the teacher. Not every student in the class participated, but about half did. Those who did not talk appeared to listen to the comments of peers. Most took some notes.

Throughout the lesson, there was an air of expectancy, of wondering what discoveries the examination of the Haymarket Riot would produce. No "right answer" for the lesson and for the meaning of the reading about the riot was predictable; the answer depended on students' "critical thinking." In the teacher's other regular-track ninth-grade classes, many of the same issues emerged in the examination of the historical event, but points were expressed in students' language rather than a standardized form. Southmoor's regular-track climate exudes spontaneity.

Differentiation at Southmoor

As a public institution, Southmoor draws students with a variety of interests from diverse neighborhoods. The comprehensive curriculum is designed to provide for these differences without partiality. In actuality, courses are not all equal, and leveling of students occurs informally, through student choice. Various teachers acknowledge this differentiation of the curriculum and, hence, of the students: "Students earn an English credit whether they elect a *hard* course like Shakespeare or an *easy* course like Sci-Fi."

In addition, curriculum differentiation occurs more formally. Southmoor has students who are not academically successful, who are not economically and culturally advantaged, and who thus do not fit the faculty's definition of the typical Southmoor student. To "meet the individual needs" of academically unsuccessful students in 1982–83, Southmoor offered a total of 12 Additional Needs classes in English, social studies, math, biology, and distributive education. Approximately 75 students, mostly freshmen and sophomores, were referred to the small, "adaptive," lower-track classes. Most were placed at the beginning of the school year, but some students were enrolled throughout the year.

How such academically unsuccessful students fare in a "heavenly" school is an important educational question, raising issues of educational equity and excellence. If Southmoor's regular-track classrooms exhibit so much purpose, academic stimulation, and easy but respectful camaraderie between teacher and students, what atmosphere and teaching role do teachers define in this academically oriented school's Additional Needs classes?

DISORDER IN A LOWER-TRACK CLASS

Staff members at Southmoor perceive Additional Needs students as troubling challenges to the prevailing definition of Southmoor's student body, its methods, and its general purpose as a college-preparatory high school. Even though students demonstrate a wide range of academic skills, diverse social backgrounds, and ambivalent behavior patterns, and even though they are not so grossly underskilled, uniformly impoverished, or isolated from the mainstream culture as lower-track students described in the literature (many of them in inner-city schools where poverty and race compound tracking's impact), teachers accentuate academically unsuccessful students' differences from Southmoor's able, affluent, college-bound, regular-track students.

So characterized, lower-track students challenge teachers' definitions of themselves as academic experts. Teachers meet the challenge ambivalently. On the one hand, they expect to act as Southmoor professionals, to "adapt" curriculum, and to set high standards. Simultaneously, however, they put the anomalous students off the scale, "at the bottom" of an educational hierarchy. Additional Needs students are "your, you know, your basic bottom"; both intellectually and behaviorally, they are "the dregs." Worse yet, in teachers' accounts, the educational hierarchy is nearly permanent: To enter Southmoor as an academically unsuccessful student is not simply to be different from the majority of the students but to be irremediably different, and teachers are not held accountable for students' instruction. Holding such contradictory role expectations, lower-track teachers direct confused and uncertain classroom encounters.

Such encounters abound in Mr. Ellison's ninth-grade, Additional Needs, social studies class. During the first semester, 16 freshmen were referred to the class, either by their eighth-grade teachers the previous spring or by their ninth-grade teachers or their high school counselors during the fall semester. Even though an aide rounds up students at the local hangouts, attendance is erratic and usually only four or five students are present. Sometimes students saunter in desultorily halfway through the class period. They scatter around the perimeter of the sea of 40 desks that fill Mr. Ellison's classroom, sitting where they will. Boys generally sit singly, against the back wall or in the front row. Girls array themselves in pairs in the outer aisles near the windows or along the blackboard. Mr. Ellison usually sits at the desk at the front of the room.

Academic Aspects

Class activity in Mr. Ellison's course is organized around daily, in-class worksheets. Teacher-made, the worksheets consist of four or five questions about a two-page reading selection, and a puzzle. The questions require an answer of several words or a sentence or two. The puzzle usually relates to the reading selection; for example, students find and circle important words mentioned in the text in a grid of letters. Worksheets are also personalized; students' names or upcoming school events are often included in the word search. As Mr. Ellison explains, he uses games to motivate academically unsuccessful students: "Puzzles make class interesting enough to the students so they can't say, 'It's boring,' without you having a good reason to say, 'Hey, I never had puzzles in school; it'd have been better if I had.' That's really giving in to them." With his regular-track students, Mr. Ellison's use of a puzzle is limited to, "Oh, maybe the day before Thanksgiving."

Additional Needs classes have small enrollments so that each student's needs can be met, but there is very little individualized instruction. Indeed, worksheets are identical, not individualized. Although students complete worksheets at varying rates, and Mr. Ellison says he uses discrete worksheets to accommodate the varied attendance and performance patterns of students, class time is often spent going over each question as a group. Thus, even though Mary may be working on question 5, Mr. Ellison will loudly discuss question 2 with Carl. He may ask for information about question 2, to which Mary, even though she has finished that question, will respond. Furthermore, Mr. Ellison rarely assigns new worksheets until everyone has completed most of an old one. Instead, students who finish early are given passes to the library or cafeteria.

Academic work in Mr. Ellison's room proceeds slowly. As one student notes to another, "Ever notice how slooow this class is?" When they enter the room, students may receive an uncompleted worksheet from the previous class period. Once or twice a week, they get a new worksheet, related to the next short reading selection in the history text. Continuity between reading selections and, therefore, between worksheets, is only broadly chronological; the text is not thematically organized. Nor does Mr. Ellison lecture or conduct cogent recitations about the readings or arrange them into units. Rather, class time is spent working through the worksheets, question by question, with accompanying discussions ranging far beyond the academic work.

Thus, progress during the semester is marked only by a series of grades on a small number of discrete worksheets. On the one day when Mr. Ellison scheduled a test, no students came to class. Mr. Ellison hypothesized that "they'd rather have just taken a 'miss' than turn around and flunk it." The next day, students took the test and, indeed, did poorly. Mr. Ellison argues that with students' erratic attendance, their range of academic skills, and the in-and-out referral process of Additional Needs classes, he cannot make or give a fair test. For the same reasons, he does not assign oral reports, research projects, book reports, or quizzes.

In general, interruptions plague Mr. Ellison's class. The teacher's interruptions of students' individual work, in the form of demands for group recitations, is paralleled by other interruptions. During the test, for example, a counselor dropped by to check on Melissa's attendance and stayed to chat with her for several minutes. In addition to their absences, students' own late arrivals interrupt class:

MAY: (loudly, stumbling against several desks) TEN MINUTES LATE!

SUE: TEN MINUTES AND ONE SECOND LATE! I'm here, but could I go get some water, my throat is sooo sore.

T: Well, ma'am, I suggest you hurry.

MAY: WHERE'S MY WORK? I want to get it done!

T: You won't finish the work I have today.

> MAY: Sheeeit! You just give it here. (She snatches the worksheet out of Mr. Ellison's hand and looks at it.) Why we do this BABY work! (Then, wheedling) You got a pencil, Mr. Ellison?
>
> SUE: I'M BACK!

In sum, academic progress is the least important aspect of Mr. Ellison's class. His worksheets offer "games," rather than lessons, to motivate students who cannot learn. Progress toward academic goals is slow and uncertain. Talk about personal affairs, simple gossip, and random items compete with talk about the academic lesson.

Social Aspects

Mr. Ellison describes many of his classroom efforts as attempts to address students' personal and social needs. He justifies the placement of Mary, "who could get B's and C's in regular classes," on the basis of "building her self-confidence." He explains that he knows "that Carl and Marvin just sit in the back of the room and talk a lot of the hour. But Marvin, especially, needs a friend, so I let it go. If I made a seating arrangement and had him up front and Carl in back, what would be accomplished?" In the classroom, Mr. Ellison often prompts students to show concern for each other. When a student is absent, he asks those present if they know if the student is sick. He encourages and joins conversations about students' personal affairs. When Cheryl was suffering from a bronchial infection and coughed through most of a class period, he solicitously advised her to "drink orange juice . . . I do, this time of year, and it really helps."

However, Mr. Ellison's attempts to "befriend students" and "establish a little family" often backfire. Students perceive his questions about an absent student's whereabouts as attendance-taking, for example. For them to answer would be to "rat" on a fellow student. Mr. Ellison himself often blurs his personal interest and his authority as the teacher. After advising Cheryl to drink orange juice, he comments further that "some students call it 'Hi-C' and they wish that were their grade." Similarly, when Mary enters class saying she is "in a good mood," Mr. Ellison responds personally, saying he is glad to hear it. But then he adds a teacherly admonition, hoping the good mood would "translate into some of your work today."

Students in the class, despite its small size and Mr. Ellison's intent, perhaps in part because of erratic attendance patterns, do not form a cohesive group. Although they usually work together on class assignments, students do not always know each other by name. Carl and Marvin worked together several days, but when Carl was absent and Mr. Ellison asked

Marvin if he had seen Carl, Marvin did not know to whom Mr. Ellison was referring. During school hours, in addition to attending classes, students may frequent the nearby candy store together, share a smoke, or, occasionally, get drunk or "high" together. However, they do not call each other after school or share weekend activities. When Dawn, a seemingly well-liked student in the class, left Southmoor for a residential drug treatment center, students paid little attention and did not write to her.

Order by One-Upmanship

Students' academic progress and the class's social cohesion are further undercut by the implicit rules governing behavior in Mr. Ellison's class. Instead of teacher-directed rules and order, the overriding rule is one of one-upmanship. Each person attempts to satisfy his or her individual needs as they become apparent. Consequently, if Sue needs help on question 5 of the worksheet, she blurts out a demand for assistance, even when discussion on another question is in progress. If her demand is not acknowledged, it is repeated, usually more loudly: "I can't find this word! - - - Ellison! (3.0) I CAN'T FIND THIS WORD, I SAID! I'm gettin' MAA-AD! (warningly)." Mr. Ellison himself interrupts students in their work. Once, moving rapidly back and forth among four students, giving 15 to 30 seconds of attention to each, Mr. Ellison monitored students' progress and provided encouragement, as teachers providing individual instruction are encouraged to do, even though his attention was unsolicited and distracting. Such competitiveness for the floor feeds the isolation of the students from one another and from Mr. Ellison as each classroom participant tries to outbid the other for attention.

Classroom participants not only compete with each other in getting and giving academic assistance but seek to out-trump each other in efforts to enliven the class. May responds to Mr. Ellison's question of why she is so loud by explaining, "I'm just making it fun - - It's so *dead* in here." Personal anecdotes, dirty jokes, and wordplay compete with talk about the lesson. For example, Mr. Ellison maintains a nonstop stream of talk, much of it a witty and ironic commentary on the academic and extra-academic activities of the students. When a student gets up to sharpen a pencil, Mr. Ellison remarks: "Fifteen minutes into the period and you just realize you need to sharpen your pencil?" The teacher-made worksheets are full of puns, some of which are quite difficult. On a crossword puzzle, one clue reads: "a word used in baseball, jewelry, and cards." Another clue is: "a vital organ or someone who hasn't died yet." (The answers are *diamond* and *liver*.) Such clues stimulate strings of additional jokes or disparaging comments from students. Similarly, a favorite trick of Mr. Ellison's is to wad up pieces of paper and fire hook shots at the wastepaper basket. His success or lack thereof provokes a stream of interruptions of the class's progress through the worksheets.

Students add to the mayhem as they belch, break wind, and throw pencils at each other. They blatantly share answers on worksheets, despite Mr. Ellison's rebuke not to "overhintify." During one class, Dawn and Sue discussed how to sneak a stick deodorant onto a teacher's desk: "He stinks so bad I can't hardly stand it. We'll tape a note on the bottle: 'hint.' How you spell 'hint'?" At that, Sue unscrews the bottle top, lifts her sweater above her armpit, and begins to apply deodorant, much to the amazement of everyone in the classroom. Students who are newly referred to the class take in these antics quietly at first, but within a day or two become participants. Clearly, the one-upmanship principle effectively undercuts the order and academic purpose expected in an educational encounter.

Mr. Ellison bases his strategy for managing the Additional Needs class on "flexibility. I never do anything normal and that way I keep them off-guard. If they think they know what I'm going to do, they sabotage it." Consequently, Mr. Ellison responds phlegmatically to interruptions of the lesson from within and without the classroom. Rather than try to limit an interruption, Mr. Ellison often prolongs it. For example, if a principal enters the classroom to check on a student's attendance, Mr. Ellison asks how he is, describes what the class is doing, or asks if the principal can guess a crossword-puzzle clue.

Paradoxically, by flowing with interruptions, Mr. Ellison achieves the appearance of control. With his mild, "flexible" manner, he simply waits for an interruption to complete itself or even encourages it to run its course. If he tried to limit the principal's interference, by briefly noting that Carl is present and accounted for, students might prolong the interruption by shouting out questions about the reason for the principal's visit or by volunteering information about their studies. Furthermore, by flowing opportunistically with classroom events, rather than trying to direct them, Mr. Ellison can select those on which he *will* take action, yet not appear powerless when he does not attend to all. Although Mr. Ellison gives the illusion of control, the random development of the lesson and the extraordinary attention paid to interruptions of all kinds preclude the coherent, ordered development of instruction.

A Caricature of Education

The unspoken principle of one-upmanship that governs much of the behavior of classroom participants promotes a sense of gamesmanship in the class. The relationship between Mr. Ellison and his students is of a teasing or lightly sarcastic nature, dominated by exchanges of jokes, insults, and anecdotes. When Mary complains rather bitterly that "this class is stupid," Mr. Ellison challenges her to write down her suggestions for improving it. Taking his challenge to heart, she quickly composes a list of eight remedies. Mr. Ellison pantomimes reluctance as he reads the list aloud to the gleeful class. The list includes many items directed at Mr. Ellison: No more "rotten" jokes, no more sports talk (football season was at its height), no more puzzles or worksheets, and "don't talk so much," to which another student amends, "That's the truth!" Mr. Ellison pretends to be crushed, but Mary pertly points out, "You asked!" However, having read the list, Mr. Ellison routinely redirects the class to the worksheet. Reading and joking about the list consumes one third of the class period, and Mary continues to comment on the stupidity of the class throughout the hour, but no changes result from Mary's suggestions.

Blatantly hostile outbursts, whether by teacher or students, are rare in Mr. Ellison's class. He works hard to respond to students with equanimity: "My rule for survival is, 'Never let them get me mad.' If I do, it's all over." He does occasionally get "het up," as students call it, and demands obedience, accusing students of the very gamesmanship he himself presents in class: "All you're doing is playing *games* with me and I don't like it. If you want to get out of this class, FOR ANY REASON, you're going to have to change your behavior. I can't just *baby-sit* you."

Students maintain their equanimity as well. One day when Sue arrives 5 minutes late, without a textbook she was supposed to return, Mr. Ellison suggests sarcastically that "perhaps we should flush your brains." Softly, seriously, almost tearfully, Sue replies, "Don't make me hate you." The minority counselor, who escorted Sue to class, defuses the situation by commenting, "Sue's cool." The girl rebounds with this support and begins to chatter about one of her latest escapades at the candy store. Mr. Ellison tells her to "quiet down." This time she playfully echoes, "Don't make me hate you." With equal gamesmanship, Mr. Ellison responds, "I haven't done anything yet. Wait till next semester. Then I start kicking your desk."

Mr. Ellison "joshes" lower-track students to establish a less authoritarian, easygoing relationship with them. His paper-wad tosses and stretched puns demonstrate that Additional Needs students should not judge him strictly as a teacher, because those are not teacherly behaviors, but should consider him a "good fellow." Nevertheless, like his attempts to be friendly, such a strategy to establish goodwill and control often goes awry. Although it may allay openly hostile and anti-educational confrontations, it creates an atmosphere of irony in which genuine educational encounters rarely happen. Mr. Ellison's gamelike, jocular behavior certainly leads to confused classroom encounters. His expressions of personal concern are undercut by their teasing tone. His evaluations of students' work are often backhanded compliments:

> How'd you do on this worksheet? Uh, I would say, uh, A minus or B plus – – What I'd probably do (teasingly), I'd flip a coin up in the air and if it comes down with a head, you know, I give you an A minus, and, uh, tails, a B. (1.0) No, I think you did pretty good. I'll have to give you that. This one's much better than the one I gave you to fix up. Can't even tell the same person did 'em, in fact.

The climate in Mr. Ellison's class, like that in other classrooms for academically unsuccessful students at Southmoor, has a curious ambiguity. It represents a strange mixture of educational order and chaos, one in which classroom activities become a game, and both teacher and students go through the motions of teaching and learning. Making academic progress on basic skills, one of the formal goals of the Additional Needs class, vies in importance with the interruption of a principal, getting in a good joke, or tossing wads of paper at a wastebasket. Although students always have a worksheet before them, making a friend sometimes takes precedence over its completion. Even so, there is little cohesion among students or between students and teacher but, instead, considerable competition and bickering. Classroom participants work hard to maintain a veneer of light sarcasm in which encounters, whether academic or social, are rarely taken seriously. As a consequence, despite special funding, the sincere concern of teachers like Mr. Ellison, students' reasonably competent academic skills, and ostensibly "adaptive" curricular and social practices, Additional Needs students drop out of classes at a rate of over 50%.*

PRODUCING PURPOSE IN REGULAR-TRACK CLASSES

Participation structure is a concept that can be used to analyze and compare the production of Pandemonium and purpose in tracked classes. It defines types of social encounters according to the patterned allocation of interactional rights and obligations of participants (Erickson, 1982; Philips, 1983). In classrooms, participation structures vary according to the

---

*Southmoor's official overall dropout rate is about 25%. No statistics are collected for lower-track students. I estimated the 50% rate in Additional Needs classes using teachers' estimates, a comparison of class lists over a 2-year period, and estimates in formal evaluations of lower-track classes that were prepared by teachers and administrators.

number of students interacting with the teacher, the academic task, and the ways in which turns at talk are allocated (Erickson, 1982; Philips, 1983). Teachers direct participation structures and students respond, thereby identifying the often implicit rules by which they are to enact their reciprocal roles.

In regular-track classrooms at Southmoor, such as the lesson about the Haymarket Riot, a participation structure predominates in which a single teacher interacts with all the students in the room. In this participation structure, which finds expression in the recitation and lecture, the teacher is the central director of classroom talk. Posing questions and assessing responses, the teacher retains control of the floor (Bellack et al., 1966; Edwards & Furlong, 1978; Mehan, 1979; Philips, 1983). Thus, he or she may choose who will talk from among the 30 participants in the recitation. The teacher's central position also allows control of the topic, its meaning, and the pace of the lesson. Thus, the teacher/whole-group participation structure, which is the norm at Southmoor, allows the academic goals of the teacher's choosing to be reached through verbal means yet in an orderly, efficient fashion.

Although classroom participants act reciprocally, taking into account the actions of others (Sacks, 1972), they are not equals. Teachers have some interactional prerogatives that students do not have. These derive from the teacher's possession of the knowledge students are deemed to need and from their adult status. Consequently, teachers direct the topic of talk; they can interrupt students; they assess students' responses (Bellack et al., 1966; Edwards & Furlong, 1978; Mehan, 1979; Philips, 1983).

However, at Southmoor, particularly in classrooms for upperclassmen and able students, teachers modify the usual participation structures to encourage student direction of classroom talk. As in the regular-track lesson about the Haymarket Riot, challenging queries to teachers' explanations are expected, invited, and common. Students sometimes respond to the talk of peers directly. Students may introduce new topics that the teacher incorporates into the lesson. These rights, and the informal teacher-student relationships that they reflect and re-create, suggest that teachers perceive older and abler students as not so different from themselves and, therefore, as able to acquire some of the prerogatives of a teacher and an adult.

Furthermore, in Southmoor's regular-track classes, it is unusual for teachers to establish more than one participation structure per class period. Except for a few minutes devoted to opening procedural matters, students and teacher interact in businesslike fashion through the 50-minute period. Use of only one participation structure increases the time spent on academic matters, because changing participation structures itself uses time, and it minimizes confusion about students' and teacher's interactional obligations in a specific classroom encounter. Furthermore, using only one participation structure, and particularly the teacher/whole-group form, reflects positive assumptions about regular-track students' age and academic ability: They are expected to have longer attention spans than children and the ability to learn through listening rather than doing. Individual seatwork, like reading or writing, is usually reserved for homework. By way of contrast, in the early elementary grades, participation structures change about 20 times per day and exhibit considerable variety, including teacher/small group, teacher/individual, and seatwork forms. Yet, by the upper elementary grades, participation structures change only 10 times per day and are more restricted in type (Philips, 1983).

In sum, in Southmoor's regular-track classes, teachers authoritatively establish one participation structure during a class period. Most often, the teacher and the whole class explore an academic topic together verbally. In such purposive yet participatory encounters, students learn that they are educationally competent and maturing adolescents, successfully maneuvering through the rite of passage that is high school (Kett, 1977).

PRODUCING CHAOS IN LOWER-TRACK CLASSES

In contrast, in Additional Needs classes, the participation structures, although of the same type as those found in any educational setting, differ in their arrangement. They shift more frequently and with less clear marking; topics are entertaining or "relevant" rather than academic. The shifts reflect uncertain direction by lower-track teachers, to which students then respond confusedly. Often their responses appear communicatively incompetent or, as teachers say, like those of "naughty fourth graders" rather than like those of intellectually competent adolescents. This unintended result is produced in the talk in Mr. Ellison's lessons and those of other Additional Needs teachers at Southmoor.

One November day Mr. Ellison and five students in the English/social studies class continued to work on worksheets begun the previous day about the bombing of Pearl Harbor. Like all of Mr. Ellison's worksheets, this one consisted of several questions and a puzzle. The class spent the first half of the period discussing the first question, their talk punctuated by lengthy personal asides, jokes, and loud bantering. Then Mr. Ellison left the room briefly to speak to a teacher in the hall. Students continued work on the next question or chatted among themselves. When Mr. Ellison returned, he entered the classroom speaking loudly:

1	T:	Uh, ANYBODY HAVE ANOTHER
		QUESTION. B⌈E –
2	TINA:	(reading the worksheet) ⌊"What"⌈ –
3	T:	⌊ – S⌈IDES –
4	TINA:	⌊"WHAT DID
5		WE DO ABOUT IT?"
6	T:	UH, I was just going to ask if you had
7		another question.
8	TINA:	Heh, heh.
9	T:	We⌈ll –
10	TINA:	⌊We went over there and beat 'em up;
11		we hit 'em in the jaws!
12	T:	Well, in other words, I would say –
13	Ss:	(beginning to chatter loudly among themselves)
14	T:	I WOULD SAY that if you would talk about
15		what the Japanese are doing. In other words,
16		they were conquering huge areas of Asia, just taking
17		'em, and, uh, adding it to their own
18		territory, uh –
19	Ss:	(continuing to chat with each other)
20	T:	Do any of you know what they called that
21		(pointing to the four circles he had drawn on
22		the board earlier to represent the Japanese
23		empire), that whole thing there. I betcha one
24		person in here at least knows what they
25		called it when . . . they took all this.
26	TINA:	They borrowed it.
27	T:	No, when they *took* the empire. What'd they
28		call their empire? (1.0) You know what
29		they called their empire?
30	BILL:	King China.
31	T:	King China, yeah.
32	Ss:	(giggling)
33	T:	Uh, Louis, you know what they called their
34		empire, you know, what the Japanese called their
35		empire, right up here? (pointing to board)
36	LOUIS:	N⌈o.
37	TINA:	⌊No.
38	T:	Do you know what they called it?
39	MARY:	No.
40	T:	Do you know what they called it?

41   MARY: They called it "theirs."
42   T: (to Cheryl) Aren't you working on
43   this (the worksheet)?
44 CHERYL: I told you.
45   T: You told me what?
46 CHERYL: I've already done it.
47   TINA: Pearl Harbor?
48   T: Uh! Uh, anybody, uh, nobody has an idea
49   what the Japanese called this thing, other people
50   were adding to Japan. In other words, if you
51   tried to draw Japan's boundary it would
52   look . . . very unusual. It would go way
53   out here in the Pacific, like that (drawing
54   on the board). They said this big area
55   here was theirs (pointing to one circle).
56   Nobody in here knows what they called it? (2.0)
57   Not a single one of you has ever heard this?
58   BILL: Nooo.
59   MARY: Probably have.
60   TINA: Probably didn't tell us anything about it.
61   T: I just don't believe this, that nobody⌈–
62   MARY: ⌊WELL, TELL US!
63   T: What?
64 CHERYL: Tell us so we do know.
65   (3.0)
66   TINA: We already know.
67   T: But nobody's telling me something they know.
68   I have to believe some of you must know this – –
68   Well, the⌈–
70   MARY: ⌊WELL, WHAT!
71   T: Well, okay, what they called it, they called
72   it the Greater (writing on the board) – – East – –
73   Asia – – Co-prosperity – – Sphere. (2.0) There.
74   MARY: What a stupid name.
75   T: No, that was, well, I thought it was very
76   official on their part, to call, to call all this
77   taking of an empire and everything. That's
78   what they called it. They said that
79   everybody in As⌈ia –
80   BILL: ⌊Who cares?
81   T: EVERYbody in Asia would prosper. Cro, er,
82   CO-prosperity. And then of course it is a sphere,

83		makes it "greater." That's what they called it,
84		Greater East Asia. What a nice way to call
85		something that's, you know, they're probably
86		killing people, taking their goodies, and then,
87		what a nice idea to call it that. (1.0) I, uh,
88		really think that that was very clever on their part
89		to give it a name.
90	MARY:	"Taking their goodies?"
91	T:	Greater East Asia - - And none of you knew that.
92	MARY:	(louder, looking disgusted) "TAKING THEIR
93		GOODIES?"
94	T:	You mean there's nobody here ever heard that?
95	CHERYL:	Well (reading from the worksheet, but
96		misreading the first word), "Why did we do about it?"
97	T:	What?
98	CHERYL:	What'd we do about it?
99	T:	What? I thought somebody would have heard
100		of it.
101	CHERYL:	Forget it.
102	T:	(turning to a late-arriving student) Here's
103		Tom. Did you, uh, run into trouble getting here,
104		uh, this morning?

This 3-minute segment of talk divides into three sections. In the first, Mr. Ellison reenters the classroom and, after several exchanges with one student, Tina, eventually establishes a teacher/whole-group participation structure that takes the form of a recitation (lines 1–23). In the second, the recitation itself unfolds (lines 24–101). Its topic, the name the Japanese gave their empire. In the third, the late arrival of a student interrupts the recitation (lines 102–104). In the 3 minutes, several types of confusion are evident: confusion about what kind of participation structure is operating; about the academic task, or topic; and, fundamentally, about how classroom participants should be acting.

Unclear and Shifting Participation Structures

More than one participation structure can and often do operate within a class at one time. For example, a teacher can help an individual student while others work on seatwork, although the teacher and student must speak quietly if other students are to "pretend" not to hear (Philips, 1983). Such is not the case in Mr. Ellison's class. One of its basic ambiguities, and one of the sources of the disorderly classroom climate, concerns whether the participation structure in operation is that of the recitation, of individual seatwork, or of small-group seatwork. Although each of Mr. Ellison's students has a worksheet and is responsible for completing it, the rules by which students are to accomplish this are uncertain because of Mr. Ellison's unclear direction.

Sometimes Mr. Ellison comes around to a student to help with a particular question, or a student goes up to his desk for help with an individual problem. If the participation structure is that of individual seatwork, teacher and student should relate on a one-to-one basis, with talk allocated on a first-come, first-served private basis according to individual needs, with students filling in worksheets. Under such a structure, talk occurs between individuals; other students are not to attend to the talk of Mr. Ellison and another student. On the other hand, some students in Mr. Ellison's class sit near friends and work together on the worksheet. If the participation structure in operation is that of small-group seatwork, the teacher should relate to two or three students at a time, as requested. However, students would also rely on each other for information, and the worksheet's completion is a joint venture. Finally, Mr. Ellison's class operated a considerable part of the time under the participation structure of the recitation. Mr. Ellison addresses one question from the worksheet to the group at large for an answer, for example. If operating under this participation structure, teacher and student should relate in a one-all ratio, with turns at talk allocated by the teacher. Talk is public, but it assists individual students in filling in the answers of the worksheet independently.

Yet, in the opening 18 lines of the segment of talk from Mr. Ellison's class, Mr. Ellison appears to direct the operation of all three participation structures at once. For example, when he reenters the classroom from the hallway, students are already working independently or in pairs on the worksheet. Loudly, Mr. Ellison interrupts the seatwork to ask if "ANY-BODY" has another question about the worksheet (line 1). His question may be an invitation for individuals—"ANYBODY"—to raise hands if they need his assistance. If one did not have a question, presumably one could continue working independently and ignore the question. Or, it could be an indication that seatwork is over and a change to a different participation structure is imminent. Still further, perhaps the class, acting as a group as it had with the first worksheet question, should now turn its attention to the review of yet "ANOTHER" question. Mr. Ellison's loud tone of voice supports this last interpretation, but who is to respond and how is not clear from Mr. Ellison's question.

Tina provides one response, by reading aloud the next question on the worksheet: "'WHAT DID WE DO ABOUT IT (the bombing of Pearl

Harbor)?'" (lines 4-5). Her response continues the ambiguity, however. She announces that, as an individual, she needs help with the second question. However, by speaking loudly (and thereby matching her reply in volume to Mr. Ellison's), she suggests that the question is problematic for and deserves the attention of the whole class.

Mr. Ellison's assessment of Tina's response, because he has already asked for questions, is an ironic reprimand: "I was just going to ask if you had another question," he says (lines 6-7). His sarcasm marks Tina's loud and persistent overlaps of his talk (lines 2; 4). Thus, it shifts the topic of talk from the question "any" student has about the worksheet to how one student, Tina, should voice hers. The shift of topic also suggests that Mr. Ellison and Tina are now engaged in a one-to-one interaction. However, it is also unclear whether Mr. Ellison will return to Tina's question ("'WHAT DID WE DO ABOUT IT?'"). Perhaps, having disapproved of her overlapping of his talk, he will again broadcast an appeal for questions to the group at large. To ensure that her question from the worksheet will not be passed over, Tina blurts out an answer to it, thus continuing her topic (lines 10-11). Again loud and public, Tina's answer revives the ambiguity about whether the participation structure involves the teacher and the whole group or the teacher and one student.

At this point (line 12), Mr. Ellison begins a series of moves that eventually establishes a participation structure involving the whole group. By lines 20-23, he asks one direct question to the whole class, to the persons "in here": "Do any of you know what they called that (the empire), that whole thing there?" The participation structure, a recitation, lasts almost 2 minutes, when there is yet another shift (lines 102-104).

In lower-track classrooms at Southmoor like Mr. Ellison's, participation structures shift much more frequently than in regular-track classrooms, and the structure in which classroom participants are to operate is often ambiguous. In a 3-minute segment of talk, for example, participation structures shift twice (lines 20; 102). This rapid fluctuation is not peculiar to the particular segment of talk transcribed or to Mr. Ellison's class. Shifts are equally frequent in one other Additional Needs class at Southmoor. In the other Additional Needs classes in which I observed, the rate of change was lower (four to five shifts per class period) but was still decidedly higher than in regular-track classrooms.

Furthermore, these ambiguous curricular practices produce some of the very "immature" or "unthinking" behaviors of lower-track students of which teachers complain. When Mr. Ellison provides worksheets for independent seatwork but interrupts students with a loud appeal for questions, students may either shout back a response or ignore him and continue working. Both the shout, as in the case of Tina (lines 4–5), and the failure to attend to group activities, as in the case of Cheryl (lines 42–46), are subsequently sanctioned.

Ambiguous Classroom Topics

The climate in classrooms for academically unsuccessful students is also disorderly because the topic of the lesson is not clearly academic and, therefore, the basis for a relationship between teacher and students is unclear. In general, an academic topic in lower-track lessons at Southmoor is replaced or undercut by entertaining games or jokes, as in Mr. Ellison's class, by topics "relevant" to students' personal lives, or by unconnected daily exercises. For example, Mr. Ellison's question about the name of the Japanese empire diverts attention from Tina's legitimate topic, which was how to answer question 2. It relates, at best, very tangentially to the day's academic lesson on Pearl Harbor. Mr. Ellison has no logical reason to introduce it, given the reading selection, the questions on the worksheet, or previous discussion.

In fact, Mr. Ellison's question is, like the entertaining puzzles on the worksheets he prepares, a joke or trick, exemplifying one-upmanship. Mr. Ellison does not really expect students to know the name, "Greater East Asia Co-prosperity Sphere." The name is not in the reading and is not common knowledge. Yet Mr. Ellison insists that the students consider the question. His repetitions of the question mark a "joshing" relationship with the students yet make students uneasy about the answer. However, the joke culminates in the students' hostile rejection of it and of its academic content. As Mr. Ellison belabors the question, forcing students to take it seriously, they respond angrily: They blame their memories (line 59) or the teacher (line 60) for their inability to answer. Finally, exasperated, they demand the answer: "WELL, TELL US!" (line 62).

This climactic moment in the recitation quickly dissolves into bitter rejection when students are at long last told the answer to Mr. Ellison's question. They assess the academic information, "The Greater East Asia Co-prosperity Sphere," as of no value: "What a stupid name" (line 74) and "Who cares?" (line 80). Their assessment is related to the double nature of the question. Students took seriously the expectation that they, as students, should know the answer, but this was a trick. Rejecting the position of having been the butt of a joke, they reject the knowledge offered by the teacher as well as his subsequent attempt to explain why the name is "official" and interesting (lines 75–89). Indeed, Mr. Ellison himself turns away from the topic and students' angry rejection of it at the first opportunity (lines 102–104). Tom's late arrival provides a "flexible" shift to a new topic and a new participation structure.

Interactional Prerogatives in an Ambiguous Encounter

In such ambiguous classroom situations, generated by frequently shifting and unclearly marked participation structures as well as bewildering mixtures of academic and nonacademic topics, the interactional prerogatives of classroom participants themselves become confused and unclear. To communicate competently in a situation, a person must first understand what the situation is. Yet in Southmoor's lower-track classrooms, the situation is, above all, not clear. It is not clearly educational, and the rules for how students should act, both in terms of their intellect and their age, are confused. Consequently, students' actions often appear stupid or immature, but their confusion mirrors teachers' uncertainty in playing their role.

In the 3 minutes of talk transcribed above, Mr. Ellison's enactment of the teacher role is decidedly curious. On the one hand, by line 20, he does have an educational point to make: The Japanese choice of a name for the empire shows their skill as propagandists. Moreover, Mr. Ellison appears very teacherly: He asks 15 questions, that most common form of teacher talk (Bellack et al., 1966; Edwards & Furlong, 1978; Mehan, 1979). On the other hand, Mr. Ellison makes his *educational* point in as *entertaining* a way as possible: He teaches by performing an elaborate trick or joke. The joke is produced through the repetition of one question (9 of Mr. Ellison's 15 elicitations are virtually identical) on a topic that is rather extraneous to the day's lesson. Usually, when teachers ask a question to which students don't rather quickly respond correctly, they offer prompts, or repairs, in the form of rephrasings or simplifications, or they give the answer themselves (Mehan, 1979; Philips, 1983). Instead, Mr. Ellison's question assumes a mocking cast that grows more onerous for the students as the recitation proceeds. Eventually, when Mr. Ellison does not modify the question to give the students a better chance to respond correctly, they reject their obligation to answer and turn the tables. They demand point-blank that Mr. Ellison himself answer: "WELL, TELL US!" (line 62).

Mr. Ellison's strange enactment of his role as teacher/trickster initiates confusion in students. The students and teacher shift into a very unusual relationship. The usual social relations in the classroom—between students and teacher and between adolescents and adult—are momentarily inverted. The students become the questioners and, especially unusual, the evaluators of the teacher, who then becomes the respondent. For instance, the students insist, three times, that Mr. Ellison tell them the name of the empire (lines 62; 64; 70). When he finally does honor their request, his answer appears so banal that they assess the information negatively. It is dismissed as "stupid" (line 74) or not worth caring about (line 80). Eventually, Cheryl, using another teacher/adult prerogative, changes the topic entirely, rejecting Mr. Ellison's topic and reintroducing Tina's original question from the worksheet (lines 95–96). However, the inversion of the social relations produces the subversion of the educational enterprise. Mr. Ellison fails to understand (line 97) and then to credit Cheryl's question (lines 99–100), just as he refused to credit students' demands that he "tell (them) so (they) do know." In essence, Mr. Ellison makes visible his power to ignore Additional Needs students, as students and as maturing adolescents. This time, however, Cheryl, already duped once in being asked to answer a trick question, exerts *her* ultimate, if self-defeating, power in response. She withdraws from the academic task, muttering disgustedly: "Forget it!" (line 101).

When a disorderly classroom climate is constructed, in part as the result of the confused direction of the teacher, the interactional prerogatives of students also become unclear. As a consequence, students exhibit behaviors that are deemed "out-of-control"; they seem not to care about, even to reject, classroom knowledge. Thus, they act toward the teacher, not as high school students should, but as "naughty fourth graders." Yet their actions are taken in account of the teacher's (Sacks, 1972).

Mr. Ellison's low expectations for the students is communicated in his offering them an entertaining trick rather than a serious academic topic and purposive direction. They respond, reciprocally, with a lack of seriousness, which, cyclically, confirms Mr. Ellison's low expectations. Furthermore, Mr. Ellison's direction of the talk reflects his own sense of uncertainty regarding the success of his professional efforts. Students respond, first, by attempting to make him teach: "Tell us so we do know!" However, ultimately, they reject him, their own role as students, and the educational encounter: "Forget it!" Cheryl says scornfully. Failing to act according to the prerogatives and obligations of students, they again confirm Mr. Ellison's expectations and keep the cycle of low expectations in motion.

Chaos in Other Lower-Track Classrooms at Southmoor

Even though other classes have distinctive histories, personalities, and curricula, lower-track teachers at Southmoor share tacitly an ambivalent role and define an uncertain tone. By using participation structures as a unit of analysis, other Additional Needs classes can be compared with Mr. Ellison's, resulting in a description that does justice to their idiosyncrasies yet captures their common form.

For example, at first glance, Mr. Thompson's Additional Needs class-room appears to be the antithesis of Mr. Ellison's. The daily lesson is invariant. During the first 35 minutes of class, all students read three or four selected articles from a national news magazine and work independently to answer 20 multiple-choice questions. This participation structure of individual seatwork is signaled by three actions: (1) Mr. Thompson says, "Lights," and a student near the door turns off the lights; (2) he turns to his left and says, "Shades," and two or three students pull down the shades; and (3) Mr. Thompson, himself, switches on the overhead projector, a soft glow suffuses the classroom, and the day's quiz appears on the screen. The second participation structure in the lesson, a quick exchange of papers and a recitative checking of answers, occupies the last 15 minutes of class and is usually signaled by Mr. Thompson's passing out red pencils. During the class period there is virtually no discussion by Mr. Thompson of the subject matter. Students may ask Mr. Thompson for individual help, but they almost never do. On the occasions when they do, Mr. Thompson often becomes impatient if the student's question is not resolved rather quickly. In contrast to the haphazard events in Mr. Ellison's Additional Needs class, therefore, Mr. Thompson's appears to be the epitome of orderliness. The participation structures in Mr. Thompson's classroom seem limited in number, clear, and regular, if not positively ritualistic.

However, ambiguity is introduced in Mr. Thompson's classroom be-cause a third participation structure, at odds with that of individual seat-work, also operates, albeit illicitly. In the third participation structure, Mr. Thompson sits at his desk at the front of the room and prepares the next day's quiz; he ignores the class and rarely looks up to monitor the class or check for questions. Meanwhile, the class, although noiseless and almost motionless, is in Pandemonium. Rather than reading or working independently on their quizzes according to the participation structure of individual seatwork, most students share answers, listen discretely to Walkman radios, do other homework, pass around food, pass around notes, mouth gossip, toss spit wads, or gaze at the ceiling. If Mr. Thompson gets up to leave the room for a few minutes, which he does often, the participation structure shifts instantly back to that of individual seatwork until he leaves the room. Despite the class's appearance of academic industry, therefore, there is considerable fluctuation and ambiguity of participation structures, as students shift between individual, bookish studiousness and concealed but rowdy group highjinks. Moreover, the contradictory participation structures resonate with students' educational ambivalence. Many maintain only the appearance of reading *Time* magazine, even when they are not engaged in surreptitious joking. They skim articles quickly, looking for answers that match questions rather than seeking to understand the text.

However, like Mr. Ellison's "flexibility," Mr. Thompson's ambiguous participation structures give him greater control over the class than if he attempted to monitor students' adherence to the lesson. A veneer of harmony is maintained so long as Mr. Thompson does not look up and students are quiet in their games.

In sum, the chaos that characterizes Mr. Ellison's lower-track social studies class also characterizes the climate in other lower-track classes at Southmoor. It is not a result of one teacher's ineptness. Nor is it necessitated by lower-track students' rambunctiousness or indifference. Rather, it arises from and re-creates teachers' uncertainties regarding their role in lower-track classes. If fed by students' confused responses, it begins with teachers' uncertain direction of participation structures. Lower-track teachers at Southmoor act with unconscious mockery toward themselves and the students. Academic tasks become games; shifting and unclearly marked participation structures reflect uncertain direction and require confused responses; teacher-student relationships are informal, as with regular-track students, but also ironical; and teachers' sarcasm resonates with students' ambivalent attitudes toward schooling and themselves. The overall atmosphere is therefore chaotic and purposeless, and encounters in Additional Needs classes become caricatures of the excellent education provided Southmoor's college-bound.

CHAPTER 5

The Ethos of
Southmoor High School

All four of the Additional Needs teachers at Southmoor whom I observed enact their teaching responsibilities with considerable confusion rather than clear enthusiasms or unwavering disdain. A pattern of ambiguous participation structures prevails in the classes, even though they vary on many other dimensions, including subject matter (one English class, two history, and one combination of English and history); size (8 to 18 students); grade level (ninth, tenth, and a combination of ninth, tenth, and eleventh); and teacher style (from motherly to casual jester to stern patriarch). Given these differences among the classes, the similarity in atmosphere and participation structure is puzzling.

Especially curious is the uncertainty of otherwise competent teachers in lower-track classes. It would be difficult to argue that lower-track teachers at Southmoor, like Mr. Ellison, are incompetent or uncaring teachers who "just can't or won't control the kids." They are experienced veterans who direct their regular classes with aplomb (if with atrocious puns!). All voice concern for the well-being of the "little family" of individuals in their lower-track classes as well as considerable despair that things do not somehow go better. Tracking would appear to be a ready explanation for the common pattern of ambivalent teaching. But how do apparently concerned teachers, meeting only irregularly, absorb and exhibit ambivalence with such consistency? Is tracking so powerful and singular a factor?

With such questions, I turn attention beyond individuals and classrooms to the larger school context in order to describe how Southmoor's culture, mediated by teachers, shapes their teaching and tracking. Thus, I argue that the ironic, aimless tenor of Southmoor's lower-track classes is sensible and potent, not simply because of invidious grouping, as critiques of tracking would predict, but because it echoes and caricatures the purpose and informality that govern Southmoor's regular-track classes. Uncertain teaching reflects individuals' struggles to integrate an intellectual's role (and their membership in a powerful, esteemed faculty) with that of a caretaker (and membership in a marginal, technical, remedial program). Furthermore, the struggles are generated and exacerbated by organizational politics: Teachers see the marginality of lower-track classes in policies and decisions that govern the administration of the classes.

TEACHING IN A "HEAVENLY" CULTURE

The culture of a school is constituted, first, by an institutional definition of the students and, second, by a bureaucratic or professional mode of operation that shapes the role of faculty members (Schlechty, 1976; Waller, 1932). Although hard to put a finger on, the cultural code is coercive in its self-evidence. It makes particular ways of behaving appear natural or commonsensical, even though they are quite arbitrary and, elsewhere, are in fact otherwise. Put another way, a school's culture sets parameters within which participants perceive and enact their roles. As they act, they re-create the culture, borrowing from its predominant, defining precepts but skewing them to fit particular circumstances and purposes. In short, culture organizes and distinguishes the world of a school from other institutions; simultaneously, it also differentiates and integrates the school's various internal domains.

The Role of the Regular-Track Teacher

Southmoor's distinctive ethos is self-assured "perfection." Although the school offers the comprehensive smorgasbord of diverse courses that Americans have come to expect, it considers itself a peerless academic institution. In such a milieu, teachers regard regular students as "nice" and as "high achievers." By social background and anticipated future, students are deemed "*easy* to teach": "The backbone of Southmoor High, er, are the children of college graduates, most of them really with advanced degrees, who intend to go on into college—and to graduate school—themselves some day." Nor is the typification ungrounded: A handmade poster displayed prominently in the teachers' lounge proclaimed Southmoor's rank among the top 15 schools in the country in number of National Merit scholars.

The emphasis on academic achievement that defines the college-bound student body defines the faculty as well. Subject matter expertise is the basis of teachers' authority in the classroom and their power in the organization. A teacher elaborated the school's and its teachers' extraordinary qualities:

Teachers here are the cream of the crop. I was told when I got a contract to teach here that it was the greatest honor. We're good –
– We care about the kids and have standards for them. We're not teaching off the cuff, from one day to the next. . . . And, nobody's running around checking up on you, seeing if you've done your job. In fact this faculty would ride any principal out on a rail who tried to interfere with what goes on in classrooms.

An assistant principal concurred in teachers' artistry and autonomy: "The faculty is a bunch of prima donnas but, damn, they do a terrific job. I don't bother them. I just let them teach."

Teachers designate themselves scholars, not mere secondary school teachers. Intellectual stature is important in a school with many professional families and with a state university in its backyard. Thus, one 30-year veteran explained his career as a reflection of his "interest in history. It grew from the stories my grandfather, who was very steeped in history, told about settling in America and recollections of his father's having come from Europe and things like that." He went on to describe an elaborate "theory of American history" and its importance to the quality of his teaching, concluding with a definition of high school's "primary" function as "intellectual":

The school is primarily an intellectual place. The foundation of education has to be that you try to teach people to improve their ability to think and, ah, that, other things, social education, and functional education, and ah, that, they're all incidental.

In short, teachers gain stature from and relish their guardianship of the "intellectual place" they see Southmoor to be. Even in casual encounters in the faculty lounge, informed, if acerbic, encounters prevail. Gathering around large wooden tables at 7 in the morning and continuing until the late hours of the afternoon, teachers discuss and debate, sharing analyses of current events, arguments regarding the school and district, and the triumphs and foibles of the day's round of classes. Administrators and district officials make a point of dropping into the lounge for a cup of coffee, recognizing it as the center of the school and the hub where crucial information will be exchanged.

Teachers' authority and subject-matter expertise also govern their classroom practices. As regular-track students give their attention to receive important information, they both confirm and fuel inspired, ebullient teaching. Sensing students' appreciation, Southmoor teachers work not only to transmit their knowledge but, as in the lesson about the Haymarket Riot (see Chapter 4), to translate it meaningfully and with sophistication into contemporary concerns. At center stage in lectures and recitations, Southmoor teachers rarely miss a chance to embellish a potentially dry lecture with anecdotes, impersonations, or jokes.

Teachers also read regular students' comments and questions, not as unpredictable, inefficient, or querulous emendations, but as added evidence of students' "high achievement" and of the appropriateness of intellectual spontaneity: Because students participate in lessons, they must understand and approve of them. Students' active contributions confirm teachers' enthusiasm for subject matter, pride in pedagogical performance, and rapport with students.

Rapport with students is also enhanced because Southmoor teachers do not set a great distance between themselves and students. Because students are moving toward college, they must value and will eventually acquire the knowledge that teachers value. Further, because teachers define students as "upper middle class, from mostly professional families," they expect them to be quick, critical thinkers who, even though they may be inexperienced, can participate courteously in debates and can formulate well-reasoned arguments.

Not surprisingly, Southmoor teachers implement planned but not rigid school lessons that combine their classical expertise with youth's experiential contributions. One teacher at Southmoor explained her test questions by emphasizing that students cannot "gear in to the book and pick out the answer." Instead, she asks students to "apply subjects to new situations" and to "make connections." Teachers can regard the "open-ended" outcomes of such lessons with equanimity because they expect that students will construct significant interpretations. Furthermore, Southmoor teachers attempt to provide a kind of gestalt of a discipline rather than bits and pieces of it. Thus, they discredit technicist, routinized, or behavioristic styles of teaching as "not what learning is all about." One teacher explained:

> D and F students would rather have hunt-up-the-answer questions. The others would probably rather have it, too, because it'd make it easier. They *think* it would. But after they get used to my type of questions, they think they're kind of neat - - - because really, down inside themselves, somewhere, they know these types of questions are not as big a chore to deal with as factual recall, you know (sing-song), "Do the odd-numbered problems."

The Role Conflict of the Lower-Track Teacher

In contrast to the certitude with which regular-track teachers at Southmoor pursue their tasks, lower-track teachers experience great conflict. Their conflict is symbolized by a brief but emotionally charged interchange that occurred one day in Mr. Ellison's Additional Needs class. Two regular-track students interrupted the class as they passed by in the hallway. They poked their heads in to ask Mr. Ellison what kind of strange class he was running. "Is this a study hall?" they wondered, observing the scattered students and their desultory engagement. Mr. Ellison's reply was noncommittal: "Not today." However, Tina, a student in the class, clarified the course: "This is a HISTORY class!" she trumpeted. Mr. Ellison then qualified her academic characterization: "Some days we are, uh, historical, some days we're hysterical." Several students in the class laughed mechanically. After that Mr. Ellison directed the regular-track students to leave and returned his attention to the Additional Needs students and the lesson.

Although the interchange produced only the most ephemeral ripple in the flow of Mr. Ellison's class, it is charged symbolically far beyond the temporal space it occupied. It marks the pervasive ambiguity with which Mr. Ellison and other Additional Needs teachers at Southmoor regard the lower-track enterprise. Sometimes, the class is "historical": an educational situation involving a teacher and students pursuing a social studies/English curriculum. As well, however, the Additional Needs class is sometimes "hysterical." This emendation suggests not a classroom but a chaotic situation in which excessively emotional adolescents are supervised by an adult caretaker. Thus, Mr. Ellison expresses, however fleetingly and obliquely, the mixed expectations he has not only for lower-track students but for his own teaching. His ambivalence stems from the contradictions between the norms that pattern regular and remedial teaching at Southmoor.

The crucial contradiction for lower-track teachers at Southmoor lies in the denial of the importance of their academic expertise in Additional Needs classes. Indeed, the phrase "lower-track teacher" is an oxymoron. Just as lower-track students are deemed unable to learn because they are so far below their regular-track peers, so lower-track teachers need not teach because there is no need in lower-track classrooms for the academic knowledge that is the foundation of the Southmoor teacher's role. Simply put, academics are the least important aspect of Additional Needs classes.

At the same time, like the "professionals" in regular-track classes, lower-track teachers have almost complete authority over what students study. However, because norms of the school discount Additional Needs students as "the dregs," the individual teacher's sense of professional accountability for such students' educational progress becomes problematic. For example, when a beginning teacher speaks about improving lower-track students' academic skills, a goal that contradicts the institutional definition, she is rebuffed by her peers.

Instead of being academic experts, lower-track teachers are defined as supervisors of the deficient and unruly: the "hysterical." Fundamentally, their job is to keep such students out of the corridors and regular classes. Yet even the role definition of caretaker is fraught with contradictions. In the first place, faculty norms at Southmoor militate against teachers being involved to any great degree in matters of discipline: Scholars should not have to "get their hands dirty by dealing with disciplinary matters," which are more properly the province of administrators. In the second place, teachers expect to get along easily with "nice" students. However, academically unsuccessful students are "unpredictable" and "immature," or they are so mature they are "13, going on 30, and won't listen to a word I say." Thus, social as well as academic relationships are uncertain at best.

In short, in lower-track classes teachers are forced to contradict their role as Southmoor teacher. To take remedial teaching or students' academic progress seriously is to contradict Southmoor's mores and to risk losing a place within the esteemed Southmoor faculty. Yet, not to take them seriously is to be unprofessional. Teachers' role conflict is not merely psychic but is manifested concretely in instructional practices, curricular topics, and classroom management.

Instructional Practices. Lower-track teachers adhere to prevailing principles of remediation when they use daily, individualized worksheets in class. As they explain, worksheets are a means of allowing academically unsuccessful students to "work at their own pace." If one student is very slow, very obstinate, or frequently absent, other students can proceed without being held back, as might be the case with a class discussion or group project. In addition, many teachers plan lessons in which there are varied activities. In this way, according to accepted remedial theory, they accommodate students' short attention spans.

However, the individualized remedial format contrasts sharply with the procedures of regular-track teaching at Southmoor. The predominant participation structure in regular-track classes is teacher/large group, wherein teachers show themselves to be teachers by performing as central actors in the classroom. Accordingly, lower-track teachers also feel compelled to direct students as a group. Sometimes, like Mr. Ellison, they interrupt individual seatwork to do so. In similarly contradictory fashion, although lower-track teachers use a variety of activities during a class period, they rarely structure them so that they are related to one another. Additional Needs students are busy, but their tasks have little coherence. In such confused provisions for individualized and varied lower-track activities, teachers borrow elements from both the Southmoor teacher role and the lower-track teacher role, often with contradictory effect.

Curricular Topics. The role conflict also affects the formal curriculum. Sometimes Additional Needs teachers emphasize the broad topics of the regular-track curriculum, but they present them at a much slower pace, in "less depth," or by using elementary school materials, as befits students who are seen as less able and less mature. Games are also part of the curriculum because students "can't complain about lessons that are fun." Thus, teachers in Additional Needs classes do not abdicate their responsibility to design a curriculum appropriate to students' needs. However, neither they nor the students who complain continually about "this baby work" see the differentiated curriculum as "real," or valid, knowledge. For example, a teacher, telling of a lower-track student who went on to a state university, did not consider it odd, despite the student's lower-track status in high school: "Well, you have to consider the college – – He's only at the state university. And, you know, he's not, he's not aiming for any great big huge job in the academic life, I'm sure." At Southmoor, only the traditionally academic counts.

Classroom Management. As with the strange amalgamations of regular- and lower-track instructional and curricular practices, teachers also skew the easy give-and-take between classroom participants that prevails in regular classes. It is caricatured in lower-track classrooms in a veneer of harmony. Thus, as with regular students, teachers joke with lower-track students, but, as in Mr. Ellison's class, such jokes can go awry. Teachers direct recitations, but as with the lesson on the Japanese empire (see Chapter 4), the group work is full of arrhythmic shout-outs and interruptions. When such interactional dissonance erupts, teachers' expectations come into play. Academically unsuccessful students are viewed as hostile, indifferent, or immature children, not as near equals, and their commitment to the educational values of teachers is deemed unlikely. To maintain the veneer—and control—teachers limit face-to-face interactions by using many films and "structured," individualized worksheets. In recitations, students' questions are not treated as important contributions to the topic, as regular-track students' questions are, but are arbitrarily rejected as nonsensical, off-the-topic, or unwelcome challenges to the teachers' authority. In teachers' views, interactions with students who are "your basic bottom" cannot be intellectual.

The give-and-take that teachers do institute in lower-track classrooms centers not on academic matters but on behavior, thus reflecting the importance lower-track teachers give to that issue. No longer claiming authority on the basis of the important knowledge they can communicate, lower-track teachers seek to establish their authority largely on the basis of an exchange of time and classroom rules for students' goodwill. By easing up on behavioral requirements, as well as on academic standards, teachers act the part of the "buddy-buddy" (Henry, 1963), or nice guy, rather than that of the academic expert. However, the modifications teachers make in classroom rules also exemplify their judgments of academically unsuccessful students. For example, lower-track classes at Southmoor rarely begin and end with the bell. Almost all start late and end early, and students are allowed to talk, find their notebooks, arrive late, eat, or go to their lockers. This relaxation of teachers' expectations for classroom behavior borrows from theories of behavior modification in that teachers adapt rules to use them as rewards. It also reflects teachers' views that academically unsuccessful students are nonlearners who need childish indulgence. As teachers make such implicit or explicit exchanges, their facial expressions usually signal disapproval or dismay. They feel compelled to make such allowances as lower-track teachers, but they distance themselves from the role because, as Southmoor teachers, they must condemn such tactics as "silly" or as bribes for persons unable to control themselves.

Goffman (1961) explains that social actors may resolve conflicts between two roles by distancing themselves from one. Lower-track teachers resolve the conflict between the Southmoor teacher role and the lower-track teacher role by distancing themselves from the latter. They adopt this solution because the educational success of Additional Needs students is only marginally important in the college-preparatory institution. Teachers will not be rewarded for their efforts with the "hard-to-teach" by the students themselves, because no lower-track student will achieve academic accolades. Other faculty members may gratefully commiserate with the teachers of lower-track students because, through their efforts, they are spared the "hard" work of dealing with such students. But regular teachers also do not actively support such efforts because the provision of classes for less able students takes scarce resources away from Southmoor's main, college-preparatory business. Indeed, lower-track teaching challenges the institution's definition of itself as an elite institution and teachers' prestigious role in it: Lower-track students do not belong in "heaven." Finally, teachers can distance themselves from the lower-track role because, as part of Southmoor's autonomous faculty, they are not held accountable for students' educational progress. Just as regular teachers are allowed to teach as they deem best, so Additional Needs teachers enjoy a high degree of curricular autonomy. One administrator voiced the prevailing ambivalence toward Additional Needs classes this way:

> Could we give them a diploma if we expanded the Additional Needs classes and they stayed in it for 4 years and got the 20 credits needed for graduation? That brings up the question of standards.

> We expect a lot of students at Southmoor. But there are no stan-
> dards in Additional Needs classes. We're just trying to get the kid in
> class; we're not worrying about what he does while he's there.

Because no one is "worrying about" what Additional Needs students do in classrooms, their teachers become mere "baby-sitters" who work to maintain control of the "hysterical" in an institution that values only high academic achievement by the self-disciplined. In lower-track classrooms, one's charges are not near equals with whom one exchanges ideas but obstreperous children with whom one exchanges indulgences.

MARGINAL LOWER-TRACK CLASSES: AN ORGANIZATIONAL ACHIEVEMENT

Southmoor's "heavenly" culture prompts not only the conflict in roles that Additional Needs teachers experience but also its resolution. In distancing themselves from lower-track teaching, teachers acknowledge the marginal importance of Additional Needs classes to the organization. One teacher explained succinctly: "Why should I care (about lower-track classes) if no one else does?"

Teachers see the marginality of Additional Needs classes in the history and structure of the classes. As Southmoor's principal remarked, the school must act "politically." Like other public schools (Meyer & Rowan, 1978), Southmoor must maintain public support and avoid public criticism. Even more than most, given the politics of Maplehurst, it cannot blatantly ignore academically unsuccessful students without risking charges of elitism, segregation, or inefficiency, yet its public also rewards the delivery of an academically rigorous program.

The school responds to the "political" dilemma in a way that makes sense, given the norms of its culture: It establishes small, temporary, "special" (Cusick, 1983; Powell et al., 1985) programs, such as Additional Needs classes, for students who do not excel in school. Administrators can point to the classes as indicators of the high school's responsiveness to all students. It expends scarce resources to offer even potential dropouts, low achievers, and "troublemakers" the classes that are "appropriate to their individual needs." At the same time, however, Additional Needs classes are only "loosely coupled" (Weick, 1978) to the main organization. Therefore, they provide an appearance of educational services but with little serious accountability for the teaching and learning that go on in them. They allow Southmoor's regular-track faculty members to continue as scholars while autonomous "professionals" determine what is best in the lower track.

Moreover, because Additional Needs classes are few in number, they substantiate the institutional myth that high achievers predominate at Southmoor.

For Additional Needs teachers, however, the organizational disregard is confusing and demoralizing:

> I: You only have six students in your Additional Needs class? Are there *enough* students at Southmoor to have Additional Needs classes?
> T: Oh, yes. More than enough.
> I: Why aren't they in your class then?
> (4.0)
> T: Well – – I don't know. (4.0) It's part of the process itself. I mean, it's unbelievable. Whether you're going to blame the teachers or the principals or the counselors. You can blame anyone you want, I suppose. That's what I'm saying, there needs to be a designated person who knows what to do (with Additional Needs referrals). Like right now, who do I see? The reading specialist? The minority counselor? There's no pattern right now for what you do. And *they* don't know either. Sometimes they say one thing is one person's responsibility, then another time, it's another's. So that's why I do what I can in my class and don't worry about it. I can't let it get me down.

Although this teacher attempts to close the classroom door and "do what (she) can," pressures from the school as a whole "get (her) down." Her individual dilemma is an institutional dilemma. It was writ large at Southmoor between 1980 and 1984 in the development and demise of five Additional Needs classes. Their history illustrates how remedial programs, although crucially important to the main organization on occasion, are not an enduring institutional responsibility.

Origins

In formal terms, Southmoor is accountable for the academic progress of all students in its catchment area. Accordingly, school members designated a rational process by which they develop "special" classes. As one put it:

> A staff member or members recognize a group of kids with a like need for whom provision should be made. They look at what help is available and try to use those programs first. Then, that person,

or persons, assumes leadership. A proposal is written. And it's discussed with the head principal or with an assistant principal. Then the head principal has to convince the higher district echelons of a need for a higher or different allocation to staff the special program.

Participants cited this general formula in characterizing the origins in 1980–81 of five new Additional Needs classes. Specifically, the classes were the organization's response to a group of 10 to 12 black girls who were troublesome "in-school truants." Because the students' skills were so low, the girls found regular classes unattractive, but rather than leaving school, they roamed the hallways. An assistant principal proposed the creation of several special classes in which the students would be taught "survival skills" at their "basic level." Ad hoc funds were found, the head principal approved the plan, and five Additional Needs classes—in English, social studies, industrial arts, math, and science—began operation almost overnight. Teachers of the classes, with two assistant principals, several counselors, and other support staff, constituted what they referred to initially as a "Fundamentals team."

However, after the first year of operation, the five classes evinced many puzzling aspects that did not match the formula for curriculum development. For example, the "group of kids with a like need" was not apparent: Students included highly skilled, regular attenders and the "eager-to-please" as well as the "basic levels," "in-school truants," and "juvenile delinquents." The classes were also uncertain in purpose. Some staff members saw their main objective as "making class a fun place where the students can feel good and will keep coming to school"; the classes existed to "give the kid positive feedback . . . and a little confidence, instead of pushing him out of school." Other staff members were adamant that they were "not being paid to be a baby-sitter." Still others described the classes as places in which students, through individualized instruction, could improve their basic skills so that they could return to the regular school program.

Not only the clients and purposes of the classes were puzzling: Lines of authority were muddied. For instance, no single staff member was identified as in charge of the five classes. The minority counselor acted as though he were in charge because he called occasional meetings of the informal "team." He explained that no one formally assigned him the role, but that he "just took the, uh, leadership on myself, kind of. It's not that hard a task, uh, and it helps the kids, you know, that I'm trying to help anyway." However, the minority counselor's assumption of the leadership role was problematic because his position in the school's formal hierarchy gave him little authority over the other members of the "team." For example, because the minority counselor was formally supervised by one of the assistant principals, his ability to direct that principal was at least qualified. Furthermore, the two assistant principals had different views of the primary purpose of the classes so that the minority counselor often found himself caught in the middle. His position in relation to the teachers was equally ambiguous: Could he insist that they individualize instruction, for example, especially given the strength of Southmoor norms for faculty autonomy?

Finally, the rational explanation of the five Additional Needs classes, although cited by almost everyone, left an important question unanswered: Why was the response to "in-school truancy" among low-skilled students so prompt in 1980–81? After all, low-skilled students had attended Southmoor for years with few special classes: Why did classes arise in this particular instance?

These questions of origin, leadership, and purpose were cast in a new light when the assistant principal most involved in starting the classes retold the tale of their beginning, with more specifics and a less formulaic emphasis:

> Yes, the classes began running first semester with a group of about 12 black girls. (The principal gets up from the easy chair in which he sits next to me, walks behind his desk, sits down, and begins speaking again.) Actually – (4.0) – Actually, on October 26, 1980 – – (He begins to shuffle through papers on his desk, muttering about finding the log of his activities) – Well, anyway, on October 26, there were three incidents in one day, and there had been a series of days with single incidents for over a week. It was a black-white thing. We had these girls who were coming to school, not going to class. Oh, they'd get their free lunch, but no attendance in classes. And, of course, they were bored. So they started fights: girl-girl fights, with whites. They'd go around to classrooms, knock on the door, and ask for a kid, the kid would come to the door, and there'd be pushing and shoving. So I gathered them all up in the Commons and said, "Look, you're not getting any credits for all this time you've been putting in here at Southmoor. If you could have a class, what would it have to be like to make you attend?"

The assistant principal's story highlights the importance of social control in the inception of the five lower-track classes. Although he acknowledges students' low academic skills and attributes truancy to them, the students come to his attention because of their uncontrolled behavior in hallways. Furthermore, their behavior is exceptionally potent because it involves race. The possibility of adverse public scrutiny resulting from interracial fighting is strong in any school, but it is particularly volatile in Maplehurst because the community's strong liberal and black constituencies watch carefully for racial discrimination. At the same time, order and safety are high priorities for Southmoor administrators because, 8 years earlier, Southmoor made headlines when a white student was raped by two black students in the school during the school day. Given this context, administrators responded with alacrity to the threat of racial "incidents" posed by the black girls. Thus, the new Additional Needs classes originated in an emergency procedure that was critical to the protection of the institution as a whole rather than in a formal, deliberative process centered on the cognitive needs of a group of special students.

Evolution

That the five Additional Needs classes originated to serve purposes of organizational order and survival was corroborated by their subsequent evolution in 1981–82.

During their first year, 1980–81, almost all participants characterized the five classes as "an overwhelming success." The principal boasted of the placement of an Additional Needs student on the Southmoor honor roll; teachers in the classes spoke feelingly of the satisfaction they derived from "seeing *these* kids learn"; many of the students, whom the school had deemed likely to drop out, completed the term and returned the following year with considerable enthusiasm. Working together, teachers and support staff focused on ensuring the "success" of the Additional Needs classes: The school psychologist wrote curriculum, the social worker arranged Friday afternoon field trips, and the assistant principals tracked down nonattenders and escorted them to class. In the first year, everyone pitched in, lower-track teachers were confident in their roles, and a potentially explosive crisis for the whole school was averted.

By 1981–82 (when I conducted a pilot study of tracking in Maplehurst's high schools), the crisis had abated yet, surprisingly, the program was in disarray. Participants expressed an awareness of the change and the developing confusion. Often wistfully, they described the second year as "so different from last year," "a little shaky," and "up for grabs." At the same time, critics from outside the program emerged who were more emphatically negative: In the analysis of one teacher, it was "an inept program . . . that is a mockery of education because the kids can't be learning anything worth knowing." An assistant principal even denied that the five Additional Needs classes were classes at all:

I mean, these classes are not classes. I want to stress that. A class is a *regular* responsibility of any school, with every department swinging its own weight and accepting the responsibility of having a class for even the kids at the very lowest level. But, Additional Needs classes! - - They're for low-skilled kids, they're a holding tank. Now I say - - I know you can take this wrong, some bleeding heart liberal will - - But I say, these kids aren't going to graduate! I mean, if they come for 4 years, what are we going to do? Give them a certificate of attendance? I mean, these classes are just a place to give them a little confidence, a little time.

The differences between the first and second years of operation reflect changes in the value of the five Additional Needs classes to the main organization. Absent a crisis of order, administrators and support staff were pulled off to put out other brush fires of a more pressing nature. An assistant principal noted the change in their ability to command symbolic and material resources from the organization when the main problem they posed was the development of an educational program:

(I won't be going to Additional Needs meetings anymore.) It's time the minority counselor ran things. I have too many other things to be involved with. We just can't afford administrators on this kind of thing.

Yet the support of administrators was essential to lower-track teachers' positive role enactment and to the program's "overwhelming success" during the first year. Administrative support protected teachers from uncertainties about their purposes and from regular faculty critics.

Demise

Following the first "successful" year, no one in the Southmoor organization worked to establish the Additional Needs classes on an educative rather than an instrumental basis: The development of curriculum for academically unsuccessful students justified considerably fewer organizational resources than did a "crisis" of control. As a result, the classes slowly atrophied. By 1983–84, all five had been deleted.

One can argue that Additional Needs classes must always be somewhat marginal at Southmoor simply because academically unsuccessful students account for such a small percentage of the student body. However, marginality is an achieved state, not an inherent one (Mehan, 1979), and the relationship between facts and culture is interactive: If there are few

Additional Needs students, only a small amount of money need be set aside to serve them; nevertheless, when a budget is small, only a few needy students can be identified and accommodated. With a different ethos, Southmoor might have made student success a high organizational priority, precisely because the number of academically unsuccessful students is small (see Wehlage et al., 1980, chap. 4, for such a decision in a similar school). The school would expend a modest percentage of its overall resources to accomplish such a goal. However, in the present cultural context, to acknowledge academically unsuccessful students would undermine the school's view of itself as a premier academic institution. It could have concrete consequences as well: Successful Additional Needs classes might attract remedial and minority students from across the Maplehurst district through the district's open enrollment policy, and such an influx would divert even more resources from college-preparatory courses.

Given Southmoor's near-"perfect" ethos, virtually no attempts were made in the second year to solidify Additional Needs classes' academic relationship to the main organization or to demand accountability regarding students' academic progress. A teacher voiced the program's marginality and its effects on her teaching:

> You know, last year I was real excited about this Additional Needs class. This year, I feel like I'm just going through the motions. This year, I'm more depressed. It seems like I just don't have the time. And this Additional Needs class is an easy class to shortcut. I hate to say it, but I know I can fake it with this class, whereas my regular classes, I have to be prepared; they'll challenge me if I'm not. The moving forces behind the classes last year, the people heading it up, put in a lot more time. I guess there was a lot of interest in getting it off the ground, but now, this planning isn't happening this year - - Why should I care if nobody else does?

Achieving Uncertain Leadership. The confused leadership of the "team" both symbolized and promoted the tenuous status of the Additional Needs classes: With no one to advocate for them, the classes lay at the mercy of other interest groups. Inconsistent leadership was not a simple result of individuals' incompetence or "burnout," given difficult students. Rather, it resulted from capricious organizational processes: a surprise merger of remedial programs developed by two assistant principals, Mr. Lear and Mr. Meyer, which was imposed by Southmoor's head principal. The merger bespeaks the culture that makes serious remedial efforts so fruitless at Southmoor.

In 1980–81, at about the same time that Mr. Meyer, along with the

minority counselor, confronted the 12 "in-school truants" and was provided with post-haste, in-house funding for five Fundamentals classes,
Mr. Lear responded to a formal, district-wide call for Additional Needs
proposals. In a 15-page document, he certified the need for what he called a
"Resource Room," or "tank," in which to place new Southmoor students
who moved in during the semester and who could not catch up in regular
classes, as well as dropouts who returned but who could not make up
missed assignments. In a Resource Room, students would earn partial
credit for work done on individualized packets. Mr. Lear's proposal was
approved at the district level and given one full-time teacher allocation for
1981–82, a significant grant in times of declining enrollments and teacher
layoffs. By contrast, the purposes of the Fundamentals classes were never
codified in writing, although participants' informal understanding of them
was that they were to keep Additional Needs students out of Southmoor's
corridors by offering them instruction at their level in "basic survival
skills."

Given these efforts, one would expect a doubling of resources devoted
to academically unsuccessful students in 1981–82, with both the Resource
Room and the five classes in operation. Instead, the Resource Room and
the five Additional Needs classes were amalgamated, or, as one faculty
member put it, each was "bastardized."

The amalgamation process further undermined faculty members' investment in remedial classes because it was not hammered out in a meeting
in which interested parties faced each other, aired their differences, and
came to a compromise. Instead, it was imposed by fiat of the head principal
three weeks after the school year started, without consultation with either
assistant principal, support staff, or any of the involved teachers. Although
the principal acted within his formal prerogatives in making a unilateral
decision, his action violated informal norms of collegiality. One of the
assistant principals explained bitterly: "An individual decision was made.
Essentially, it was *his* (the head principal's) decision, as I understand it. *I*
was not consulted."

By acting singlehandedly, the head principal undercut the Additional
Needs classes, reducing funds, muddying teaching assignments, and exclud-
ing faculty members and administrators from a critical decision. Yet, at the
same time, the principal's action enhanced his own power. Because any
Southmoor principal must coexist with the very strong, long-lived, and
independent Southmoor academicians, as well as a large administrative
staff and a knowledgeable community, all find their power tenuous at best.
In addition, the current principal is not well regarded. One teacher echoed
the comments of many in the school when she characterized him as vain
and unimaginative but powerful:

> Who runs the school? Well, the principal makes the final deci-
> sions − − You know, the kind of person he is, he hates it when
> anyone does something without him knowing about it. Like, we
> printed up a program for Fine Art Week. Another teacher looked at
> it and said, "Oh, my God, you don't have his name as principal on
> the cover." That kind of thing. But no, I don't think he thinks for
> himself. He has no mission, no master plan for the school, no idea
> where the school will be in 10 years.

Another teacher praised the principal backhandedly as "smart enough to
leave us alone to run the school."

First, therefore, in merging the Resource Room with the five Additional Needs classes, the head principal checked a subordinate on his staff
and reasserted his own control over teaching allocations. In 1980–81,
Mr. Lear threatened the head principal when he "found" extra, in-house
teaching resources for Mr. Meyer's five Additional Needs classes.
Mr. Lear's "find" reportedly angered the head because it infringed on a
domain—teaching allocations—that the principal considered his alone.
Furthermore, when the Resource Room proposal was funded by the central
district office, Mr. Lear had an allocation of his own to dispense for what
everyone referred to as "Lear's program."

By using the allocation for the Resource Room to continue the five
Additional Needs classes, the principal also enhanced his standing with
many of Southmoor's regular teachers: Like the politician's pledge to hold
the line on taxes, the principal's move enacted concretely his assertion that
no special programs, such as Additional Needs classes, would ever cut into
the regular education allocations at Southmoor. It was another example of
the principal's efforts to cater to the faculty's autonomy and its devotion to
a traditional curriculum.

The principal's action also reserved power to his office. He often took
an unpredictable interest in less autonomous programs outside the core
academic departments, such as special education, vocational education, English as a Second Language, or Additional Needs classes. Regular Southmoor teachers, with considerable administrative protection, disdained such
classes as "not part of what Southmoor is all about." Because regular faculty
were uninvolved in "special" programs, the principal could manipulate the
teaching allocations with little scrutiny. The head also garnered support
from special teachers and from junior faculty by protecting their jobs: Had
the Resource Room allocation been used to hire one new teacher, all five
Additional Needs teachers would have had to teach part-time at other
schools. Finally, by associating himself with special classes, the principal
increased his standing with his district-level superiors, for whom such

classes *were* a priority, given the additional monies, legalities, and active interest groups they involve.

The principal's arbitrary amalgamation of the two programs also enhanced the power of his office by dividing two of his assistants. A "power struggle"—as both assistant principals characterized their disagreement—developed over the goals of the merged classes. Given the reality of a dictated merger, Mr. Meyer and Mr. Lear at first reacted by trying to achieve the aims of both the Resource Room and the Additional Needs classes. They changed the name of the "team" to reflect the amalgamation: Resource Fundamentals. However, they did not rethink the contradictory aims and methods of the two remedial proposals. The Resource Room was conceived as a temporary room for individuals, staffed by one teacher trained in the development of individualized instructional packets. But the Fundamentals team emphasized the group more than the individual and envisioned a series of self-contained classes. Because neither assistant principal had more formal authority than the other, a stalemate resulted, and the five classes of 1981–82 remained a confused, confusing conglomerate.

Gradually, over 2 months, both assistant principals withdrew, leaving the five classes without their crucial support. Mr. Meyer asserted that he would refuse to write the evaluation report required by the district administration to continue the five Additional Needs classes, using the Resource Room monies. Mr. Lear withdrew as well, to wait until the need for a Resource Room "resurfaced":

> I will not seek renewal of the allocation we now have. One year of deception is enough – – Basically, you know, I feel the allocation is being misused. We tried to adapt the five classes to my Resource Room proposal – – This was no problem to me – – But I have been unsuccessful in working with my colleagues. Since my name is on the proposal, I am planning to write a letter to the district Additional Needs Committee so that they know that the proposal has not been implemented as indicated.

Although both principals were originally interested in promoting Additional Needs classes, both deserted the classes as they experienced Southmoor's "political" realities.

Teachers and support staff were also drawn into the "power struggle." Information about it was not guarded, and people became privy to parts of it based on fortuitousness, persistence, or loyalties. Because all had incomplete information, however, groundless internal rifts formed in the "team." Thus, several teachers saw Mr. Lear as having "been against the idea of

Additional Needs classes from the beginning." An exactly opposite perception was held by the school psychologist, who saw Mr. Lear as "instrumental in getting the program off the ground." Such internal cleavages promoted Byzantine battles, and the remedial classes were weakened by the infighting. At the same time, the internal machinations deflected attention from the role of the head principal and from the organizational processes and precepts that worked against the success of lower-track classes.

Producing Ambiguous Goals. Divisiveness and ambiguity also characterized the goals of the five Additional Needs classes. As in all school programs, instrumental and educative goals compete. But in this case, an overlay of race exacerbated the tension, which, because of racial taboos and the Southmoor context, could not be acknowledged. As a result, the program's goals remained vague and politics superseded pedagogy.

The impact of the unspoken, uncertain goals on teachers and on program success was exemplified by the minority counselor's position. Although he assumed the role of team leader in 1980 and most staff members continued to name him as leader in 1981-82, the head principal (in another unpredictable intervention in special classes) designated the reading specialist in charge of the program "for political reasons":

> The reading specialist has taken over the Additional Needs classes now (1981-82). I tried to give it to the two assistant principals, but they don't have the curricular time. But she'll work with them - - I don't want to downplay their role. . . . The minority counselor has been active too. But I don't want people to believe it's a black program. There's another political thing in there.

Faculty members also implicitly acknowledged the importance of curbing belief that "it's a black program." They responded to questions about the overrepresentation of minorities in lower-track classes with the quick retort that race was not an issue in referrals and then quickly changed the topic. A counselor characterized black and white students at Southmoor as "polarized, but we don't have a really defined racial problem because of the healthy attitudes of our staff and the fact that kids come from professional homes." More grandiloquently, the head principal described Southmoor as Maplehurst's "most cosmopolitan high school - - Racial disturbances are, well, just about nil here."

If Southmoor staff members did not express direct concern about racial inequity, if few were overtly prejudiced, and if many were well-meaning, race flowed like an undercurrent in the "heavenly" high school. Demographics may have contributed to the perceptions at Southmoor:

Eighty-eight percent of the student body is white; blacks constitute about half of the minority population (although the proportion of black students is rising at Southmoor and throughout the Maplehurst district); there are only 5 minority faculty members among the approximately 125 teachers. Just one minority student in a class can constitute statistical overrepresentation.

However, participants at Southmoor also worked to keep race submerged, even though silence interfered with their making sense of school events.* However, teachers sense that things were "different *this* year," but they could not examine the difference because it required identifying racial strife as a factor in the origins of the Additional Needs classes. Thus, when I asked a usually well-informed source whether Additional Needs classes were a response to a "racial incident," she pooh-poohed the notion and characterized the events as "mere monkey business." A black college student who assisted the minority counselor said he didn't understand the question when I asked if he saw any significance in blacks being overrepresented in some of the five Additional Needs classes: "There's no problem with a class being mostly black. A class is a class. It doesn't matter who's in it."

The minority counselor's informal, uncertain position exemplified and, ironically, sometimes contributed to the racial undercurrent. For example, to deserve his role as leader, the minority counselor presented

---

*Taboos operate in classrooms as well (for another case study of racial taboos in schools, see Clement, Harding, & Eisenhart, 1979). Southmoor teachers deny that the overrepresentation of minority students negatively affects educational encounters in the five Additional Needs classes. Rather, students benefit from the placement because of their low skills. Certainly, there are no explicit references by teachers to students' race. Although I did not systematically investigate how the issue of race is made visible by classroom participants in classroom talk, I did note that lower-track teachers consistently pay more personal attention to lower-track students who are white. For example, teachers much more frequently comment on a white student's new haircut or bad cold and refrain from such personal comments to black students. Erickson and Schultz (1982), examining counseling interviews, demonstrate that the chitchat, rather than the formal topics of interviews, carries information about minority and ethnic membership. For instance, counselors may mention the score of a game in the Catholic basketball league, thereby unconsciously signaling to the interviewee an interest in Catholic activities. Erickson and Schultz go on to show that if counselor and interviewee can establish that they are joint members of a special group, such as Catholics, the counselor will provide the student with better guidance. Similar processes may be at work in lower-track classrooms in Maplehurst. In them, personal topics often replace academic topics as the focus of classroom talk. Blacks may therefore be twice excluded in lower-track classrooms. Like white students, they do not receive the substantive academic content that regular-track students do. In addition, unlike their white lower-track peers, they may also not participate in personalized encounters.

himself as having important expertise that others did not have: As a member of a minority group, he understood the students in the Additional Needs classes. However, in making this claim, the minority counselor simultaneously undermined his power by isolating himself from most of the members of the team, who were white.

An interchange with one of the teachers captures the paradox of the minority counselor's position:

> T: If the Additional Needs students are 5 minutes late, I mark them present. I make them leave if they come late and cause a distraction.
>
> MC: When you make them leave, send them to my office, okay? I'll talk to them before I send them back to class.
>
> T: Well, if they're really disrupting, throwing things or whatever, they pull the regular kids off and *they* start disrupting. Then all I do is baby-sit - - - I'm not being paid to be a baby-sitter!
>
> MC: Well, I'll talk to them. They may just need jacking up or whatever before class.

Here, the minority counselor confronted a teacher about sending students out of class (and, thus, into the halls where they caused trouble for the school as a whole). He also implied that he could "jack up" the students so that they would be able to return to class and behave appropriately. The counselor did not suggest that the teacher, a member of Southmoor's esteemed faculty, could interact constructively with academically unsuccessful, minority students. Instead, the teacher appeared as a functionary who marked attendance and monitored classes.

The minority counselor carried racial expertise to another level when he purported to have information about Maplehurst's black community. In particular, he warned:

> Some of these Additional Needs students are not the typical Maplehurst kid - - - Teachers have their notions about how kids should act in class but these kids are different. Some are from inner cities. They're used to policemen in the schools. Things are different here. . . . But the fact is, the kids in Additional Needs classes *are* here and they have to be serviced in some way. The tensions that could go on in the school - - - - I don't mean to scare you or anything - - - But this is a period at Southmoor when if we don't do something, who knows what could happen? I mean, gangs haven't really developed yet here, but - -.

Information about gangs was very "scary" at Southmoor. It was accessible to most staff members principally through the minority counselor, who gained power and position by providing the information. The minority counselor played a similarly interpretive role in the administration: As the only knowledgeable expert on minority affairs, he secured funds for Additional Needs classes by claiming that there were "different," potentially dangerous, blacks with urgent "special needs."

Through no conscious intent on his part, however, the minority counselor's expert knowledge also undermined the educative goals of the Additional Needs classes. First, the counselor's description of Additional Needs students stressed their differences, particularly the disciplinary problems they posed. Such clients would have little appeal to Southmoor's academic experts who disdain disciplinary responsibilities. Second, the more the minority counselor acted as an expert, the more teachers simply deferred to his expertise, distanced themselves from the lower-track teacher role, and "sent the student to [his] office." Yet the counselor was dependent on committed, informed teachers for success because there were simply too many students for him to deal with. Finally, the minority counselor's administrative advocacy was ineffectual unless there was a crisis: Like teachers, the administrators simply expected the expert counselor to take care of the "political problem" that minority students represented. In short, taboos, heightened by the "political" salience of race at Southmoor and in Maplehurst, silenced discussions about the purposes of the Additional Needs classes and exacerbated the role conflict of lower-track teachers.

Marginal Structures That Structure Marginality. Southmoor's culture informed (and was reinforced by) the birth, life, and death of the five Additional Needs classes. Hastily inaugurated in 1980 and adventitiously dismantled by 1983–84, the five were structurally and symbolically marginal to the institution. Lower-track teachers grasped their borderline status in concrete facts such as fluctuating funding, inconsistent leadership, and capricious mergers. At the same time, as these events delimited teachers' efforts, their limited teaching reiterated the marginality of the classes.

Fundamentally, teachers saw that "no one else cares" and asked, "Why should I?" Only in a crisis of order did Additional Needs classes become critical to Southmoor. In one such crisis, the institution demonstrated that it could be "overwhelmingly successful" with academically unsuccessful students. However, after the crisis, the evolution and demise of the five Additional Needs classes indicate the ephemeral status of the academic progress of unsuccessful students within the "heavenly" culture of the institution.

CHAPTER 6

Discipline and Distance in Lower-Track Classrooms

In the next two chapters, I develop a double comparison of tracking to pursue further the questions developed in Chapters 4 and 5 about the effects of tracking on the climate and teaching in regular- and lower-track classes. I compare the two at Marshall much as I did at Southmoor, but I add as well a comparison of lower-track classes across the two high schools. Specifically, the comparison poses the question of whether the mechanism of tracking prompts similar results in both high schools. Do chaos and confusion differentiate Marshall's lower-track classes as they did Southmoor's?

The double comparison challenges the traditional formulation of tracking in which lower-track classes are presumed to be both clearly distinguishable from regular-track classes and clearly similar to each other. As I describe in this chapter, track levels do correlate the differences in classroom climate and teaching at Marshall. However, as at Southmoor, lower-track classes also share features of the school's regular-track classes and are therefore understandable as *versions* of these classes. Accordingly, as I discuss in Chapter 7, lower-track classrooms at Marshall, although different from regular-track classes, are also strikingly different from Southmoor's lower-track classes. As the double comparison elucidates, the crucial point is that the significance of tracking is not invariant but relational: Teachers and students in classrooms will construct idiosyncratic versions and meanings of tracking which, however, will partake of and affect stable meanings from wider contexts, specifically from schools' cultures.

To set the stage for discussion of lower-track classroom life at Marshall, I begin with a general description of the orderly high school that sits just 20 minutes across town from Southmoor. I then narrow the focus to one Additional Needs classroom, Mr. Bauer's, to provide a detailed description of the explicit and implicit principles that govern lower-track life within the Marshall organization. Finally, in the third section, I focus again, as in Chapter 4, on classroom processes, including participation structures, to trace how classroom participants produce the regimented climate that distinguishes Marshall's lower-track classes. I document that, as an exemplar of the other three, equally formulaic Additional Needs classes at Marshall in which I also observed, Mr. Bauer's class both differs from and is similar to the school's orderly but hardly regimented regular-track classes. It is a hyperbolic translation of the regular-track atmosphere: The "practical," "no-nonsense" climate in regular-track classes is rendered "basic" and "structured" in the school's lower track.

MARSHALL HIGH SCHOOL

Marshall is a high school very like Southmoor. The two schools are similar in size, physical resources, staffing patterns, administrative policies from the district office, and the seniority and qualifications of faculty members. In many surveys, they would be classified together as a type.

At the same time, the two schools also differ in some objective dimensions. For example, although Marshall's student body, like Southmoor's, is overwhelmingly white and middle class, Marshall has a greater proportion of parents who are skilled and unskilled workers and a smaller proportion of professional parents, as well as a smaller minority population (fewer than 3% versus Southmoor's 12%). Similarly, Marshall's curriculum is as expansive and comprehensive as Southmoor's, but Marshall devotes a greater proportion of the schedule to vocational and special education courses (still, however, sending over 40% of its seniors to higher education). A final contrast: Tracking is more overt and extensive at Marshall. In contrast to Southmoor's student handbook, Marshall's clearly labels college-preparatory and non-college-preparatory courses. Approximately 25% of Marshall's ninth graders find spaces in lower-track classes, whereas the figure is 10% at Southmoor.

These objective features undergird, although they do not determine, the distinctively different cultures of the two schools and their curricular manifestations. Therefore, one can ask of Marshall, as of Southmoor, what this "no-nonsense" high school makes of its academically unsuccessful students. One might expect, for example, that Marshall's culture inspires more satisfaction among the members, because the school commits more resources to academically unsuccessful students in contrast to Southmoor's rather single-minded focus on academics.

Curiously, however, and despite the apparently better balance between educational equity and excellence, Marshall's culture is one of pedestrian competence rather than exalted confidence. Accordingly, educative procedures are set in place, but, for teachers as well as for students, minimal expectations prevail. In contrast to Southmoor, teaching at Marshall is not a prestigious occupation but a job performed punctiliously. Teachers do everything they are supposed to do to earn their salaries: They plan curricula, conduct classes, support school policies, and keep order. However, many perform these duties with little enthusiasm or investment of self. As one teacher, who taught several years at both Southmoor and Marshall, put it, "You don't have to *believe* in your job at Marshall."

Teachers act compliantly, if rather mechanically, partly as a reflection of the specialized function defined for them in Marshall's bureaucracy. In contrast to Southmoor's "prima donnas," few Marshall teachers openly or often express dissent from school-wide policies. Rather, they "cooperate" as members of the "team," particularly by upholding Marshall's "tradition of discipline": Within their own ranks and with students, procedure is paramount. Faculty members insist on punctuality, regular attendance, cleanliness in the hallways, and "respectful" behavior, but place rather less stress on the substantive issues of academics or governance that confront them. Many regular teachers also adapt to a restricted classroom role, deferring to "specialists" to deal with learning disabilities, reading problems, truancy, and the like. Thus, publicly they adhere to the informally promoted but pervasive model of direct instruction sponsored by Marshall's very large reading, special education, and vocational education departments. Only privately do academic teachers complain that "real education" is supplanted in the emphasis on basic skills, the addition of vocational and career units to academic courses, and the administrative push to get all regularly attending students through high school regardless of achievement. Feeling that their prerogatives are restricted and their contributions to the school are undervalued, Marshall teachers act competently to convey basic skills and facts, but they often mask the "depth" and "excitement" that their subject matters can inspire.

Teachers' low opinion of their role reciprocates the acknowledged view of Marshall's student body as "homogeneous" and "typically blue-collar kids." Seen as financially comfortable, such students are presumed to value "practical" educational endeavors, particularly those that directly ensure continued material prosperity and high-paying jobs. Hence, teachers interpret regular students' concern with grades as a desire to get lower car insurance rates or a $50 reward from a parent rather than as engagement with ideas for their own sake or concern about the quality of schoolwork. Teachers expect that very few of the students respect the academic knowledge teachers have and value and that even fewer will go on to college to acquire it. Given perceptions of serious differences, the boundaries between teachers and students are strongly maintained. The basis for teachers' authority is not the important knowledge they have to transmit, as at Southmoor, but their hierarchical role in the school organization. Principally, teachers' authority is defined as the power to certify that students have spent time in classrooms.

Hence, within Marshall's businesslike culture, constituted by the interactions between definitions of a bureaucratic mode of operation and of students as "your typical blue-collar kids," teachers do their job, but, in contrast to teachers at "heavenly" Southmoor, they do not "believe" in it. Teaching at Marshall is decidedly competent, in the sense that teachers are punctual, prepared, and in control; some curricular units are as innovative as any I saw in the Maplehurst district. However, even with regular-track classes, teachers withhold themselves, preferring not to be judged as teachers, because the role commands relatively little respect by virtue of being considered cerebral, inconsequential, and poorly paid.

A Regular-Track Lesson at Marshall

Compared with the spirit and spontaneity with which Southmoor's regular-track classes discuss broadly conceived academic topics, as in Mr. Robinson's lesson about the Haymarket Riot that I described in Chapter 4, Mr. Bauer's 10th-grade world history class at Marshall, although explicitly designated by the teacher as "open ended," was rather closed.

Mr. Bauer directed his students to "do some research" on questions about the rise of fascist governments in Germany and Italy by reading as homework several pages in a standard chronological text. The next day, in discussing the "research," students were instructed to describe conditions common to both and, hence, fundamental to fascism. Mr. Bauer emphasized the open-endedness of the lesson to his regular-track classes: Every class "will fill the board with different information." Furthermore, he urged full participation because "the class that puts more up on the board may be at more of an advantage on the exam next Friday. So it is really up to each class to do its best." However, despite Mr. Bauer's prediction that three history classes would "fill the board with different information," the charts in each contained much the same information, and the phrasing of all was almost identical. The uniformity resulted from Mr. Bauer's strict management of the discussion and students' response to that management.

As students began to answer Mr. Bauer's questions about the conditions in Italy that led to Mussolini's ascension to power, for example, they quickly realized from Mr. Bauer's responses that the desired answers were ones that echoed the phrases in the text. At first students put answers in their own words, but Mr. Bauer restated them or asked for clarification, so that words from the textbook were eventually elicited. Moreover, Mr. Bauer's topics unfolded in the order of their appearance in the reading selection. After several exchanges, students simply began reading phrases directly from the text. For example, the conditions surrounding Mussolini's rise were simplified to short, clipped responses: "poverty," "employment," "social unrest." When students asked questions that developed from the recitation—"Why *did* the Germans blame the Jews for their problems?"— they were deflected with comments like, "That's a topic for a dissertation! If we go into that right now, we won't get through with our chart."

Thus, although Mr. Bauer intended an "open" lesson using inductive learning processes, the lesson was a reiteration of facts from the book. Student initiations were tabled or downgraded. Questions were set aside in the interests of efficiency. Students reciprocated the teacher's role enactment by routinizing their participation and limiting their questions. In contrast to the joint endeavor in "critical thinking" about the Haymarket Riot in Mr. Robinson's classroom, Mr. Bauer's lesson presented more clearly the teacher's dominance and distance, both in his direction of the discussion and in his insistence that there was one Right Answer for every question.

This is not to suggest that Southmoor lessons are totally open-ended or that teachers there do not have ideas they want students to learn. Furthermore, many teachers at Marshall draw students into livelier discussions than Mr. Bauer's. However, the informal ambience and confident exploration of wide-ranging academic topics are more characteristic of lessons at Southmoor, and Mr. Bauer's disciplined, stylized coverage of the textbook is more common at Marshall.

THE REGIMENTED CLIMATE
IN LOWER-TRACK CLASSROOMS

The distance regular teachers at Marshall establish between their role and their person assumes a decidedly strained tenor in classes for academically unsuccessful students: Neutrally, even guardedly, students and teachers go through the motions of education. However, aloofness does not result in disorganized teaching at Marshall, as it does in lower-track classrooms at Southmoor and in those described in many qualitative studies (Furlong, 1977; Hargreaves, 1967; Hargreaves et al., 1975; Lacey, 1970; Leacock, 1969; McDermott & Aron, 1978; Metz, 1978; Schwartz, 1981; Willis, 1977). Instead, Marshall's lower-track teachers are superorganized, even if highly impersonal. They act as taskmasters to lower-track adolescents whom they see as so different from themselves and from regular students that they are "uncivilized." Disciplined and disciplining, lower-track lessons at Marshall are distinguished by the control teachers maintain.

Control takes innocuous forms, one of which is control of time. Thus, when the clock hand jerks to 8:03, signaling the beginning of Mr. Bauer's Additional Needs history class, silence reigns. Immediately, Mr. Bauer asks the ninth graders to take out their books and homework. The 15 students do so amid some minor bustling. With a smooth "okey-dokey, heeeere we go," Mr. Bauer begins the review of questions from the end of the chapter in the textbook. The review proceeds steadily through about half the class period. When the text questions have been checked, Mr. Bauer asks students to take out their answers to the reading-skills questions. There is again some minor shuffling as students find their papers. The reading-skills questions, like those from the text, require short, factual answers drawn directly from the reading selection, and they are reviewed in a similarly efficient fashion. When the second review is completed, Mr. Bauer announces the total points for the homework assignment, students add up their scores, and Mr. Bauer records them, calling students by name for their scores. With somewhat less than half the class period remaining, Mr. Bauer hands out the next day's reading-skills worksheet and assigns the reading of the next chapter in the text, along with the questions at the end of it. Students work independently and quietly on the homework assignment until 1 or 2 minutes before the period's end. At 8:53 on the electric clock, they stand and leave quickly and noisily.

An Invariant Routine

Mr. Bauer directs his invariant routine almost every day of the week. It is interrupted only by unit tests that come about once every 4 or 5 weeks; by reviews for unit tests that proceed from study sheets similar to the homework and reading-skills assignments; or by a film or slides day, usually on the second and fourth Fridays of the month. Mr. Bauer both acknowledged and justified the routine when he remarked in an interview that on one occasion during the school year he had allowed students to work on their homework together in small groups, but "it just didn't work."

Profound orderliness governs interactions between classroom participants as well as curricular sequences. Moreover, impersonality undergirds order, and student-teacher exchanges seem to involve no one's will or opinion. For example, the unfolding of a lesson follows the impartial order of the questions at the end of the chapter in the easy-to-read text, not Mr. Bauer's directives. Mr. Bauer sometimes accentuates the neutrality: He announced once that students should never have a question about what the homework assignment is, even if they are absent, because "it's always the next chapter in the book."

Similarly smooth are the homework reviews that consume about half of each class meeting. Codelike, they require little personal improvisation with language or knowledge. Mr. Bauer can indicate the activity as well as the question to which he wants an answer simply by stating the page and the number of the question: "Awright, page 20, part 1, number 1." Students match their responses to Mr. Bauer's questions. After the teacher designates a respondent, the student cites a letter to signify the answer: "B." If the student's answer is incorrect, Mr. Bauer blandly calls on another student for another letter. After a correct answer, Mr. Bauer may repeat the question and answer, but he quotes directly from the text:

T: Number 4.
S: A.
T: (reading the question from the text) "Which area had more railroads?" A. Yes. "The North – – had more railroads."

Even when talk involves more than a codified exchange of homework answers, it remains neutralized; even though it is centered on the teacher, his dominance is muted. For instance, Mr. Bauer frequently interrupts the homework exchange to elaborate on topics in minilectures, which furnish additional information or relate a topic to an earlier lesson. During the elaborations, students sit quietly, apparently listening. However, none take notes on the exposition and few pose questions. Nor are students ever expected to provide similar elaborations on subjects themselves, say, on unit tests or in verbal responses.

Sometimes Mr. Bauer's minilectures evolve into a recitation. Then students participate by answering the questions the teacher poses. Usually, Mr. Bauer asks "easy" questions concerning generally known facts rather than questions about history. Although intended to engage students, monitor their attentiveness, or expand their understanding, the questions elicit only hesitant and brief responses. For example, when reviewing questions about the French and Indian War, Mr. Bauer interrupted the routine with a prosaic analog to present-day Canada and bilingualism. He asked how many students had traveled to Canada and when several raised their hands, he continued: "Did you notice anything as you drove along the highway?" A girl noted, "It wasn't very exciting." Mr. Bauer frowned slightly and narrowed his question: "I mean the road signs." Then a boy volunteered that the mileage is given in miles and kilometers. Mr. Bauer responded: "Right! I loved going 100 kilometers an hour." The class murmured appreciatively. Mr. Bauer then added that the signs are in two languages.

Similarly, in talking about the Great Basin, Mr. Bauer asked what a basin is. When no one attempted an answer, he hinted, "That's where you do your dishes, girls - - Boys, of course (winking), never do dishes." Solemnly, succinctly, a student guessed that a basin is a "sink." Mr. Bauer then proceeded with his lecture about U.S. geography. However, he commented on the limited student-teacher exchange: "Sometimes I feel like a dentist pulling teeth, trying to get you to answer."

In a regularized but remote fashion, then, Mr. Bauer and his Additional Needs class work their way steadfastly through the daily regimen of 15 or 20 short-answer questions from the text and the reading skills questions. There is almost no talking among the students and very little eye contact. All face Mr. Bauer at the front of the room or look at their papers. Students very rarely volunteer personal opinions or experiences that are germane to the lesson. Rather, like Mr. Bauer, they also withhold themselves: They work as directed but ask few questions and issue few requests for further explanation. No one ever disputes an answer that has been validated by Mr. Bauer. Indeed, even when Mr. Bauer indicates that a student's answer is wrong, the student does not question his judgment.

Yet Mr. Bauer's routine is not heavy-handed. Rather, because of Mr. Bauer's management of the classroom, its flow appears natural. For example, he allows few free moments during which classes can become disorderly. He admonishes students to "keep at it until that (clock) dial says you're done." Students may greet the daily homework assignment or the announcement of a test with mild groans, but there are no firm protests. Very occasionally, Mr. Bauer foregoes homework, but he does not fully relinquish the routine or his prerogative to insist on it: "I'll give you a break tonight - - but we'll work in class tomorrow to catch up."

In 6 months, I saw only one instance where students explicitly questioned Mr. Bauer's routinized curriculum. After about 2 months of school, as Mr. Bauer passed out the usual homework questions, a boy asked him, "Will we get through this *whole* book this year?" Mr. Bauer replied, rather proudly, "The whooole thing, I promise you." Then a girl chimed in, somewhat plaintively, with her own question: "Won't we have no filmstrips, or anything?" Phlegmatically, Mr. Bauer promised to "work in some of those every other Friday or so."

Even the entry of a new student of considerable "reputation" did not crack the order. Replete with sucker sticks in his mouth, grin on his face, and swagger in his step, Dick sauntered into class about halfway through the period during the second week of school. Students in the class glanced at each other and some rolled their eyes. A few commented, softly but excitedly, "Dick's going to be in here?" Dick handed Mr. Bauer a yellow slip and looked up and down the class. Mr. Bauer commented laconically, but pointedly, "I kinda expected you last Friday." Dick replied coolly that he was getting his schedule changed. Mr. Bauer persisted, letting Dick know that he knew Dick had skipped class on Friday: "You mean I got a copy of your schedule before you did?" Then Mr. Bauer added mildly, "Better get rid of that sucker before I get ahold of it." At first, Dick appeared not to hear, but with a sharp reiteration of the command by Mr. Bauer, he deposited the sucker in the wastebasket. Mr. Bauer directed Dick to the front seat of the fourth row. Dick sat in the front seat of the fifth row and began looking around the room, smiling and nodding at friends. Firmly, but lightly, Mr. Bauer repeated: "FOURTH row. If you don't come closer, we'll get the idea you're trying to avoid us." In full control, Mr. Bauer then proceeded with the lesson. Thereafter, the only trouble Dick made in class was to give persistent wrong answers and grin slyly as he did. Even that behavior diminished in frequency, so that by the end of the semester Dick vied for the highest average in the class.

A "Tradition of Discipline"

Given the disarray that frequently characterizes lower-track class-rooms, Mr. Bauer's quiet, orderly, industrious class appears a very model of remedial education. However, there is an edge to Marshall's lower-track order that Mr. Bauer and other lower-track teachers acknowledge implicitly both in the degree of their control and in the careful unobtrusiveness with which they exercise it. Even though teachers set clear directions and voice positive expectations, they are nervous and doubt their efficacy with Additional Needs students, whom they see as very different from themselves in their hostility to schooling.

One teacher commented matter-of-factly on his responsibilities with "untrained" students: "Additional Needs students are like puppy dogs: They're likeable, and I like to see them grow up over the year, but they've got to be trained." Another noted that students "are behavior problems (who come from families in which) both parents work and don't have time to supervise the kid." A third concurred: "Additional Needs students haven't been socialized to the middle-class Marshall classroom." (This remark indicates that Marshall classrooms *should* be "middle-class" in demeanor.) Thus, because students are "unsocialized," teachers anticipate "explosions" if such students are "set off." They act as solicitous but properly watchful taskmasters because they see lower-track students not as children who simply have not yet "learned better" but as large, near-adults, who are present in school against their will and who are virtually unamen-able to teachers' influence. Simultaneously, they both protect themselves and uphold Marshall's "tradition of discipline" by using discretion in directing students who offer the possibility of open conflict. In particular, they present a neutralized school situation, one that appears to be of no one's making and for which no one can be blamed.

Accordingly, within Marshall's businesslike ethos, teachers define the high school experience for Additional Needs students as a straightforward matter of time, training, and transition: "High school is different from middle school; there you were used to moving from grade to grade without doing too much, but here, you have to earn credits to move from grade to grade." Therefore, in Additional Needs courses designed to "ease the traumatic change from middle school," teachers provide "practical," sequenced exercises, and students who practice are promised they will progress.

Furthermore, the scholastic transition and training correspond to a developmental rite of passage. Teachers exhort lower-track adolescents repeatedly to "be reasonable - - The ball is in your court now." To "grow up and act (their) age," students must "work hard." They must practice being on time, attending regularly, bringing the proper "tools" (notebooks and pencils), and making the necessary "effort."

Finally, high school represents the means for a successful transition to adulthood and the economy by students who, in the Marshall vernacular, are "young people moving into the world of work." The student handbook explicates the pragmatic connection between school life and later life: In classrooms, students will "not only progress through sequential learning patterns but also develop life-long habits of achievement, responsibility, and punctuality." More colloquially, lower-track teachers intone the "relevance" of schooling: "The work habits you learn here are the work habits you will need later."

On the one hand, then, Marshall teachers define education as a neutral, unmysterious, "practical" endeavor. Any serious aspirant, regardless of talent or track, may succeed through perseverance. Marshall teachers assure Additional Needs students repeatedly of their ability to make progress toward scholastic, vocational, and life goals if they attend regularly and practice on sequenced, skills-based lessons "at the student's level."

On the other hand, for all of its efficient regularities, the climate in Marshall's Additional Needs classes is laced with tension and unpredictability. Even though teachers admonish lower-track students toward academic competence and adult independence, they also wonder if lower-track students progress or simply run in place. Disheartened, if disciplined, teachers complain that a Marshall education "allows too many good students to be underachievers" and that it "enables" poor students to maintain inadequate learning behaviors yet still graduate.

PRODUCING A REGIMENTED CLIMATE

Pedagogical maxims admonish novice teachers that the first days of the school year are an important time for setting a classroom's tone: "Don't smile 'til Christmas" (Ryan, 1970). At the beginning, then, experienced teachers state and demonstrate many of the procedures they will expect students to follow during succeeding months. Sometimes, teachers offer explicit reasons for rules. If successfully inculcated, the initial orientation provides a taken-for-granted procedural base. From it, students and teachers can move efficiently and harmoniously to academic endeavors (Edwards & Furlong, 1978).

However, the balance between good management and meaningful education requires tact as well as resolve, and instrumental concerns easily overshadow academics when dealing with the unpredictable, uninitiated, raw recruits of a culture. The predominance of control may not be readily apparent, particularly when it is embedded technically in curriculum (Apple, 1979; 1983), as when teachers use films, notetaking, or individualized assignments to circumscribe the time-consuming, not to mention excited, debates that controversial topics and divergent perspectives can unleash. When unobtrusive but unequivocal, orderliness can take on a life of its own, with unintended costs in the diminution of humane inquiry.

I examine the first days of the school year in Mr. Bauer's Additional Needs class to analyze how teacher and students balance instrumental and educative purposes to produce Marshall's distinctive lower-track regimen. The "basic" content and the rationalized, "structured" form of lower-track lessons reflect and sustain the orderly but strained climate, teaching by remote control, and the very student disengagement that "adaptive" Additional Needs lessons are officially designed to preempt.

Day 1: Defining a Clear Work Routine

On the first day of school, Mr. Bauer stresses his role as distant taskmaster, able to oversee dispassionately the headway that lower-track students make toward school and future success. He makes explicit his "expectations." With colloquial stories, he depicts the reasonableness of classroom routines. Matter-of-factly, he provides the "structure" that academically unsuccessful students presumably require. Throughout, he relies tacitly on a long-established theory of direct instruction (see Bloom, 1981, e.g.) whose salience at Marshall is particularly strong. The theory posits that if students are told explicitly what to perform, they will be able to concentrate without confusion on the clear-cut tasks that are constitutive of academic mastery.

Enacting elements of the theory, Mr. Bauer begins by citing his "expectations – – the things that will cause you to get credit from me and move ahead, or not to get credit." To earn a credit, first of all, students must be trained in "good work habits." One of the most important of these is punctuality: "It's *irritating* when someone says he's going to be somewhere at a certain time and he's late. . . . If this gets to be a serious problem, you may have to make up the time you miss with me after school." A second and related "work habit" is attendance. Students are admonished not to "cut, it's a waste of your time."

Mr. Bauer drives home his message about the importance of developing good, clock-related "work habits" by telling a fable, one of his low-key devices for inculcating procedures. He begins by asking about the unemployment rate. A student suggests its level as "about 10%." Somewhat taken aback by the student's knowledge, Mr. Bauer launches nevertheless into his illustrative story:

> You know, I play tennis, and at the club, the bartender had a job opening. He was getting six or seven calls an hour about that job. That's the kind of times we live in. Now, suppose an employer called me about some students. Say, one student, student A, has been absent 50 times and tardy 60 times. (He makes a chart of the students on the blackboard.) Student B, never absent or tardy. Student C, oh, absent 4 times and tardy 7. Student D, 45 and 30. Student E, 13 and 23. Now, who's not going to get my recommendation? (He begins to draw lines through students A, D, and E.) And, kids, I'm not even talking about educational qualifications, just about work habits, about showing up and being dependable. As young people going out into the world – I hope the unemployment rate will get better, but – – – As young people moving into the world of work, it's important for you to get into good work habits now.

"Good work habits," which will pay off after high school as good job habits, are also instilled through the assignment and assessment of daily, individual homework, Mr. Bauer lectures. Indeed, he points out that school assignments, like job assignments, are "not made on Friday – – No work for the weekend." Appealing further to Marshall students' presumably "practical" orientation, he notes that students will not be required to work on the tasks at home, because time is provided in class, just as many jobs require no extra at-home hours. The work is assessed every day. Each individual's "points," along with unit test grades, are averaged and measured against an objective standard: "You always know where you stand – – And with my system, everyone in the class can get an

A – – – or everyone can get an F. . . . *Your* grade doesn't depend on anyone else's."

By the end of the first class period, Mr. Bauer has made clear both his "expectations" and, implicitly, the impartial, down-to-earth "work" routine that daily lessons will follow: School success begins with adherence to classroom procedures. Accordingly, from the very first day, Mr. Bauer casually assumes direction of the classroom, doing all the talking except for the one student's response to the question about the unemployment rate. He "structures" seating neutrally according to the alphabet, drawing the 15 students, scattered by their choice around the room, mostly at the back and around the edges, into a grid of five rows of desks, three deep, centered on him. He explicitly identifies punctuality, attendance, and following rules as commonsensical indicators of scholastic accomplishment. And, on the first day, he makes the first homework assignment and sets students working. Then, throughout the first week of class, he reiterates the themes from the first day: Plain and simple "work habits" are the means and ends of lower-track classes. Teachers in other lower-track classrooms repeat a similar message, even using some of the same phrases.

Day 2: A Reassuring Redefinition of Academics

On the second day of the new school year, Mr. Bauer lectures about the content of the Additional Needs American history course and its relation to school success:

> Now, I want to talk this hour about history. As far as I'm concerned, being a teacher, I'm in the people business. And history is people. But in this particular ninth-grade history class, we're less concerned about history and more concerned about improving your reading skills, graph skills, and your map-reading skills. Would you believe, last year I had a student who had trouble remembering that the top of the map is North?! So we are going to learn geography, too. And I hope we are going to see some reading-test improvement. We're going to start with U.S. history from the beginning. From a historical viewpoint, we'll move rapidly. But from a reading standpoint, we'll take our time. You know, I like to think if we give you a bit every day, you'll get better over the long haul. But it takes patience and practice.

Here, Mr. Bauer predicts positively that students with histories of academic failure "will get better" as they study reading, a subject that matters. With a cursory nod to graduation requirements and the course title that will appear on students' transcripts, Mr. Bauer leaves behind the sweep of "American history" for fundamentals: "reading skills, graph skills, and your map-reading skills." Mr. Bauer's comments imply a hierarchy of knowledge: Only with the "basics" in hand can Additional Needs students proceed to harder subjects, higher-order thinking skills, and regular-track classes.

In similar fashion, the teacher goes on to demystify processes of knowing. Borrowing from a long tradition in curriculum, particularly remedial curriculum, he renders mind building as transparent as bodybuilding.* Just as he worked determinedly to improve his tennis game over the summer, Mr. Bauer soliloquizes, so students should persevere in improving their reading skills through daily "bits" of practice. Reassuringly for lower-track students who may doubt the value of scholastic endeavors and their ability to perform them satisfactorily, Mr. Bauer's requirements are straightforward and within the reach of all: "patience and practice."

So important is patient practice that Mr. Bauer's "talk this hour about history" renders *what* students read less important then *how* they read. History, it turns out, is important principally as a medium for teaching skills. At length the teacher urges students to use the SQRRR reading method: "I want you to write SQRRR in your notebook - - Take a *fulllll* page - - I want the letters to stick out like a sore thumb so you remember them." Then Mr. Bauer moves letter by letter through the acronym to explain the method. Before one reads, he intones, one "warms up" by Surveying the selection, noticing chapter titles and headings of sections, pictures, or charts. These details "help you figure out what you are going to read about." One also asks oneself Questions about the reading selection. As Mr. Bauer explains, this means looking at the questions at the end of the chapter: "If you don't have anything to look for when you're reading, if you're not set, you won't find anything." After this preparation, one actually Reads. However, reading is always directed and instrumental. With a rhetorical question, Mr. Bauer indicates that one does not read for surprises or the pleasures of reading itself: "What do you read *for* when you read? For the answers to the questions you or the book or your teacher has created." The last two letters of SQRRR, Recite and Review, emphasize the importance of repetition as a feature of learning, as it is in physical training (and in "good work habits"). After Reading, one Recites, or "says again," the answers to the questions in the text. One does this by "writing the answers, it's the same thing as reciting." In Mr. Bauer's class, the daily,

---

*The tradition of mental discipline, with its metaphor of mind as muscle, is described by Kliebard, 1982.

oral review of homework answers adds an additional repetition of the factual, textual material on top of students' initial reading and reciting.

But the last "R," Review, is given the most importance. Mr. Bauer explains why review is so important, again using a story, one in which the connection between physical and learning exercises justifies the routinized, elementary content in Additional Needs classes:

> Back in the 60s, kids came to school saying, "Oh, American history, we've done that before - - I did geography in eighth grade - - I did it once." Now, if you are on a baseball team, you'll do a lot of reviewing during batting practice. You've heard of Ted Williams, the "greatest natural hitter in baseball"? It's his last game, he's batting .400. Doesn't have to play the doubleheader, so he can go out with a lifetime average of .400. But he WANTS to play anyway. What happens? He gets seven hits with nine times at bat and goes out with .406. "Greatest natural hitter?" (2.0) Talent? (1.0) If you mean by that that he went out for batting practice one-half hour early and stayed one-half hour late! Talent? Naww, he WORKED at it. You gotta review. Your brain works like this. You get an idea, it triggers some cells, if you never get that idea again, it goes away. If you hit that brain cell over and over again, it doesn't disappear. You may never be as good a reader as Ted Williams was a hitter, but you will get better.

In presenting the SQRRR method, Mr. Bauer redefines and reduces "American history." Rather than an interpretive endeavor to understand and frame multivocal accounts of the past, history becomes a vehicle, instrumentally important for reading-skills instruction. The simplified, 25-year-old textbook is chosen for its reading level rather than its historical merits. Class time allocations reflect the reading emphasis: "From a historical viewpoint, we'll move rapidly. But from a reading standpoint, we'll take our time." Furthermore, Mr. Bauer's explication of the SQRRR acronym mitigates any difficulties of skill development as well. Training the mind, like training Ted Williams's batting, may hinge somewhat on talent and thought. But more important in Mr. Bauer's scheme is the daily, repetitive effort: "If you hit that brain cell over and over again, an idea doesn't disappear." The kind of idea, students' assessment or manipulation of it, or their engagement with it do not figure in Mr. Bauer's homilies.

With this redefinition of history, Mr. Bauer converts potentially controversial or confusing content and public, divergent interpretations into reassuringly clear, noncontroversial, individualized skills training. Neither he nor students have to care or worry about maneuvering through history's mazes; it is secondary to their central endeavor of developing "basic" reading skills.

Days 3 and 4: Neutralizing Teacher Control

On the third and fourth days of the first week of school, Mr. Bauer leads students through their homework assignments, putting into practice the routines he has already described. Without domineering, he directs two regularly alternating participation structures: Both limit students' verbal participation and thereby contribute to the orderly but disengaged classroom climate (see Chapter 3 for participation structures).

The teacher/whole-class participation structure comes to life in codified reviews of homework, teacher minilectures, and short-answer group recitations. Few structures provide so efficiently for good order and coverage of content. By and large, students work quietly. They mark their answers to end-of-the-chapter questions, answer briefly if called on, and listen (or at least appear to listen). Given students' quiescent role, the teacher's activity appears natural. He specifies questions and evaluates answers, selects speakers and topics, and generally engineers classroom talk.

Adding to the taken-for-granted quality of Mr. Bauer's central position is his markedly phlegmatic enactment of teaching. The unfolding of homework reviews follows the given order of the questions in the textbook. His neutralized control depends also on what he and students do *not* do. For example, Mr. Bauer simply does not encourage students to contribute information. He asks them few questions; those he asks require brief, usually one-word responses. When a correct answer is not forthcoming, rather than clarifying with the student the reasons for the wrong answer, he moves on easily to another student for another chance at the answer. Mr. Bauer also limits questions that might prompt divergent student responses. Thus, he often skips the one open-ended question at the end of each chapter. Or, if he assigns it, the answer receives little or no discussion in the homework review. On the question, "Do you agree that the U.S. is a melting pot?" Mr. Bauer comments: "Everybody gets two points for that one. Any answer you have is right, because this is an 'AGREE' question."

The teacher/whole-class participation structure usually predominates for 25 to 35 minutes of a class period. It alternates with the student-seatwork participation structure, manifested most commonly in students' working silently and individually on worksheetlike tasks that will furnish the following day's homework review. This privatized discourse form accounts for virtually all of the remaining time.

The second participation structure operates as a variant on the implicit "treaties" that teachers and students negotiate in Marshall's regular classes, as well as in many other classrooms across the country (Cusick, 1983; McNeil, 1986; Powell et al., 1985; Sedlak et al., 1986; Sizer, 1985). Thus, in Mr. Bauer's class, students contribute to the maintenance of distance and routines as they exchange compliant behavior for relatively innocuous academic demands from the teacher. They work quietly through the class period, methodically retrieving factual information from the simplified text, knowing that if they finish they will have no homework that evening. Mr. Bauer sits at his desk for the most part, preparing future lessons and saving energy for the remainder of a long day.

Using time in these ways, both teacher and students give the appearance to each other and to outsiders of being engaged with an academic discipline in a disciplined fashion. Mr. Bauer's class appears legitimately historical, particularly in contrast to Southmoor's "hysteria": Mr. Bauer establishes participation structures very unambiguously and therefore with little confusion, shifts between structures are predictable as part of the invariant routine, and the topics look educative and worklike rather than gamelike or indulgent.

At the same time, however, Marshall teachers' direction of the participation structures of recitation and seatwork also minimizes their and students' sustained engagement with consequential knowledge and with each other. Ambiguously, the achievement of order both serves and undermines educative purposes.

Day 5: Ambiguous Interactional Prerogatives

On the fifth day of the new school year, Mr. Bauer presents a lesson that exemplifies the oblique dynamic of remote control in Marshall's Additional Needs classrooms: In a paradoxical interaction, dispassionate orderliness both regulates and provides for teacher and student edginess, which in turn prompts teachers' perceptions that an even more impersonal regimen is required. Central to the dynamic and its unintended consequences is the ambiguity of the teacher's control over knowledge.

All teachers control knowledge. Even in inductively organized lessons (Edwards & Furlong, 1978) or in open classrooms (Sharp & Green, 1975), they work to shape students' meanings to fit somewhat the meanings they have planned as a lesson's outcome (Bellack et al., 1966; Mehan, 1979). Explicitly and self-consciously, teachers premeditate outcomes to render knowledge accessible to students, to meet standards for accuracy, and to cover material efficiently. Less explicit or conscious, however, is teachers' control of school knowledge to secure behavioral control. For instance, teachers rarely comment that they plan lessons that cover facts rather than interpretations because factual lessons evoke fewer time-consuming questions, just as they rarely describe the use of individual worksheets as providing fewer opportunities for students to learn that school knowledge is controversial rather than univocal.

In Mr. Bauer's Additional Needs class, restricting knowledge to restrain behavior and safeguard teacher authority is carried a notch further than in his regular-track classes. Mr. Bauer initiated the process on the second day of class, when he replaced arguable history with reassuringly straightforward reading skills. On the fifth day, he extends the reduction further to include the "easy" rudiments as well. In Additional Needs classes, knowledge inheres in singular, arbitrary Right Answers, and students know by guessing the "bit" that the teacher happens to have in mind.

This redefinition of school success as a lucky guess results in an ambiguous rather than a clearly educative or alienating situation, as Mr. Bauer's fifth-day lesson illustrates (recall, also, the "Trivia Listening Quiz" in Chapter 1 and the lesson about the name of the Japanese empire in Chapter 4). In it, Mr. Bauer returns to the SQRRR method of reading to instruct students directly in Questioning. Specifically, Mr. Bauer wants to give over more class time to reading skills and to have students become "active readers": readers who ask questions as they read. He accepts the notion that self-generated questions will focus students' reading of texts and thereby enhance comprehension. Thus, on the fifth day of class, Mr. Bauer adds a reading-skills worksheet to the daily homework assignment. Before reading the chapter or answering the questions at the end, students will skim the chapter's 10 to 15 paragraphs and "create" one question for each paragraph.

After the class completes checking the previous day's homework, Mr. Bauer begins instruction in "active reading" by directing students' attention to the next chapter in the textbook: "Look at the first paragraph of the chapter and read the first sentence, JUST THE FIRST SENTENCE, of the paragraph and create a question. (2.0). Who can make a question based on that first sentence? (The chapter concerns Cortez's conquest of Mexico; the first sentence reads, "The central and eastern parts of Mexico were ruled by an Indian people called the Aztecs.") A boy volunteers: "What are Aztecs?" Mr. Bauer accepts this response, saying to the whole class, "Okay, write that down, 'What are Aztecs?'"

This auspicious beginning is short-lived, however, as student questions for subsequent paragraphs prove unacceptable. After pausing momentarily while students write down the first question, Mr. Bauer resumes: "Now, read the first sentence of paragraph 2. To yourself. (1.0). Now, can somebody create a question for me?" (The sentence in the text is: "Many young men came from Spain to the New World to seek their fortunes.") This time the student's suggestion, "What kind of fortunes were they looking for?" does not match the question Mr. Bauer would pose. Mr. Bauer's evaluation makes this clear: "*I* would have asked a different question."

Mr. Bauer then points students' "creativity" in the right direction by reminding them of a question-making formula: "Let's remember, what are the five basic questions?" Collectively, in unison, students list "who, what, where, when, and how." "What kind" is not in the list and, therefore, is not the right kind of question. Smoothly, with no further discussion about the use of wh-questions—and with no repercussions for the student who posed the wrong initial question—Mr. Bauer directs class attention back to the first sentence of paragraph 2: "Who can make another question?" (A girl responds with a question that fits the wh-question strategy and that Mr. Bauer accepts: "*Who* are these explorers?"

Even pointed in the right direction with the wh-formula in hand, however, students run into difficulty again as they try to guess the answer that the teacher wants. The first sentence of the third paragraph presents trouble: "Cortez had been able to conquer the powerful Aztecs with only 600 men." Using one of the "five basic questions" and, therefore, operating with Mr. Bauer's framework of meaning, a student creates the question, "Who was Cortez?" But Mr. Bauer objects, saying, "Now look at that sentence again: (reading aloud from the text) 'Cortez could [sic] conquer powerful Aztecs with only 600 men.' Anybody want to take another one of the five?" With no discussion as to how one selects from among the five interrogatives, a second student randomly "takes another": "*When* did Cortez do this?" Again, this is not the answer Mr. Bauer has in mind. Dissatisfied, he hints: "I've got a feeling the author wants you to ask that hard question, you know the one I mean?" With this prompt, the third attempt is successful. Mr. Bauer comments: "Good. '*How* did Cortez conquer them?' I would suggest you use the 'how.'"

Mr. Bauer and the class continue through the first six of the ten paragraphs of the chapter in a similarly busy if daunting routine. Told to "create" questions, students "try," but they find that they are to use preformulated questions. Even a formula is no guarantee but itself depends on the already-found questions of the teacher. Students' "effort" begins to wane in the face of repeated failures. They become testy. Mr. Bauer calls attention to the ambiguity of students' prerogatives as they begin working individually to "create" questions for the chapter's last four paragraphs. Rather than "active reading" of the text, he suggests that students "try hard to be mind readers of the author – – think what topic the author is trying to tell you about in that first sentence."

In short, Mr. Bauer renders lower-track reading as "mind reading." The mind to be read is not the student's own as it engages with a history text but the teacher's (or the author's, as the teacher interprets the author). Indeed, after several days of "active reading" of daily chapters, Mr. Bauer gives up requiring students to generate lists of questions. He explains that he is "dissatisfied with the students' questions: They don't know how to ask good questions, and *it's less chancy* if the reading teacher and I do it" (my emphasis). Thus, in conjunction with a reading specialist, Mr. Bauer assures that the questions generated will match The Right Answer that he has in mind. Nonetheless, Mr. Bauer hopes that "if the students practice answering our questions, some of it (generating questions) will seep into their heads."

Most of the questions for the reading-skills worksheets give practice in basic reading skills. None are open-ended, interpretative, or evaluative but, like almost all the chapter questions, concern retrieval of factual content directly from the text. Such worksheets "hit a brain cell over and over again." The reading-skill questions provide yet another repetition of the textbook's history facts, because students review the content when they write answers as homework and, again, when they recite the answers orally in class.

However, although redundant practice may have worked for Ted Williams as Mr. Bauer's fable implied, it has mixed effects for Mr. Bauer's ninth graders. It affects quite inconsistently students' "batting averages" on history quizzes and grade reports. It also both invites and discourages students' willingness to come out for extra practice. In the main, redundancy provides experience in "trying hard" to guess factual "bits" of school knowledge. Because the significance and validity of such knowledge appear beyond anyone's control, its effects are paradoxical: Both engagement and disengagement in lucky lessons make sense. On the one hand, guessing is easy. Moreover, because incorrect answers signal a lack of luck, not students' lack of talent or effort, success by luck assuages lower-track students' anxiety about academic participation. Teachers are also absolved. They have simplified and structured knowledge to provide even the most unsuccessful, recalcitrant students with neutral formulae for success: All students have to do is refer to facts, an answer sheet, commonsense knowledge, or "what the author has in mind."

Yet, on the other hand, lucky lessons lead teachers to worry that the redefinition renders historical study trivial. Moreover, they doubt their efficacy in the face of students' lack of mastery even with persistent repetitions; their lackadaisical responses to "What are Aztecs?" or whether A or C is correct; and their emergent anger when even though they comply with formulae for "creating" questions, their success is not algorithmic after all. Ironically, students' disregard for trivialized school knowledge requires teachers to "pull teeth" to secure their attention: Remote control justifies even more remote control as, in a catch-22, lower-track teaching ambiguously engages students and turns them away.

The efficient, regimented climate in Mr. Bauer's Additional Needs American history classroom is characteristic of the other lower-track classes in which I observed at Marshall. In both word and deed, veteran teachers set forth the principles of time and training. They arrange the classroom situation as an invariant but commonsensical routine; they reconstruct a complex, "bookish" body of knowledge as reassuringly simple, step-by-step, "practical" skills; and they dominate classroom talk without domineering. In short, they teach by remote control, without calling attention to themselves as teachers.

The teaching is mirrored in an equally double-edged student role: Lower-track students are sometimes comfortably acquiescent, sometimes aggressively passive as they demonstrate habit formation or work quietly at individual seatwork. Paradoxically, remote control both regulates and feeds their unpredictability: "Easy" lessons "at the student's level" promise success, but because the lessons are controlling and trivial, they also justify disengagement. As a result, for all their orderliness, Marshall's lower-track classrooms simmer.

CHAPTER 7

The Ethos of
Marshall High School:
A Comparison

Simple explanations are insufficient for understanding how regimented, remote teaching makes sense to Marshall's experienced, conscientious lower-track teachers. Examining Mr. Bauer's psyche for stress, his biography for burnout, or his idiosyncratic style for authoritarianism will not suffice, because the same dynamics of time and training also structured teaching in the other three lower-track classes in which I observed at Marshall. Nor is the organizational factor, tracking, a sufficient explanation, because Marshall's impersonal regimen differs so strikingly from Southmoor's lower-track chaos. Furthermore, a simple correspondence between the type of school and classroom contexts can also be discounted. Indeed, because Marshall, in contrast to Southmoor, devotes considerable resources to remedial classes, lower-track teachers' disheartened enactments are rather surprising. Finally, routinized lower-track teaching is also not a straightforward reproduction of community mores. Although Marshall offers Additional Needs students the "practical," disciplined lessons that working class communities purportedly demand, the students' engagement with the curriculum is as tentative as the teachers'.

A relational analysis does provide understanding of the complexity of lower-track teaching. Accordingly, in the first part of this chapter, I compare the regimented, remote teaching in lower-track classes like Mr. Bauer's with that in teachers' orderly, evenhanded, regular-track classes. I show that the similarities and differences in tracked classes are, like jazz performances (the metaphor appears in Erickson & Schultz, 1982), oblique improvisations on themes in Marshall's "nothing-out-of-the-ordinary" culture. Marshall's teachers find themselves caught in a number of dilemmas that, like Southmoor teachers, they resolve by distancing themselves from the lower-track role.

148

However, because Maplehurst's two high schools differ culturally, distance at Marshall results in precise, hands-off, lower-track teaching, whereas at Southmoor the result is chaotic caretaking. Therefore, in the second half of the chapter, I broaden the relational analysis further to compare the two schools and the community contexts that shape (and are shaped by) them. Although the school differences might appear structural—skills-based education in a working-class school and academic education in a middle-class school—people in schools interpret structures such as social class and filter their significance in accord with local conditions. As a result, the meaning of curriculum differentiation arises in a complex *interaction* of differentiation within a school (through tracking) and differences between schools (through school cultures).

TEACHING AT "NOTHING-OUT-OF-THE-ORDINARY" MARSHALL

Marshall High School is comparable to Southmoor on many of the objective measures used to characterize organizations, but its culture is different. Grounded in a definition of students as different from white-collar teachers and in a bureaucratic, hierarchical mode of operation, it emphasizes competence and coordination rather than preeminence. However, competence and coordination are problematic, and the school is riven by internal feuds over models of instruction ("practical" and skills-based versus abstract academics), purposes (discipline versus educational engagement), and organizational imperatives ("team" membership versus professional judgment).

In such a milieu, teachers, particularly teachers of traditional academic subjects such as English and social studies, are not kingpins. Indeed, the struggles over purpose and program lead teachers to doubt that either students or the school values their contributions. As a result, teachers hold limited expectations for themselves as well as for their "blue-collar" students. Regular-track classes are distinguished by consistent teaching, coordinated curricula, and composed teacher-student relationships in accord with bureaucratic accountability, but, because teachers do not "believe" in their role, the climate is uninspired.

Teachers' doubts and the institutional definitions and dilemmas in which they are grounded are exaggerated in Additional Needs classes, so that the reserved, regular-track routine becomes regimented remote control. Lower-track teachers at Marshall suffer a double assault on their status. First, as instructors in English and social studies, they are mere academicians rather than "practical" educators. Second, they confront very different students in lower-track classes, yet they lack the credentials of remedial specialists who presumably know the "practical" strategies that will work with academically unsuccessful students. On two counts then—academic role *and* lower-track role—Additional Needs teachers are discredited.

As a result, whereas it is sensible from Southmoor teachers' perspectives to resolve lower-track role conflict by distancing themselves from a marginalized Additional Needs role and by embracing a powerful, high-status, regular-track role, Marshall's Additional Needs teachers are hamstrung. As outsiders to specialized departments in reading, special education, and vocational education, they doubt many of the merits attributed to a "no-nonsense," skills-based model of education. However, as besieged academicians facing unpredictable lower-track students, they have no strong, equally certain alternative to which they can turn. Thus constrained, they use direct instruction but they are ambivalent: Remote-control teaching is the concrete result.

"Unsocialized" Students

At Marshall, even regular-track students are deemed quite different from teachers. Because of their "blue-collar" backgrounds, Marshall students "don't see *learning* as important":

> Education is expedient, it's only a credential. There's a provincial attitude toward education – – It should get you something. . . . I see so many bright young women – – Their parents are happy if they go to business college.

Another teacher commented regretfully on regular-track students' (and peers') lack of interest in academic subjects and the effect on his confidence:

> Students don't come in after class to talk about issues that came up in class. . . . Stimulation from other faculty is more work-related than intellectual: We talk about policy and programs, not novels. . . . I was convinced of my teaching ability because of my earlier experience at Southmoor.

Teachers perceive lower-track students as even more different than Marshall's instrumentally oriented, regular-track students:

> In general, lower-level kids are distracted. In class there are callouts. They're up walking around the room when they shouldn't be.

They haven't been socialized to the middle-class Marshall classroom. They're really uncivilized, I guess you could say. . . . That's what prevents them from being in regular-track classes - - Take Jean. She has only negative interactions with boys. She's really into female liberation and talks in class about it - - She's emotionally disturbed. I would guess that maybe her attitude toward boys is related to some males in her family and so she's resentful of males in general - - If she had one of her temper tantrums in a regular class, they'd laugh her right out of it.

Another teacher concurred in lower-track students' lack of "socialization":

There's a disintegration of the family - - No demands from home. There is no leadership at home. Dad sits in front of the tube and guzzles beer. There is no experience from home - - Parents send their kids to school and say, "Here, you (the school) do it."

Thus, in contrast to Marshall's "nice, well-behaved (regular-track) kids who want to get a diploma so they can get a job and settle down," lower-track students are considered not only unskilled but antagonistic toward all schoolwork. Accordingly, lower-track teachers vacillate, regarding their students alternately as trainees *and* as beyond training.

Academic Socialization. Teachers rely on and re-create the definition of lower-track students as academically "unsocialized" when they design, deliver, and assess "basic," "structured" remedial lessons, such as Mr. Bauer's. For example, Mr. Reed's tenth-grade Additional Needs history class talked about the bombing of the U.S.S. *Maine* after reading a three-page description of the event in a text that the teacher assessed as at a seventh- or eighth-grade level. At first, discussion was halting and restive as the teacher, proceeding much as Mr. Bauer did in the "active reading" exercises, drilled students in reviewing the main facts of the article, paragraph by paragraph:

> T: How much information is in that first paragraph?
> (5.0 seconds of silence)
> T: *What things are you told in that first paragraph?*
> (7.0)
> T: NOW THIS IS FOR YOU TO RESPOND - - EVERY HAND should be up to say, "I've got this piece of information from that paragraph."
> (5.0)

T: KEN! Give me some information from the paragraph!
KEN: Cuba is a Spanish colony.

Shortly after this tense, halting beginning, as it became apparent that no one really knows what happened to the U.S.S. *Maine*, student interest quickened. The students began to discuss the contradictory evidence avidly. For example, there was a facsimile of a newspaper of the time in the textbook, with a graphic picture of the explosion. Students ruminated about how a reporter could take a photo at night, how anyone could have been on the scene so fortuitously, that maybe it wasn't a photo, how an eyewitness could draw such a scene, and so forth. For a while, they encouraged the teacher in a discussion of the more general issue of yellow journalism and its application to press coverage of modern events. The discussion was animated, even sophisticated, and contrasted sharply with students' usual lethargy during recitations of more narrowly defined topics, such as "How much information is in that first paragraph?"

After the class, Mr. Reed and I talked about how Additional Needs students can be classified as unskilled and "anti-intellectual" when they respond positively to such a "bookish" school lesson (for other examples of marginal students' active engagement with school knowledge, see Heath & Branscombe, 1985; Valli, 1990; and Wehlage et al., 1980). Neither simplistic nor cynical, Mr. Reed began by agreeing that the class did very well in the discussion. But he then cautioned that he had worried both that the discussion would "never get off the ground" and that, once off the ground, it would "get out of hand." Mr. Reed went on to acknowledge students' good oral skills and their preference for group work, but he followed the praise by derogating their reading abilities and expressing his fear that group interactions would become "shout outs":

> They cannot read things and recognize those kinds of things happening either. . . . Sure, once they start talking about it, for one day, and especially like, like Arthur is really sharp. But he is, ah, so off-the-wall socially, and behaviorally, and so on. And he just can't relate to people. . . . He gets mad, then he starts to talk back, they start shouting out and nobody can hear anything.

After Mr. Reed explained his worries about group discussions, he proceeded to list other problems, one after another, that Additional Needs students present. For instance, he predicted that students would be totally unable to recall the discussion the next day: "We'll be back to ground zero tomorrow. That's the biggest difference with these kids. You can't develop a topic with them over time." In addition to having attention spans or memories limited to one class period, none of the students would be able to write a reasonable answer to an essay question or give an oral report about the U.S.S. *Maine*. In sum, although Mr. Reed noted students' multifaceted performances, he adhered to institutionally acknowledged mores that mark students' distance from the norm: No matter how well Additional Needs students perform one task, such as lively, thoughtful discussion, Mr. Reed and other lower-track teachers counter with another deficiency.

Nevertheless, Marshall teachers are guarded in telling Additional Needs students of their academic deficiencies:

> BRETT: (receiving a new worksheet) Is this work the same as in your other classes?
> (5.0)
> ARTHUR: Isn't this class easier?
> (3.0)
> T: The - work - in this class - is designed for, uh - - this class.
> (5.0)
> BRETT: Is there a *harder* class, put it that way.
> T: It's harder for some of you - - You need to get quiet and get to work now.

Teachers explain that "if Additional Needs students knew how low they are, they'd be devastated." But the impact on teaching might be equally "devastating": If provided "realistic" information, discouraged students might refuse to acquiesce in lessons altogether. Then, quite literally, teachers would find teaching impossible.

Behavioral Socialization. Teachers also use the phrase "unsocialized to the classroom" to connote lower-track students' troublesome behavior. In contrast to regular-track classes, whose students are "tolerant of school - -they sit back and let the teacher teach," lower-track classes "hang from the chandeliers," are a "circus," or are replete with "distractions," "call-outs," even "explosions":

> You can't have a short fuse and work with these kids - - They can be frustrating. And physical size, that plays a part, you know, especially at the ninth-grade level. If you're bigger, they have to listen.

Contrarily, however, lower-track classes are also deemed annoyingly blasé. For example, Mr. Bauer and Mr. Reed often complain that the problem in lower-track classrooms is to get students to talk at all. These seemingly contradictory characterizations have in common their notable difference from the characterization of the regular student as "passive" and compliant. Both, paradoxically, fuel the lower-track emphasis on control.

Teachers' recurrent, ambivalent comments about the need for order make sense within Marshall's culture where, even though order is paramount, the possibility of disorder is perceived as an ever present threat. Therefore, on the one hand, teachers know that if their classes "explode," organizational as well as pedagogical and personal repercussions will follow. The daily regimen, the invariant routines, and a classroom arrangement that runs on its own without question are all efforts to forestall the "any one thing that can set students off." On the other hand, teachers also recognize possible unintended consequences of the "tight discipline" they feel compelled to provide: "But sometimes some of these things are inhibiting to learning. . . . 'Nothing out of the ordinary'—lockstep—characterizes Marshall." They also worry that rigid disciplinary procedures "push out" students.

Overall, teachers' efforts to control "trouble" are successful: In contrast to Southmoor's, Marshall's hallways are quiet and free of debris after lunch; classes that occasionally overstep the bounds of civility are rather easily hushed; and when announcements are made on the public intercom, lower-track students sit quietly, whereas at Southmoor, announcements are usually drowned out by raucous catcalls.

However, "blowups," as some teachers call them, do occur and with powerful, alienating effect. For instance, in a 10th-grade history class, Gary could not find the North Sea on the map in the textbook in order to transfer its name to a mimeographed map worksheet. At first, the teacher berated Gary for his inattention to the maps. The student reciprocated with loud belligerence of his own: "I *am* looking! YOU wrote the map wrong! How do you expect us to do this when you wrote the map wrong!" The teacher admitted having omitted Luxembourg from the mimeographed map. Even so, as the teacher continued to try to help Gary find the North Sea, the student continued to have trouble. Finally, with increasingly hostile retorts from Gary, the teacher walked to the far side of the room to help another student. Gary continued to mutter intermittently. Students around him then turned quickly in their desks to show him how to mark his map. When a second student, in a querulous tone, raised another map question, students around him quickly helped him find his place too, perhaps themselves fearing a second "explosion." Although no one mentioned it, tension in the room was palpable throughout the hour, and teacher and students treated each other gingerly.

Although the occurrence was unique in the class during my 6 months of observation, the incident suggests the degree of anger that can flash to the surface in Marshall's lower-track classes. At least on occasion, students can be directly confrontational. Equally bitter, Gary's teacher reciprocated cuttingly: "Gary should be removed from the classroom. He's drug-involved; I don't know why we bother."

The teacher's assessment that Gary is so far beyond the pale that he should be "removed," even from Marshall's lower-track classes, is matched by pessimism regarding his ability to influence Gary. Other teachers suggest dispiritedly that time more than training—what one called "the maturity factor"—is critical for students' intellectual and civil development. For example, one teacher claimed that he is "realistic" in his negative assessment of the impact of his teaching:

> I don't judge *my* success and failure by *students'* success and failure. I had a kid in an Additional Needs class a couple of years ago. He flunked the course. Dropped out of school. He came back last year and told me, "You know, I could have passed that course." Some of these kids just need a few years to grow up.

Aggressive Passivity. Teachers' doubts about students and self are fed by perceptions that students are not only intellectually deficient but fundamentally hostile. Individually and as a group, lower-track students act with *aggressive passivity.* As a result, from teachers' perspectives, "trouble" is not limited to occasional personality conflicts or to a few isolated "blow-ups" such as Gary's but is always a possibility. They always expect bland acquiescence to slip to adamantine silence, recalcitrance in answering even the simplest of questions (as in the opening of the lesson about the U.S.S. *Maine*), stoniness in reaction to their jokes, or superciliousness in the face of their enthusiasm: "They're a sea of blank faces - - I want to shake them to wake them up."

Seen from this perspective, students' failure to have learned the rules of either reading or "respect" is as much an indication of their unwillingness to learn as of their inability. Thus, although teachers describe lower-track teaching as impartial time and training, they experience it as a tedious, if subterranean, struggle. A faculty member described his ongoing "battle with Joe":

> He talks back to me! He got mad at me 3 months ago - He's classified ED (emotionally disturbed), by the way - - And he won't let go of the anger. . . . It started with some writing assignment. He

has a physical problem of some kind, but no one told me. So he felt picked on when I asked him to recopy the theme. He's *very* defensive about this, you can see - - I said to him, "Let's work this out," but he won't talk about it.

Students also understand the struggle. Two girls, echoing sentiments expressed by other lower-track students, described their aggressively passive stance toward teachers:

> PATTY: The first quarter and stuff, Mr. Bradley gave us lots of freedom, I think more than I think a regular class should get. And, um, I don't know, just lately he's been really tightening up on us, so -
>
> I: I wanted to ask you a little bit about um, whether, what you have to do to get along with Mr. Bradley.
>
> PATTY: I had to bend. I had to bend, kind of. Not much, you know, but I had to control what I said. 'Cause I get carried away sometimes - - talking. . . .
>
> I: What about you, Tiffany? Is there any kind of thing that you have to do [-
>
> TIFFANY: [I [don't.
>
> I: -to [get along with him?
>
> TIFFANY: I don't.
>
> I: You [don't? You don't be[nd for him?
>
> TIFFANY: [No, I won't. [I don't like that.
>
> PATTY: I mean, he starts yelling - [
>
> TIFFANY: [Except for real big things, I don't. And if he doesn't like it, then he yells at me.
>
> PATTY: You just ignore him.
>
> TIFFANY: I'm not trying to be mean. Yeah, I *do* ignore him.
>
> PATTY: Yeah, he started yelling at me the other day, and I just sat there, like.

As the "battle" lines suggest, aggressive passivity places limits on Marshall teachers' omnipotence, prompts the guardedness with which they teach, and thus contributes to the remote control that distinguishes Marshall's lower-track classes. Mr. Reed's students refused to countenance his commanding, trivial questions regarding the first paragraph about the U.S.S. *Maine*; Mr. Bauer's balked as their luck failed at guessing the wh-question that he had in mind about the Aztecs; Mr. Bradley's lesson in group communication stalled over perspectives on power.

Thus, even though Marshall teachers are not tyrants and Additional

Needs classes exhibit few of the usually cited signs of outrageous, outraged lower-track antagonism and resistance (Cusick, 1973; Hargreaves et al., 1975; McNeil, 1986; Metz, 1978; Rosenbaum, 1976; Schwartz, 1981; Willis, 1977), students nevertheless act cohesively in the invariance of their stolid response. Teachers remark on the "negative peer group," whether lower-track students join in lessons or tune them out. Different from "passive" regular-track students, Marshall's lower-track students also differ from Southmoor's Additional Needs students who see teachers as capricious and inscrutable perhaps but also as worthy of moderate good feeling. At Marshall, Additional Needs students view teachers with as much disparagement as teachers view students: Teachers are fools or arbitrary "policemen. . . . They all like to boss you . . . they're just looking for a 'bust.'" Or, as a teacher who had worked at both schools put it, "At Southmoor, a teacher can have a 'following' (of students). Here (at Marshall), the teacher is 'the enemy'" (see Wolcott, 1974).

Counterreaction: Depersonalized Teaching. In response to students and school, lower-track teachers reduce the content of lessons, in part because it is a "realistic" response to students' academic skill deficits, but also because lessons about factual tidbits limit the possibility that public differences in opinions and angry confrontations will emerge. They individualize assignments, in part because the technique accommodates differences in ability but also because seatwork forestalls the unnerving "explosions" that the "negative peer group" can generate. Depersonalized, taken-for-granted routines both uphold Marshall's "tradition of discipline" and protect teachers from classroom critics.

Circularly, however, regimented remote-control teaching also sustains Marshall's culture and the definition of Additional Needs students as academically and behaviorally different. For example, even though lower-track students work quietly on apparently educational lessons, their fluctuating homework grades and mixed test scores suggest that they take little from them. Teachers respond ambivalently to students' continued failure. Occasionally, privately, some worry about the unintended consequences of the skills-based model of instruction. They imagine that remedial exercises insult or bore adolescents who, even if they lack "basic" decoding skills in reading, may nevertheless have knowledge of the world or higher-order comprehension skills. Furthermore, when Additional Needs students spend almost all their time on skill development, they miss opportunities to learn the language and interactional skills associated with scholarship in the academic disciplines and success in regular-track classes. Accordingly, students who experience history as a series of incontrovertible dates, names, and places, may take the facts as an index for the certainty of historical knowledge, for the teacher's command of it, and for the student's proper reciprocal role as memorizer (Edwards, 1978).

Most often, however, because it is congruent with the institutionally acknowledged definitions of students and of Marshall's "practical" purposes, teachers' response to students' continued failure is to blame students for insufficient diligence and to press harder on time and training. When a student failed to turn in a worksheet that required identifying in a word or two more than 80 "People of the 1920s," the teacher's interpretation was not that the exercise was tedious but that the student was "slipping up" and "not being consistent - - She's bright but she doesn't keep at it." However, the more teachers press "uncivilized" students to "keep at it" in routinized, depersonalized lessons, the more aggressively passive students become. The "sea of blank faces" deepens and teachers find themselves increasingly unable to teach. As I explain in the next section, teachers recognize, at least intuitively, some perverse effects of the standard skills curriculum, but, within Marshall's bureaucracy, they feel compelled to use it.

A Bureaucratic Mode of Operation

Both regular- and lower-track teaching mirror the second constitutive element of Marshall's "nothing-out-of-the-ordinary" culture: a bureaucratic organizational mode based on three principles of scientific management.* First, the school strives for certitude while denying ambivalence and contradictions. Thus, all persons in the organization have clearly delineated roles, or specializations. So long as everyone "cooperates" and is a "good team player," as Marshall's principal puts it, the school will function harmoniously and efficiently. Second, the organization is compelled to produce. Allocating almost as many teachers to special as to traditional departments, the school guarantees the preparation of all students for their ostensibly predictable futures through "practical," disciplined, direct instruction. Finally, questions about the organization are not encouraged. Marshall's emphasis lies in the orderly production of graduates, not in debate about relationships between the means and ends of production. Persistent questions are referred to committees or superiors in Marshall's hierarchical structure where distant administrators have more decision-making power than teachers, just as teachers direct students with little equivocation.

Even though cooperation is touted in Marshall's distinctive bureaucracy, conflict abounds: Programs compete; the faculty is "noncohesive";

---

*For a description of the scientific management model, see Kliebard, 1977a.

the administration is decentered. Members of the weak, fragmented teaching faculty acknowledge both the conflict and the ethos of officialism that attempts to manage it by retreating to their individual classrooms, avoiding public debate about school-wide policies, and striving to be "good team players." Indeed, many avoid public encounters altogether, even over coffee: In contrast to the hubbub in the faculty lounge at Southmoor, Marshall's is virtually deserted except for a table of lively kitchen workers. One teacher explained that he never went to the faculty lounge, even at lunchtime, because he would see people with whom he had "extreme differences philosophically. There are some teachers, they're so off-the-wall - - So I eat in my room."

Communication fails on a larger scale as well. A teacher explained an effort to revive a "faculty senate" that would express "a faculty perspective" on "major issues" and demand administrative responses:

> It worked reasonably well for a while. Um, we would, we would get concerns and draft questions and so on and address them to Dick (the head principal) and get some kind of response. And for a while that wasn't bad, except in areas where some kind of major decision had to be made. Like, uh, rule enforcement. And then we never got that satisfactory a response. We ran our own survey once, and the results of it as far as the faculty perceiving the administration as supportive of the faculty - - did not come across. And Dick and the assistant principal were very upset by this. Because they thought they were doing a better job, and they really kind of resented the survey that we did. And since that point, we've had very poor responses from Dick on things - - unless it's something like, ah, buying a coffee maker for the lounge or something.

Thus, the basis for Marshall teachers' authority is not the important knowledge they have to transmit or their "professional" power and responsibility, as at Southmoor, but their hierarchical role in a "practical," "lockstep" organization. Calculating and complying with bureaucratic imperatives of accountability and coordination, regular teachers provide consistently solid if straightforward lessons: Teachers are methodical without being martinets and determined but not rigid.

The school's bureaucratic mode of operation also influences teaching in Additional Needs classes. Whereas Southmoor's classes for academically unsuccessful students are small, restricted, and at the school's margins, Marshall's are at its heart. The efficient system provides differentiated, standardized places for different individuals.

Ironically, however, the support for producing graduates contributes to lower-track teachers' role conflict: Accountability and a standardized technology compromise teachers' professional independence and expertise at the same time that "by-the-book" mores gloss over rather than elucidate the "noncohesive" faculty's disagreements. In such a milieu, lower-track teachers protect themselves from censure by going through the motions of organizational membership and classroom instruction.

An Elective Lower Track. One might expect Marshall's Additional Needs teachers to feel encouraged in their work because lower-track classes form a large, integral component in the school's curriculum. Four sections each of Additional Needs English and social studies are taught regularly to about 25% of the freshman class. Moreover, the ninth-grade courses articulate with Additional Needs courses for students in the upper classes. The classes do not come and go with special funding, as at Southmoor. Special monies augment rather than supplant academic departments' regular allocations for a complete lower track. As a result, lower-track classes command a steady stream of students, and students can satisfy virtually all their graduation requirements in lower-track courses.

Not only does the extensive, lower-track curriculum confirm Marshall's definition of students as interested in a "practical," "easy" education (just as the absence of classes at Southmoor reflects institutionally acknowledged presumptions that few students in the college-preparatory high school want or need remedial courses), but the regularized provision also indicates that lower-track courses are an integral rather than a marginal part of Marshall teachers' jobs. Accordingly, teachers' five-class assignments balance regular- and lower-track classes: typically, two (or three) lower-track classes and three (or two) regular-track classes. Because lower-track teaching is a routine part of almost all teachers' loads, it does not carry the stigma that it does at Southmoor. At the same time, it lacks some of the pressures of regular teaching at Marshall:

> I guess I find Additional Needs kids fun to work with - - You know, they're like puppy dogs, they need a pat on the head. More able students, if things don't go well, they look more for a scapegoat, they want to find someone—like the teacher—to blame it on.

However, if lower-track classes are not marginal to Marshall's main organization, lower-track teachers nevertheless experience role conflict. In an inverted twist on Southmoor teachers' conflict, Marshall's lower-track teachers question whether they should provide such "easy," "practical" educations to students, but the school culture also leaves them uncertain in making the case for "bookish" studies.

Teachers' ambivalence is manifested organizationally. The school struggles to provide differentiated programs for all students, including those headed to work and those headed to college. But academic teachers worry that "easy" skills are overemphasized and serious academics are deemphasized by what several call Marshall's pervasive "anti-intellectualism." Almost every adult with whom I spoke portrayed the community as "anti-intellectual." Several cited the large, supportive crowds that sports activities draw in contrast to the small turnout at Parents Visitation Night. One teacher complained: "I worked on the Parent Advisory Council. No one ever wanted to discuss the quality of instruction. It was all sports and pep club." At the same time, some faculty members also portray colleagues as uninterested in ideas. Factions of "elitists" and "anti-intellectuals" snipe at each other: One teacher claimed he had to start reading the sports page to be viewed "as a 'man' and get any respect in the faculty lounge," whereas another spoke superciliously of a teacher who "uses a five-dollar word every chance he gets, when a half-dollar word would do just fine."

Worries about the lack of appreciation for academic pursuits center particularly on a school policy that allows any student to elect a lower-track course. In Marshall's "consumerism," as an administrator termed it, Additional Needs classes are neutral equivalents of regular-track classes: "We don't describe them as 'dummy' courses," one teacher explained. In the same vein, a counselor reported that she would not hesitate to "switch a kid to (lower-track) Social Psych 2934 instead of (regular-track) 2933 without telling him if I thought he needed the low level. He would never know (because the numbers are so similar)."

And, indeed, Marshall students voice little compunction about electing lower-track classes. They often refer to "the good deal" of "dropping down" to a lower-track level from a regular-track class. In an interview, a student complained: "History stinks. . . . Who *cares* about crap in the past? It's boring. And the tests! I'll read the assignment and I'll get half the quiz wrong - - I think I'm just gonna go in a lower class." By contrast, a Southmoor student agonized over her lower-track placement: "My dad said, 'How many of those Additional Needs classes are you in?' And I just said, 'History,' because that's the only one. And he said, 'Well, that's good' - - 'cause I'm not in a whole bunch of these lower classes."

In the face of a laissez-faire economy, Marshall teachers fear that if they insist on rigor or a less "practical" orientation, they will find themselves without students, because any student may take "the good deal" and "drop down to an easier," equally legitimate, equally credit-conferring course. Even students in Additional Needs classes who begin to flounder can be accommodated further in the school's large special education department or in "low-low" courses.

Therefore, perversely, the emphasis on producing graduates hinders teachers' ability to teach. As a teacher recounted explosively, he cannot demand much from lower-track students:

> Tracking ENABLES drug abuse. It ENABLES truancy. It fosters students' dropping out of academic pursuits. Life here is so easy for students that they can be "high" all day or absent half the semester and still pass, and tracking is part of the reason why.

An equally frustrated guidance counselor agreed that allowing able or "lazy" students to elect lower-track classes without accurate information about the significance of their choices promotes students' underachievement and diminishes the value of the "hard work" education to which many teachers subscribe: "I saw a transfer student with a drug habit and scores on the Iowa Basics in the 98th percentile, and she was *allowed* to sign up for lower-track classes." When I asked who "allowed" the registration, the counselor replied pointedly: "The administrative stance was not there."

Thus, at Marshall, as at many other American high schools (Cusick, 1983; Jackson, 1981; Powell et al., 1985; Rosenbaum, 1976, chap. 6), choice is deemed crucial to educational success and, if students choose lower-track classes, lower-track education must be what the school should provide. Circularly, because enrollment in "practical," "easy" classes *is* high, Marshall's image of itself as an efficient, responsive school that serves "typical blue-collar kids" who are uninterested in "abstract," "bookish" endeavors is validated. One administrator explained the double-bind with the querulousness that is characteristic at Marshall:

> We have Harvard material here, too, but what can we do if the kid elects to take Additional Needs English instead of Survey of British Lit? We have a consumer economy operating and kids have the freedom to handicap themselves with a second-rate education.

"Consumerism" also handicaps teachers. It undermines their morale and leaves them feeling that their intellectual expertise is undervalued, that their jobs are, literally, on the line, and that their position within Marshall is besieged. From their perspective, the school itself is "anti-intellectual," and their colleagues are unwilling or unable to take a stand in defining education as something one earns by means other than clock punching and for purposes other than materialism or vocationalism.

A *"Noncohesive" Faculty.* The counselor's angry story of a bright, troubled student who was "allowed to sign up for lower-track classes" by a vaguely identified "administration" is symptomatic of the lack of consensus in the Marshall "team," as well as of members' reluctance to confront each other with their conflicts. In contrast to the single-minded, self-assured pursuit of academic excellence at Southmoor and the constant verbal interchanges among teachers, students, and administrators that reinforce that school's solidarity, Marshall is "noncohesive."

No group within the high school has the political or cultural means to resolve the profound, internal rifts. Formally, teachers are subordinate to the administrators. In addition, they are also split along disciplinary and ideological lines, with individuals and departments competing for symbolic domination, funds, and students.

The teaching faculty's "noncohesiveness" is exemplified numerically: About 45% of Marshall's teachers work in three nontraditional departments: reading, special education, and vocational education. Furthermore, these specialist departments, especially special education, have grown at a time when declining enrollments have taken their toll in traditional staff positions. According to an administrator, Marshall had "one special ed teacher and eight kids in 1969. Today special ed is the largest department at Marshall *by far* and there are over 200 kids. There is *tremendous* resentment by academic teachers!"

The faculty conflict is deepened by Marshall's history. Since the school's founding in the 1960s, academic teachers have experienced a dramatic shift in status. According to the saga of institutional origins (Clark, 1972; Jelinek, Smircich, & Hirsch, 1983), the school's first principal was "a great intellectual who was at Southmoor for years." He "raided" other Maplehurst high schools for "the best teachers in the city to bring them to Marshall." However, since his tenure ended, "The school has changed - - - It used to provide a quality education, but not anymore." Moreover, within the ethos of compartmentalization, the storytellers are able to see only differences rather than common ground. Thus, they do not countenance an even worse scenario: Marshall High could have died of declining enrollments had not the growth of the special departments saved the school—and academicians' jobs—by maintaining a sufficiently large student body to justify the organization's efficiency.

The split between specialists and academicians is crosscut by a technological split. The special departments of reading, special education, and vocational education are associated with the predominant, transmission model of instruction. The model presumes that teaching and learning are transparent, linear processes: Learning follows from repetitive practice in discrete, self-evident, step-by-step tasks; teaching is the work of technical specialists, each with a particular area of expertise, who design and direct appropriate exercises. Used correctly, the model promises immediate, concrete returns: What you study in school is what you will need later on the job, as a "functional" adult, or as a law-abiding citizen. The model's power at Marshall derives from its resonance with the school's production ethos, the differentiation between and among teacher-specialists and student-trainees, and efficient, accountable order.

English and social studies teachers, many of whom know different models of instruction, are defensive rather than deliberative: Given Marshall's officialism and "teamsmanship," they find it hard to argue against the straightforward model. The milieu renders them equally inarticulate about a contrasting conception of teaching as the promotion of students' interpretations of complex, enduring, human activities. The contrasting model suffers from "elitist" overtones that contravene Marshall's emphasis on the "practical," just as it also risks violating disciplined teacher-student relationships because it assumes classroom interactions and differences of opinion. At the same time, despite the consequences of regimented lessons—students' aggressively passive and mixed academic performances—teachers are unsure that liberal forms of education can appeal to or work with lower-track or "blue-collar kids."

In short, Marshall's bureaucratic mode of operation—manifested in the growth of the special departments, the predominance of a transmission model of instruction, "consumerism," and "anti-intellectualism"—confirms regular- and lower-track academic teachers' sense that their place within the school organization is increasingly questionable. Several characterize themselves explicitly as "outsiders": They say that they do what they believe best in their classrooms and leave life in the school to others. They are unwilling to identify a "faculty leader," they demur to "speak for others here," and they avow that "there's no point in talking, we'd just be angrier than we already are." Like insurgents, teachers snipe at each other and the administration. They trade insults about being a poor "team player" who, in raising publicly questions about curriculum and pedagogy, simply "makes matters worse than they already are." A teacher noted the convoluted dynamic of bureaucratic control and conflict that feeds the "noncohesive" faculty members' irresolution:

> It's hard to get a feeling of unity because we don't ever meet as a whole faculty and really discuss things that are on people's minds. And I think there's a fear that, boy, if you open issues up, it's going to get worse. . . . You get some real bad personality situations and, of course, nobody wants that, but you lose some real input that people have, too.

In short, teachers are as guarded with each other in the organization as they are with students in classrooms.

An Organizational "Team." Marshall's administrators are equally uncertain in their authority. Maintaining a low profile, they work "by committee," defer decisions to "downtown," or justify policy decisions with statements that point beyond themselves, as when programs are rationalized as "what the community wants." Thus, administrators are also guarded and remain at a distance. In contrast to Southmoor, where teachers do not hesitate to voice concerns directly to each other, department chairs, principals, or district coordinators, Marshall teachers complain that issues are simply shuffled from departmental chairpersons to the "administrative cabinet" to committees to "downtown."

One of the most significant features of the Marshall "team" is that its quarterback plays from the sidelines. Even though Mr. Day, Marshall's head principal for 3 years, sits at the pinnacle of the formal hierarchy, he describes his role as that of "facilitator":

> I'm not sure it's the *best* thing, but I'm responsible for securing resources and helping in areas where help is needed. I'd like to say it's strong instructional leadership. I find, however, that I don't do as much of that as I'd like to do. . . . Personally, I want to be viewed as someone who's open and accessible. . . . I don't see myself as being innovative, as running a model school, being the person who provides the impetus for change. I see myself as being much more reactive than I'd like to be.

Thus, speaking "realistically," Mr. Day limits his principalship to financial management, general help, and listening. He rarely gives questions a straight answer but promises instead to "check with downtown to see what has happened with that."

His tentative, "reactive" leadership, although intended to promote "openness" and engagement in organization agenda, feeds (and reflects) Marshall's fragmented system. For example, key to Mr. Day's "facilitation" is his decision to govern by committee: "Running Marshall is a collective thing." Embodying the theory of participatory management, Mr. Day established an "administrative cabinet" consisting of department chairpersons and administrative staff to advise him in running the school. However, the arrangement also provides Mr. Day with power he might not have otherwise: By bringing together the fractious department heads who, in contrast to Southmoor's, "do not coalesce, philosophically or politically" in responding to administrative policies, Mr. Day sets himself up as a necessary arbitrator. With a nod of approval, he can "rescue" department chairpersons as they vie with each other for limited resources. Thus, governance by committee and the appearance of low-key leadership, rather than signaling a limit to Mr. Day's power, may actually enhance the little he has.

A comparison with Southmoor's principal illustrates the convoluted interrelationship between organizational leadership and organizational ethos. For example, both men worked within the same formal district and institutional constraints to provide for computer education, a high-visibility curricular innovation in the early 1980s. At Southmoor, the principal determined unilaterally that all of the school's capital improvement budget (including departmental budgets) would be used to add a large, elegant, glassed-in, wood-framed computer center to the Math and Science Resource Center. Set in the center of the third floor, the lab presents passers-by with a clear view of 25 glowing computers, manned by 25 or more industrious students. The scene is guaranteed to impress anyone with the quality of high-tech instruction at Southmoor; the lab's architecture, congruent with the rest of the building, suggests the comfortable fit between the curriculum of the future and Southmoor's classical program. Even department heads whose funds were appropriated for the project admitted the lab's symbolic value in reassuring highly educated parents that the school is excellent.

By contrast, Mr. Day worked to "facilitate" the diverse interest groups represented on his advisory "administrative cabinet." Agreeing to spread Marshall's budget around, the cabinet allocated only limited funds for computers. As a result, computer education at Marshall scattered eight machines on assorted lab tables in an old science room. A plastic curtain protected them from dust. Students could use the machines only when individual teachers could find time to take them to the room. I heard of no challenges from parents or teachers.

In faculty meetings, too, the principals at the two schools exhibit different styles of leadership, each consonant with his school's bureaucratic or "professional" mode of operation. For example, at Marshall, meetings are infrequent and mundane. At one, Mr. Day opened the session by apologizing for beginning 3 minutes late (thus recognizing norms of punctuality); he routinely reminded teachers to turn in their charity pledge cards (instrumental business); he asked for announcements (there were two, both procedural); then he began the agenda (during which teachers sat with as much aggressive passivity as lower-track students). A comparable gathering at Southmoor began late; involved noisy, sarcastic jokes; and produced lively interchanges between and among the principal and various teachers (although most concerned minor business).

Mr. Day notes faculty members' as well as his own unhappiness with the role he feels he has to perform. Teachers complain that he "hides in the front office" and that "he doesn't exercise that kind of forceful leadership we need to get going educationally." Some analyze Mr. Day's remote leadership as an effort to balance the school's warring factions: "He's a team player – – and appears indecisive; I'd guess he's being careful not to offend the people who think we should have easy classes and those who don't." Others see Mr. Day's invisibility less generously as a signal of a growing distrust and disparate goals between Marshall's teachers and administrators. Both views confirm the apparently limited jurisdiction Mr. Day exerts over the divided Marshall "team." The principal himself doubts that he can change: "If I had a chance to step back and really put my time into certain areas differently – – I do have fair leeway at that – – but I don't see that I can do what I'd like to do."

In sum, the general uncertainty at Marshall about the kind of institution it is and the kind of education it offers is pervasive. However, it is not a subject for public debate. Rather, uncertainty is tacitly acknowledged; It is managed but not resolved in a bureaucratic system that emphasizes productivity, compartmentalization, coordination and, as with any good "team," playing along with rather than questioning procedure.

Ironically, however, even though Marshall's brand of bureaucracy promises certitude, it exacerbates uncertainty and keeps members on the defensive. The school-wide ethos permeates classroom and collegial relationships, maintaining conflict by silencing its discussion. Thus, lower-track teachers who worry that a skills-based mode of instruction is inadequate face a catch-22. If they operate according to precepts of time and training, many miseducative if unintended consequences result: "Life here is so easy for students that they can be "high" all day . . . and still pass." Students' aggressive passivity matches teachers' remote-control teaching and both set limits on their engagement with school knowledge. However, lower-track teachers find refutation or rejection of the model unthinkable. Alternative models risk loss of students who can always find an "easier" class to "drop down to," of civil (or at least controlled) relationships with peers, and even of teachers' jobs. Teachers' demoralization is simply compounded by administrative practices in which clear answers are rarely given, teachers' advice is rarely sought, and decisions are limited to the trivial (a coffee maker for the lounge) or are made by a remote cabinet, invisible "facilitator," or "downtown."

Thus, academic teachers at Marshall, especially in Additional Needs classes where students challenge teachers' sense of self and status, distance themselves from the lower-track role: They calculate their performance according to the "team" rules, knowing that the classes are crucial to their jobs. But, simultaneously, they act with little "belief" that the work they perform is valued by the "uncivilized" lower-track students, the "no-nonsense" institution, or the "anti-intellectual" community.

A COMPARISON OF MARSHALL AND SOUTHMOOR

In this concluding section, I bring together the strands of classroom climate, teaching, tracking, and school culture that weave through this and the three preceding chapters. Turning outward, I compare Marshall's and Southmoor's cultures and their relationships to their local communities, just as earlier I looked inward to trace the relationship between the institutions and individuals in classrooms. The comparison documents that the scholastic and the social orders present tangled "strata of meaning" (Geertz, 1973, p. 9) rather than strictly neutral or straightforwardly reproductive patterns. The order of a school is a contextualized translation: It is indeed related to the social order, but the relationship is oblique, not deterministic.

For example, in analyzing data at the beginning of my study in Maplehurst's schools, I saw the relationship between the educational order and the social order as rather clearly reproductive. Poor and minority students were overrepresented in lower-track classes; observations, like that in Mr. Bradley's group discussion about group communication, suggested a preponderant emphasis in Additional Needs classes on "keeping order" rather than on education; teachers characterized lower-track students invidiously, as academically "inept," "from families that don't care about education," and as dull or disorderly in attitude.

However, as I looked longer and contemplated the data further, evidence emerged that contradicted the simple formula that lower-track classes further disadvantage already socially disadvantaged students. I began to notice the mixed messages in teachers' characterizations of students and their dismay when things did not go well. Furthermore, the vast majority of Maplehurst's Additional Needs students are white, middle class, and not as academically disadvantaged or uninterested as Maplehurst teachers' typifications suggest or as other studies of tracking indicate. Indeed, as the analysis of Mr. Ellison's "hysterical" history lesson about the Japanese bombing of Pearl Harbor suggests, students' apparent dull or disorderly behavior is produced on account of teachers' ambiguous, inconsistent direction of lower-track lessons. Similarly, the pervasive emphasis in Mr. Bauer's routines on subordinate ways of knowing, such as guessing what the teacher has in mind, is punctuated by teachers' interpretations of even competent performance as a fluke or as a challenge to Marshall's "tradition of discipline." Accordingly, the school order, through tracking, appeared to have considerable autonomy after all: Relatively advantaged students, classed as lower track by the schools and presented with a differentiated lower-track curriculum, responded with lower-track obstreperousness.

Moving to yet another level, however, if the differences between lower- and regular-track classes at Southmoor and Marshall suggested the crucial—and largely negative—importance for students' careers of the educational structure of tracking, dramatic differences between the lower-track chaos at Southmoor and the regimentation at Marshall suggested that tracking, in and of itself, was hardly determinative. Consequently, I moved beyond the lower- versus regular-track classroom comparisons to an examination of the classes' institutional contexts, reasoning that the contexts might explain similarities among all the lower-track classes in one school and their differences from the lower-track classes at the second school.

The Cultures of Two Schools

Initially, I understood the chief difference between the two schools to lie in the socioeconomic status of the student bodies: "blue-collar" Marshall and "upper-middle-class, largely professional" Southmoor. However, the evidence on which these distinctions, like so many others, rested also proved ambiguous as I continued to observe and participate in the schools. The mixed data regarding differences in the school's student bodies, coupled with disjunctions between and among my observations and faculty members' reports, directed my attention to symbolic as well as structural differences between the schools.

Thus, I begin to delineate and compare the cultures of the two high schools and to seek the mechanisms that link institutionally acknowledged precepts of students and of organizational modes to particular practices in regular- and lower-track classrooms. As I have recounted, each of Maplehurst's high schools perceives itself as serving a particular kind of student, even though both serve diverse student bodies. Faculty members at Marshall identify students as "your typical blue-collar kid," whereas at Southmoor, the student body is from "upper-middle-class, largely professional families." These social class characterizations are echoed, often verbatim, by faculty members within each of the organizations. They are sociocultural constructions: Teachers' definitions of students reflect their participation in the culture of the educational organization and are, simultaneously, one of its defining elements.

Explicit reference to students' socioeconomic status merges with academic and behavioral characteristics to form the constellation of traits by which teachers identify students (Keddie, 1971). Maplehurst teachers do not consider information about students' family backgrounds inappropriate in determinations of educational needs or interests, any more than they would omit reference to students' academic performance or behavior. It is a commonsensical category, explaining present academic success and probable educational aspirations and destinations.

Teachers enact the definition of the typical student, as well as a particular teaching role, in school lessons. First, as they explain, the curriculum provides that knowledge that students "want" and/or "need." However, although teachers talk about meeting the "individual educational needs" of students through the curriculum, its design is largely taken for granted, rarely based on formal diagnoses, and seldom implemented in an individualized assignment for each student. At the same time, faculty members also explain the curriculum by referring to the demands of parents and the community, although here, too, I heard about few formal organizational structures or conversations with parents that facilitate communication about the community's wishes in regard to curriculum. Nevertheless, Marshall faculty members consistently reiterate the view that the skills-based curriculum is not simply a pedagogical choice but is necessary because "this working class community wants a practical education . . . (and a) tightly disciplined school." Similarly, Southmoor's faculty members assert that the "largely professional . . . parents demand a rigorous academic program" but loose disciplinary standards: "They want a college campus atmosphere."

In short, the culture of a school shapes teachers' understanding both of their professional or bureaucratic mode and of students, and it is itself shaped by those definitions as faculty members enact them in school lessons and organizational procedures. It is linked to the larger social order by staff members' acknowledged perceptions of the social class of the school's typical student and of the educational demands of the community. At the same time, the culture is reflected and recreated in classrooms as teachers provide the school's version of a curriculum appropriate for students of a particular social class. Thus, curricular differences between Marshall and Southmoor translate principles of social differentiation. Faculty members enact a school's stereotype of class differences. Like Mr. Robinson in the Haymarket Riot lesson, Southmoor's "professionals" follow an educational norm of self-confident engagement with academics for students they perceive to be from "upper-middle-class, largely professional families." In contrast, like Mr. Bauer in the lesson about fascism, Marshall's "good team players" adhere to an educational norm of punctilious coverage of "practical" skills for "your typical blue-collar kid."

The Independence of School Cultures and Teachers' Perceptions

The "down-to-earth," skills-based, regular education at Marshall and the "heavenly," academic, regular education at Southmoor, provided to meet the needs and plans of students headed for "jobs" or "graduate school," suggest that Maplehurst's high schools are linked rather deterministically to the social order. Southmoor's intellectualism is consonant with the large proportion of students with college-educated parents (about 60%), whereas Marshall's "anti-intellectualism" responds to the large proportion of children of skilled workers (about 40%).

However, the correspondence between the institutional definitions, individuals' perceptions, and objective measures is not necessarily straightforward. A remarkable instance of the independence of institutional cultures occurred at Marshall High School. Several years ago, the school ran a survey to identify the occupations of parents. Respondents selected from 10 occupational categories, such as skilled worker, professional, semiskilled worker, retailer, and so on. With the raw data collected, two categories, skilled and semiskilled, were collapsed for purposes of interpretation. The final report concluded that the skilled/semiskilled category, constituting 40% of the respondents, predominated among Marshall's families. These objective data seem to confirm the school's definition of its students as "your typical blue-collar kids" and therefore to corroborate the appropriateness of a skills-based curriculum.

In the interpretation of the raw data, however, two other occupational categories, professional and semiprofessional, were not combined. Had these categories been collapsed as the skilled and semiskilled categories were, they would have represented 38% of the respondents, a proportion of families almost as large as the skilled/semiskilled workers. Such a tabulation of the objective data was not visible to the surveyors, however. Given the extant institutional definition of the students as "blue collar," tabulators saw the numbers—the objective facts—according to the order of the institution's culture.

Similarly, if less dramatically, at Southmoor there is simply a dearth of talk about the 41% of the students who do not plan to go to college. A fundamental lack of support for programs for low-achieving or average students is taken for granted as a fact of Southmoor life. Thus, a school counselor noted:

Even though we have students here who can't write, teachers have a skewed perspective and lose sight of the fact. . . . Departments ought to be responsible for offering courses for all the kids, not just advanced courses, but it's up for grabs. I don't know if Mr. Davis (the head principal) would push. The overall functioning of the school is his number one concern. It's hard to know what he'll go to bat for. If there's special money, he might.

The faculty's "number one concern" for the "overall functioning of the school" is less ambivalent than the principal's: They are vigilant regarding resources for "high achievers." For example, a frequent comment in the faculty lounge is that it is "criminal to take resources away from good students and spend them on students who really don't care about education anyway." Faculty members also successfully argued that the grades of Additional Needs and special education students were inflated and should be weighted differently in computing grade-point averages. Otherwise, the averages of special students might shift the class standing of regular students so that they would be ineligible for admission to more competitive branches of the state university. Thus, although many students at South-moor do not fit the institutional definition of "high achievers . . . from . . . largely professional families . . . (headed for) graduate school," the power-ful faculty acts on the assumption that teaching to "the best and the brightest" is justifiable. As one teacher commented:

It's good, if you're going to err, to err from the standpoint of too many people thinking that they are in the professional class, or in the Harvard class, as opposed to the other, whatever. There are some people who should be going into that, that end up not doing it. And the school continues to be run in the interest of that group, even though it isn't the majority.

Therefore, although faculty members at Marshall and Southmoor *perceive* social-class distinctions in students, build educational programs that take into account the sociocultural differences they select, and thereby provide for the reproduction of the social-class differences, teachers' per-ceptions are circumscribed by the ethos of each school. Their perceptions are not necessarily direct responses to the objective status of students. Whether Marshall's community is in fact "blue-collar" and "wants" a skills-based, practical education and whether Southmoor's community is "upper middle class" and "wants" a preponderantly academic education appear to matter less than notions that teachers within each school acknowledge about each community's social characteristics and its presumed educational preferences. Although only partly based in the reality of the communities, the notions function as an ever-present reality within the two schools.

Lower-Track Classes: Chaotic and Regimented

Direct instruction at Marshall and the classical curriculum at South-moor acknowledge (and re-create) each school's stereotype of perceived social-class differences in the Maplehurst community. Regular-track students at Marshall receive the education that students proceeding directly to adult work or vocational-technical school "need" and "want" even though many teachers feel uneasy with it, a significant portion of the population at the school is upper middle class, and more than 40% of the seniors are college bound. Southmoor's regular-track students, in contrast, receive an education that prepares 59% of the seniors for a college and, often, a graduate education. Presumably, they also go on to white-collar and professional jobs, even though a significantly large number of the students (34% of the seniors) will attend vocational-technical schools or go directly to work.

The educational norm at each high school, varying according to a typification of regular-track students' sociocultural characteristics, becomes the basis for differentiation *within* each school as well as for the differentiation between the schools. Lower-track students in Marshall's regimented Additional Needs classes and in Southmoor's chaotic ones receive an education that is a *version* of each school's regular educational norm. Hence, the surprising difference between Additional Needs classes at the two schools, like the differences between regular-track classes, can be understood as the result of teacher's mediation of distinctive institutional cultures.

At Marshall, lower-track classes resemble regular-track classes in that school as much as or more than they resemble lower-track classes at Southmoor. The "no-nonsense," disciplined norm for regular-track, "blue-collar kids" who are presumed to be disdainful of education's abstract value is exaggerated in regimented lower-track classes, where students are not only "blue-collar" but, beyond that, are "uncivilized." Teachers who enact their regular role with competent aloofness, offering unquestionably "practical" exercises, insisting on punctuality and respect, and limiting spontaneous discussions and controversy, act as impersonal, relentless task-masters in their lower-track classes. Therefore, through invariant, unengaging, and noncontroversial routines, the "unsocialized" lower-track students at Marshall experience an impassive role: They answer straight-forward questions when called on or work quietly and individually at seatwork. Although the instrumental norm guides regular-track students' school experiences, pointing them toward work or vocational-technical schooling that leads directly to work, it points Marshall's lower-track students toward immediate entry into routinized jobs and little further education.

At the same time, the routine, the dominance of the teacher, and the impersonal relations in the classroom also make the student's role unexacting and safe. Lower-track students, who have reason to worry about their success in school, can simply sit back and listen. As a result, for many students, Marshall's lower-track classes are not stigmatizing but represent a shrewd choice on their part: Students say they have "conned" the credentialing system by electing lower-track classes. Teachers tell of able students who do poorly on tests or in classes just so they will be able to stay in lower-track classes. Ironically, the school and the "adaptive" lower-track curriculum contribute to the construction of students' shrewdness as well as their choices, and to their lowered educational expectations and achievement.

Teachers at Southmoor, like teachers at Marshall, also perceive lower-track students in relation to regular-track students within the school rather than in terms of their "individual educational needs." At Southmoor, they are "the dregs." Consequently, their instruction is deemed impossible, teachers are not held accountable for it, and academic progress is the least important aspect of Additional Needs classes. Lower-track classes present a caricature of the school's norm of academic excellence. Thus, in such classes, an academic curriculum has little value because students are irremediably "basic," and it is replaced by a curriculum of games and puzzles. Ostensibly motivating, the puzzles are also oddly similar to the exploratory, unstructured lessons developed in Southmoor's regular classes: Students are expected to catch on to clues for crossword puzzles rather than deduce them in some strategic fashion, much as regular, "easy-to-teach" students "see the connections between ideas (rather than just doing) hunt-up-the-answers."

Accordingly, lower-track students at Southmoor receive a boisterous, gamelike education, reminiscent in its requirements of the carefree days of elementary school. Such classes, like regular-track classes, suspend students in time. However, Additional Needs classes direct students neither toward further education nor toward vocations. Students sense the purposelessness of the educational caricature, and despite considerable academic and social advantages, they drop out of Southmoor at a considerably higher rate than their backgrounds would predict.

The independence of Maplehurst's faculty members' ideas and the concrete enactment of those ideas in curricula add to the evidence that teachers and schools can create environments in which precepts of social

differentiation are modified. However, the cultural nature of the constructions produced in Maplehurst's high schools suggests as well the difficulties
and limits attendant on creating such environments.

A cultural and curricular analysis suggests the profoundly complex,
interactive nature of the relationship between social and curricular differentiation. The meaning of the practice is not understandable by pointing
unilaterally to prejudiced teachers, inept students, structural practices like
tracking, or material constraints, like the socioeconomic characteristics of
the community, although each is important. Rather, the meaning of curriculum differentiation is always contextualized, as teachers mediate both
institutional and societal variables in their direction of classroom lessons. It
is not contextualized in a predetermined fashion, however, but is selectively
wrought, according to typifications that are peculiar within an organization
and a community. In Maplehurst, teachers' perceptions of students' social
characteristics not only reflect the school culture, but they are profoundly
circumscribed by that culture, as it assumes a life of its own.

Part IV

DEFINING THE LOWER-TRACK CURRICULUM

CHAPTER 8

How Teachers Interpret School Knowledge

In addition to defining the student's role and the classroom climate and teacher's role, teachers have the prerogative and the responsibility to define the curriculum. When the bell rings at the beginning of a class, all ears and eyes turn expectantly to the person at the front of the room, listening for the familiar, "Awright! What we are going to do today is . . ." In setting the lesson, the teacher simultaneously establishes order, as 25 or so individuals orient to one task. Students may groan after the topic is announced, denounce an activity as "boring," or "tune out" completely. But even though students' responses influence the meaning of the curriculum, their power as students does not include its determination.

To portray the lower-track curriculum and its significance for teachers and students, I reexamine the eight Maplehurst classes, asking what knowledge and what ways of knowing characterize lower-track lessons. Is the knowledge different from that in regular-track lessons? What influences the selection of knowledge, and what circumstances—of classroom, institution, and community—affect (and are affected by) teachers' and students' responses to it? Do lower-track lessons have their intended, explicit effect of "motivating" and "catching up" remedial students? Or, do they subvert "equal access to knowledge" (Goodlad, 1984) and promote school resistance and failure? In short, does school knowledge—however unremarkable it may appear to participants in and out of school—make a difference?

In considering the planned curriculum here and, in Chapter 9, the curriculum that students experience and evaluate, I sift through its artifacts: course syllabi and lesson plans, instructional materials, teachers' stated and tacit purposes and their performances, students' perspectives, classroom participants' interactions, and organizational and community contexts. Rather than taking any one of these as *the* curriculum, I seek the principles that tie together the "piled-up structures" (Geertz, 1973, p. 7) of curriculum to give it meaning.

Those principles are cultural and political, not simply cognitive, logi-cal, or technical (Kliebard, 1977b). Schools impart the knowledge a culture deems worthy and, because U.S. culture is paradoxical as well as diverse, struggles over curriculum are omnipresent and convoluted. In the 20th century, four interest groups have competed for dominance to designate the worthy knowledge that schools should impart: traditional humanists argue the value of the time-honored classics; child developmentalists, the value of children's interests; social-efficiency experts, the value of practical skills; and social meliorists urge the value of the knowledge that is required to transform society (Kliebard, 1986). Although struggles among the four interest groups often take the form of abstruse scholarship or idealized commission reports, they nonetheless shape the regular high school curric-ulum. In Maplehurst, as I will describe, the competing traditions also inform the lower-track curriculum.

Symbolic and scholarly discourses affect the high school curriculum as teachers' everyday talk in and about school lessons translates them and as teachers use the idealized platforms and theoretical formulations for par-ticular, locally sensible purposes. Thus, the rationales with which teachers justify their lessons, including lower-track lessons, are translations of the broader, traditional arguments. Furthermore, no matter how colloquial, teachers' translations are culturally and curricularly consequential because they bring elements of the wider discourse to life in mundane school lessons. And, although more obliquely and unpredictably than is usually acknowledged, school experiences in turn influence the wider debates: Students will not only furnish the achievement and occupational data for future commissions, but, more importantly, they are the future citizens whose understanding of public institutions will have been forged in schools.

THE LOWER-TRACK CURRICULUM IN MAPLEHURST

In defining the curriculum in Southmoor's and Marshall's Additional Needs classes—what will count as knowledge and as ways of knowing—individual teachers have considerable latitude. Indeed, they are charged to develop "adaptive" curricula.

Despite their considerable autonomy, however, Maplehurst teachers give scant attention to curricular concerns when they ruminate on Addi-tional Needs courses. Unlike Keddie's (1971) teachers who operated dur-ing the curriculum development heyday of the 1960s and who saw as problems both lower-track students and lower-track knowledge, the prob-lematic issue for Maplehurst's teachers (in the early 1980s) is getting through the day. Thus, teachers talk at length about students and their "needs," but substantive course topics, activities, texts, and teaching are virtually axiomatic. Lower-track knowledge operates as institutionalized common sense (Geertz, 1983; Sarason, 1971). In the culture of the school, everyone, with little reflection, knows the knowledge that particular kinds of students "need."

If Southmoor and Marshall teachers seldom reflect explicitly on the lower-track curriculum, school knowledge is nevertheless a critical ingredient in the production of curricular and social differentiation. However tacitly, knowledge is the stuff over which teachers and students struggle: They use it to construct differentiated roles for themselves and each other and different meanings for the educational enterprise in which they are bound.

In Maplehurst these constructions exhibit regular if unremarked patterns. As I describe in this chapter, the *content* of the lower-track curriculum follows three rationales, whereas its *form* is common across classrooms. These patterns distinguish lower-track from regular-track lessons in the two Maplehurst high schools and distinguish the lower-track lessons in each school from each other.

THE CONTENT OF THE LOWER-TRACK CURRICULUM: THREE PATTERNS

Although we speak of *the* lower-track curriculum, the content in Maplehurst's eight classes varies according to three patterns. The patterns reflect locally meaningful distinctions regarding curriculum differentiation and, as well, they echo broader, on-going debates about the knowledge that is worth teaching in school. In the first lower-track pattern, the topics of the formal curriculum are deemed "the same" as those in teachers' regular-track classes although they are covered in "less detail." Maintaining that all students are in school to study traditional subject matter, Maplehurst's lower-track teachers mirror the classical orientation of academicians. By contrast, in the second pattern, an emphasis on reading skills supersedes an emphasis on the substance of the discipline. Here, Maplehurst teachers articulate elements of the position of the social efficiency experts, who argue that the curriculum should emphasize the "practical" skills that students will need in life. Then, in the third pattern, topics are chosen for their "relevance" and differ from those in regular-track classes. Lower-track teachers, like the child developmentalists, foreground the interests and needs of academically unsuccessful adolescents in designating what schools should teach. As the more detailed descriptions that follow will illustrate, the three patterns are not mutually exclusive. Elements from all echo across the eight classes at one time or another. However, sorting the classes clarifies the tangled patterns that underlie the complex particularities of individual remedial lessons.

Pattern 1: A Skeleton of Regular Coursework

The first model of differentiated curriculum content—and, historically, a very common and tenacious one (Krug, 1960; Westbury, 1988a)—offers a skeleton of parallel, regular-track coursework. By this model, all school lessons should impart the time-honored subjects of the Western tradition, although, to accommodate lower-track students, remedial lessons provide "less detail," "less depth," and "fewer connections." Thus, Maplehurst faculty members explain that their regular- and lower-track classes follow "the same" course outline but, in the latter, the "pace is slower."

Although this content modification reflects traditional scholastic assumptions about valued knowledge and its distribution, Maplehurst teachers attribute it explicitly to the "needs" of a particular kind of lower-track student: the "slow" student. Such students "want to do well, but they just don't have the mental equipment." They "lack basic skills, especially in reading." However, they have "good going-to-school skills": They attend regularly and, compared with lower-track "delinquents," they present few discipline problems.

Given "good" behavior, teachers assume that lower-track students will benefit from the "bookish" curriculum offered to regular-track students, if only it is moderately differentiated and "made easier." To these academic benefits of a skeletal curriculum, they add social benefits: Because Additional Needs students study the same topics as their peers, they "do not feel so set apart. . . . They can sit at the lunch table with their other friends in ninth grade and say they're reading *Jane Eyre* too."

Thus, in the skeletal pattern, Maplehurst teachers express the ambivalence about tracking's segregative aspects and about whether all students should or can study the traditional curriculum that has centered curriculum debate throughout the 20th century (Cohen, 1985; Kliebard, 1986). Teachers assuage their doubts by differentiating lower-track lessons but asserting that the differentiation is imperceptible.

Three of the eight classrooms I observed adhere principally to the skeletal model. Mr. Robinson's lower-track course at Southmoor, titled American History, 1865–1945, includes the same units that his regular ninth-grade history course follows: post-Civil War industrialization, the settling of the West, the rise of big business and labor unions, and turn-of-the-century immigration. Similarly, Ms. Mitchell's ninth-grade Additional

Needs English class at Southmoor parallels regular-track units, such as *To Kill a Mockingbird, Jane Eyre*, grammar, paragraph writing, and Greek and Roman mythology. At Marshall, Mr. Bradley's Additional Needs English class includes *Romeo and Juliet, To Kill a Mockingbird*, a raft of short stories, and paragraph writing.

The three classes share activities and films as well as topics with teachers' parallel regular-track classes. For example, the skeletal curriculum is distinguished from other lower-track models in Maplehurst and in other public schools (Metz, 1978; Oakes, 1985; Schwartz, 1981) by its emphasis on public recitation and grand, "open-ended" questions. Maplehurst teachers explain that "discussion" accommodates remedial students' good oral skills, allows adolescents to engage with serious topics and "higher-order thinking," and compensates for their poor reading and writing skills. It also corresponds to teachers' relatively relaxed view of "slow" students' "attitudes." Similarly, lower-track students join their regular-track peers in large assemblies to see Gregory Peck as Atticus and Kirk Douglas as Odysseus in popular, filmed renditions of high culture's literary classics.

However, using identical recitations and films can also lead to negligible, even negative, results rather than to "equal access to knowledge." For example, lower-track talk differs from the subject- and student-centered discourse of the regular-track, especially at Southmoor. When Mr. Bradley asks the "open" question, "Why is it important to read Shakespeare today?" his answer is tellingly closed: "'Because he wrote the most and he wrote the best.' That's all you have to put." Similarly, Mr. Robinson speaks of requiring lower-track students to respond to essay questions on examinations. However, he tells students the question, insists that they compose an answer together, writes the composition on the blackboard, instructs students to copy it, and expects them to repeat the answer verbatim on the next day's exam. In short, despite public interchanges and nontrivial topics, these interactions are limited and childish.

By the same token, at Southmoor, Additional Needs students entered class, noticed a projector, and asked if they were going to have a film. The teacher responded, "Oh, well, okay, I wasn't going to show you this one, but since I have it for my regular classes, you might as well see it too." The film, a difficult piece about Greek civilization, was replete with images of marble statues, a convoluted text, strains of Middle Eastern music, and a lugubrious narrator. As often happens in lower-track classes at Southmoor, chaos erupted during the showing. While the teacher studiously shuffled through papers at the front of the room below the screen, students gave the film their own meaning by moving the projector cart bit by bit so that the film was half on and half off the screen, first at one side, then at the top, then on the other side. Stifled guffaws about "pot" greeted narrative references to the Greeks' "herbal crafts," and shots of nude goddesses evoked cruder references.

Lower-track teachers may use films, even when they are not apropos, because they are pedagogically recommended as a change of pace for lower-track students whose attention presumably wanders; because ordering a film for a specific date may have to be done a year ahead; or because films often have a mesmerizing effect on unruly students (and, despite teachers' characterizations, students in skeletal classes are often unruly). Nevertheless, students who saw the Greek film may have learned little about Greek mythology except that the subject is an *esoteric* joke that has little to do with them. Thus, even when skeletal topics, talk, and films are "the same" as those listed on regular-track syllabi, they can be enacted differently and may carry far different meaning.

Mediating contexts of school and track, teachers also modify activities and texts. For example, the three skeletal classes differ from each other in their balance of academic content and skills as teachers translate differences in the cultures and educational norms of the two high schools. For example, Southmoor's handbook notes that regular ninth-grade English includes "all types of literature (and) the composition of paragraphs and themes." Therefore, skeletal versions retain the *humanist's* focus on subject matter and give only marginal attention to *"technical"* matters, such as vocabulary development, spelling, and composition rules, even though Southmoor teachers recognize insufficiencies in lower-track students' reading and writing skills.

Indeed, although Southmoor teachers demonstrate basic skills, the instruction is so erratic that it competes with students' academic attentiveness. For example, when working as a group to compose a paragraph about the results of the Civil War, Mr. Robinson's class generated the sentence: "Now, industries like textiles, iron, and steel led to the growth of cities." At "textiles," Mr. Robinson paused in his writing at the blackboard and punned: "Textiles! That's easy to spell. Those are those large *tiles* they raise down in *Tex*as." Similarly, in other writing assignments, "population" was "POP!ulation," "machines" were contrasted with "pa-chines" and "kid-chines," and the "spe*cific*" was "not the At*lantic* or the Pa*cific*." Mr. Robinson's puns make class lively and informal, in accord with Southmoor's norms for "spontaneity," teacher showmanship, and classroom camaraderie, and they may provide students with spelling heuristics. But they also set off a string of responsive, chaotic comments and jokes by students so that group high jinks undermine sustained thinking about industrialization.

By contrast, Mr. Bradley's skeletal class, a version of ninth-grade English that Marshall's handbook describes less grandiloquently than

Southmoor's as "reading and writing skills improvement," includes regular-track academic topics but pays consistent attention as well to skills instruction and learning schemata. However, Mr. Bradley moves to a different extreme than Mr. Robinson: He renders complex, academic subjects as simple, straightforward techniques. For example, writing a paragraph involves "following a strict formula: If you follow it, you'll get an A every time." First, students should write a "thesis statement"; next, they "support the thesis with details," usually in three sentences; then they write a "concluding statement." Similarly formulaic is Mr. Bradley's explanation of the use of transition words. The teacher hands out a list of about 25 "linking expressions," including words such as *therefore* and *furthermore* and phrases such as "in the first place." He instructs students to use two items from the list when writing a paragraph. However, just as he does not emphasize that composition entails having an idea as well as a format, so he does not discuss the meanings of the "linking expressions" or why students would use one rather than another. Consequently, when several students complete the assignment, they choose transition words arbitrarily and the paragraphs are senseless, albeit formulaically correct. If Southmoor's instruction in language skills is haphazard, Marshall's instruction in composition is routinized.

Lower-track modifications of "the same" topics mix curricular differentiation with broader social precepts of age and with school-specific values. Teachers regard students' "slow" intellect as concomitant with "slow" development, and they turn to lower-track materials and activities reminiscent of those used in elementary school. Such lessons add to the confusion that adolescents already face in the uncertain rite of passage to adulthood. For example, Ms. Mitchell explains that she selects "easy" versions of the classics to accommodate lower-track students' reading skills. She assures that lessons can go forward by refusing to allow "immature" students to take textbooks from the room "because you (students) will forget them at home." However, although students can decode the very old, "easy-to-read" edition of *Jane Eyre*, it lacks the style and complex story line that enchant readers of the original and distinguish it as a classic. In some instances, the text is so simplified that it is incoherent, and Ms. Mitchell must tell students what the book says. Moreover, by not allowing students to take books home, she makes the use of shortened versions necessary: There is simply insufficient class time to move through all of *Jane Eyre* if students are not asked to read "in depth" as homework.

As in elementary schools, teachers also use games to supplement lessons, particularly in Southmoor's lower track. Deemed "motivating" and "fun," as well as curricularly innovative (Feldman & Seifman, 1969; Henry, 1963; Shaver & Berlak, 1968), games nevertheless bear uncertainly on substantive topics because Maplehurst teachers use them quasi-scholastically and as a kind of bribe. Thus, after the unit on industrialization, students in Mr. Robinson's class spent several days enthusiastically playing Monopoly; however, the relationship between the game and the "Captains of Industry" went unexplained. More earnestly but still in a relaxed mode, Mr. Bradley's Additional Needs class at Marshall routinely spent Fridays in a "free reading day." Students used the time to "practice reading" texts they brought to class or, if they forgot, old copies of *National Geographic* or *Reader's Digest* which Mr. Bradley kept on hand, assuming that some students would forget.

In sum, skeletonizing the regular curriculum begs the questions about whether an undifferentiated curriculum is either desirable or possible. If one compares course syllabi or surveys teachers, regular and skeletal curricula might appear "the same," but examining the curriculum-in-use suggests significant differences. Moreover, such an examination exposes the irreducible dilemmas in trying to foster "equal access to knowledge." Indeed, it suggests that standardized requirements for all students can contradict equality: Some students cannot read *Jane Eyre*, but offering them a plot summary hardly provides them with knowledge that is humane, high status, or even educative. Perversely, it might convince students that the time-honored classics are shams.

Maplehurst teachers acknowledge the dilemmas and embed them in skeletal lessons: They present traditional content but "with less depth"; they provide "spontaneity" but withhold the coordination that makes entertaining games and films intellectually meaningful; they protect unskilled students from failure by limiting demands for reading and writing, even though they thereby do not ask students to use and possibly improve their skills; and they encourage student participation in public discourse but then severely delimit it. Even when activities are borrowed directly from the regular-track curriculum, they are often caricatured, as when teachers "challenge" students with "more conceptual" essay questions but insist on rote responses. Thus, the skeletal pattern reflects and maintains the long-standing uncertainty about whether traditional knowledge, if slightly modified, can contribute to all students' educational progress.

Pattern 2: Skills More Than Substance

The second pattern of content differentiation emphasizes instruction in skills. In this pattern, exemplified at Marshall in the history classes of Mr. Reed and Mr. Bauer, academic subject matter is superseded by utilitarian "basics," so that *what* students study is less germane than *how*. As in arguments for a socially efficient, scientifically designed, regular curriculum that "works" to prepare students for their measured places in society, a lower-track curriculum should meet students' "needs" for functional literacy, civic duty, and direct job preparation and should not waste time providing "the garden variety of citizen" (Tyler, 1949, p. 26) with liberal study of the academic disciplines.

As described in Chapter 6, this pattern reflects a hierarchical notion of bodies of knowledge, cognition, and information in which "foundations" are prerequisite to advanced subjects and complex operations. As in the skeletal pattern, age and intellect are again conjoined, and the academic hierarchy mirrors cultural understandings about how people progress up the "ladder of life" (Perin, 1977). In the age-graded curriculum, youngsters should learn the "basics"—the three R's—in elementary school; if adolescents are poor readers, then, like early elementary students, they must master fundamental reading skills before they can go on, like upper elementary students, to read in history or literature. As one Additional Needs teacher explained explicitly to his ninth graders: "One reason you're in this class instead of another history class is you don't read as well as you should. This class is designed for that."

Cognitive skills are ranked as well as subjects. Echoing formal taxonomies (e.g., Bloom, Hastings, & Madaus, 1971), Maplehurst teachers stipulate that answering true-false or matching questions is "more basic than eventually succeeding on multiple-choice or even essay questions." In contrast to skeletal classes, skills classes use worksheets that rarely include even modified essay questions. Instead, as in elementary school, instruction proceeds through repetitious drill and practice on clear-cut facts. Repetition maintains standards and, as one teacher noted encouragingly before a quiz, the possibility of eventual mastery: "I want to emphasize – – If you don't remember (the answers), don't be discouraged. You may get the same question on another quiz and then you'll get a second shot at it. We'll come back and back and back with things – – so all of you have a chance to do well."

Finally, facts themselves are ranked, much as they are in currently popular tests of cultural literacy (Hirsch, 1987) and in debates about minimum competencies (Finn, 1989). Teachers assert that specific items reflect the "basic information that an educated person ought to know—and that many students at Marshall do not come to us knowing." Consequently, teachers drill and test students on definitions of words (*isthmus, revolution*), names of people or places (the governor of the state, Moscow), and facts of civics (the names of the branches of government). Acting efficiently and with purpose, they pay little attention to the complexities of revolutions, the contradictions of tripartite government, or the aspects of topics that students find engrossing or problematic. For Marshall's "uncivilized" Additional Needs students, "practical" subjects, "basic" skills, and the rudiments of civilization are both the minimum standards on which teachers insist and the best that they can expect.

Given students' intellectual "immaturity," coupled however with their increasing interest in adulthood, the world of work, and material rewards, teachers act as grim, distant taskmasters rather than as persuasive pundits as they hurry to "socialize" students to Marshall's "tradition of discipline," much as children are made to swallow medicine that is good for them. As one teacher protested: "In the feeder schools, there's a tendency to minimize the skills. There are no demands made on the kids. They can laugh and giggle their way through eight grades. So I guess the high school finds itself in the business of teaching skills."

Concomitantly, skills teachers express less explicit concern than skeletal teachers for lower-track students' feelings of self-esteem or for their separation from regular-track peers. Skill deficits are treated "realistically," as facts of life that objective tests reveal dispassionately and to which a differentiated curriculum is a "necessary," efficient response: "Students *are* different, after all." By the same token, the school demands little commitment from "blue-collar" students who may not acknowledge the value of scholastic endeavors: All it requires is "effort."

Both to ensure "effort" and to disperse resistance, teachers provide worksheets that students complete individually. Emphasizing students' step-by-step improvement, they "structure" courses so that daily assignments, graded precisely with a number, are as important to a final semester grade as unit tests. As a result, the most significant feature of skills classrooms is the absence of talk. In contrast to the public, often playful, banter in skeletal classes, at least one-third of each skills class is devoted to silent, privatized drill. The talking that does occur is usually either a ritualistic review of answers or a monotoned minilecture.

Although students in both Mr. Bauer's and Mr. Reed's classes receive graduation credits in history, historical insight is of secondary importance to the rigorous retrieval of specific bits of information. As described in Chapter 6, a reading text, "written on a low reading level to help those students who have difficulties in reading and work study habits," constitutes historical studies in Mr. Bauer's nearly invariant routine: Films and games are rare; exams repeat the facts covered in chapters and on worksheets; students are expected to "do their jobs."

Mr. Reed's class offers considerably more variety than Mr. Bauer's. For example, students use several texts, including "relevant" novels (*Animal Farm*, *The Bridges of Toko-Ri*), rather than marching through a single history textbook, chapter by chapter. Occasionally, games, films, and personalized recitations replace bland worksheets: "Why do you get into fights with your peers? Are your reasons like those of nations going to war?" Such variety mitigates the regimentation that prevails in Marshall's lower-track classes.

Nonetheless, even with these variations, concerns for "discipline," "structure," and routinized procedures predominate in Mr. Reed's class, as in Mr. Bauer's. A dramatic illustration of the preponderance of order—both intellectual and behavioral—occurred during what first appeared to be a lively, "inquiry" (Bruner, 1977) lesson. After outlining the events leading to the Great Crash of 1929 and explaining some of the vocabulary words associated with the stock market (e.g., *shares, dividends, stockbroker*), Mr. Reed and his class spent 3 days buying and selling in the "Stock Market Game." Mr. Reed acted as a broker on the New York Stock Exchange, taking messages over an old-fashioned telephone, handling transactions, and announcing changes in prices and payment of dividends. Beginning with an amount of cash, students could buy or sell stock in AT&T, Ford, or Florida Lands. With each transaction, they had to balance their bank accounts. The 3-day activity, which allowed students to experience the processes of the market, ended with its crash.

Most students found the activity interesting and played competitively and enthusiastically. The class was slightly noisier and more informal than usual, as students moved about the room, compared notes, and made stock transactions. To keep up students' interest and enthusiasm, as well as to convey the market's risks, Mr. Reed asserted repeatedly that "anything can happen on the market."

As it turned out, however, Mr. Reed's scenario was completely fore-ordained. Regardless of how students traded stocks, the market behaved in exactly the same way in both of Mr. Reed's lower-track classes. Students accidentally discovered this regularity. In their enthusiasm for the activity, they talked to members of the earlier class to find out how their transactions were going. They then came to their own class, ready to buy wisely on the basis of "insider information" from the earlier class. Mr. Reed became very angry when he realized what was going on and denied that the market was predictable. His anger bothered some students so much that they decided not to act on the "insider information." Ironically, through their enthusiasm and engagement, students were spoiling Mr. Reed's game. However, events did unfold exactly according to the schedule used in the earlier class, and students who used "insider information" made a killing. They whispered gleefully, but discretely, that they "just *knew* Florida Lands would go up and then fall."

In sum, in the skills pattern, "basics," efficiency, and "structure" precede liberal study in the traditional bodies of knowledge. Class activities are orderly and individualized. In contrast to the flamboyant, ungraded public recitations of skeletal classes where academic progress is difficult to measure, skills classes appear industriously schooled, and many lower-track students and teachers take satisfaction in marking their individual progress through the steady stream of activities.

Yet, at the same time, teachers also complain about "apathetic" students who treat history as a mere requirement to get through on the way to a "practical" credential. Students themselves experience a catch-22: If they reject routinized lessons because they find them demeaning, they may be forced upward into "harder" regular-track classes, downward into stigmatized special education classes, or outward from school altogether. But if they comply with skills lessons, they engage, however busily, with trivia. In either case, students miss experiences with the humane understanding that history records. Therefore, the skills model leaves unresolved the question of whether efficiency and "basics" are the proper foundation for a lower-track curriculum.

Pattern 3: A "Relevant" Curriculum

In the third, "relevant," pattern of content differentiation, a scholastic curriculum, academic or skills-based, is deemed unacceptable to or unsuitable for academically unsuccessful students. Like developmentalists who argue that the regular curriculum should be based on the needs and interests of children, remedial teachers using this model substitute interesting, motivating topics, including some that they consider personally (if not intellectually) germane. In the three classrooms that adhere to this pattern, teachers hope that "relevant" content will mitigate the recalcitrant, remedial students' aversion to the classroom (including hostility to its teacher representatives) and return them to the straight and narrow.

This modification reflects a complex notion of academically unsuccessful students as near-adult and "anti-intellectual": Students are "13, going on 30, and won't listen to a thing I say." Teachers perceive that students reject school because, given their life experiences and adultlike interests, "abstract" lessons do not make sense to them. It is unfair to hold such students to a "bookish" standard: "The teacher (in an Additional Needs class) is under some pressure to design some kind of curriculum that is going to be different from the familiar environment in which the kid has failed already."

Yet, teachers also say that academically unsuccessful students need to be set straight in their "attitudes." Therefore, in place of the "familiar environment," teachers recommend personalized, quasi-therapeutic lessons that address issues that are self-evidently important to "street-smart" students' present and future lives: drugs, safe sex, adolescents' legal rights, nutrition, budgeting, job applications, or social and political issues such as racial prejudice. Blending sympathy with censure, teachers turn from academics and school skills to moralisms (Leacock, 1969) as they adopt the empathetic but all-knowing stance of counselor to the "troubled."

In "relevant" courses, teachers voice few expectations that students will return to regular-track classes, and there is almost no articulation between the lower-track and other courses in the high school. Rather, the courses represent "last-ditch efforts" to give oppositional, disadvantaged students a few "survival skills," a few more months in a "protective environment," or one more credit toward a graduation that no one deems likely. Concomitantly, teachers see themselves as unable to persuade students of the value of academic subject matter. Indeed, teachers vigorously insist on the uselessness of academics for lower-track students, and, just as vigorously, attribute such doubts to students. Instead of academic knowledge, teachers preach the value of "life skills."

As a result, the relationship between teachers, students, and school knowledge is marked by a strange cycle of invasiveness and distance, or what one teacher characterized as "tough love." Teachers "reach out to" students by designing lessons that presumably correspond to their interests and needs. However, the apposite topics also risk insulting lower-track students. Confronted with units on drugs or child abuse, students may infer that teachers think that they use drugs or that they will be abusive parents. Teachers' "relevant" lessons may appear meddlesome rather than empathetic, especially since teachers often disapprove of or are dismayed by students' interests. In response, students reject teachers' expertise on extra-intellectual matters (Werthman, 1963). Questions about teachers' authority over personal style (hair length, clothing, or the meaning of friendship) and political values (prejudice, legalization of marijuana, or juvenile rights) spill over into questioning their authority regarding traditional knowledge. In the face of such "trouble," teachers shy away from direct instruction and sustained engagement: As in the skills pattern, they uphold standards and discipline by providing large chunks of class time for students to work privately and silently on simple worksheets. Ironically, lower-track "trouble" centers precisely around the "relevant" knowledge that teachers select with such high hopes.

The dynamics and activities of "relevant" lessons vary in the classrooms of Mr. Thompson and Mr. Ellison at Southmoor and Ms. Campbell at Marshall. For example, Mr. Thompson first designed his 10th-grade history course around a local newspaper and later a national news magazine, because both are "fundamental to a kid's daily existence. Most people have a, a newspaper or *Time* in their home, and they're familiar with their parents reading it - - And so it's something that really is, ah, that the kids grow up with." Although Mr. Thompson rarely teaches students directly about current events, he considers the daily quiz of 20 questions about articles from *Time* an indication that he has met his teaching responsibilities: "The kids see I've done my job (by preparing the quiz) and they have to do theirs. It's not a free-air day (like some lower-track classes)."

"To do their (jobs)," students spend 35 minutes every day working individually to answer the objective, multiple-choice questions. The classroom is silent, except for the hum of the overhead projector on which the quiz is displayed. However, if Mr. Thompson's curriculum shares features of the skills model, it differs from it in its subterranean chaos: Albeit quietly, students engage in surreptitious pantomimes, constant note passing, radio listening, and daydreaming, while Mr. Thompson concentrates on the next day's quiz at his desk at the front of the room (see also, discussion in Chapter 4).

Mr. Thompson's curriculum is also distinguished from perfunctory skills lessons by its largely unspoken emphasis on "attitude." Given "relevant" topics, students must act as though they care. Hence, during the last 15 minutes of class, when papers are exchanged and answers are checked aloud, students clamor for turns to answer to show their enthusiasm. Similarly, they exhibit the right "attitude" when they accept without question Mr. Thompson's mellifluous pronouncements: "No, class! I will NOT accept A. The ONLY correct answer is B."

The emphasis on "attitude" is explicit in Mr. Thompson's final examination. Although he and other teachers avoid tests in "relevant" classes because they will be "exercises in failure," or because students' attendance is so erratic that they cannot participate in summary activities, school policy requires that all courses have a 2-hour final, so Mr. Thompson complies.

A sophomore, Susan, described the values-clarification game that Mr. Thompson used as the "relevant" final examination for the 10th-grade American history class. When students arrived for the test, they drew from a box slips of paper with the names of characters from "Charlie's Angels," "M*A*S*H*," and other television programs. Wondering what to make of the names, students were told only to "find their group – – I guess we were supposed to catch on to the names." After considerable mayhem, five groups "found" themselves. Then the teacher provided each group with the Stranded-on-the-Moon exercise, in which students were supposed to work to reach consensus about the 3 items from a list of 15 that they would need if their imaginary spaceship crashed on the moon. The exercise required no knowledge of history, although some general knowledge was useful; for example, the candle could be eliminated from the list because it would not burn in the moon's oxygen-free environment.

According to Susan, once students understood the assignment, their reactions to the examination were mixed. Some played with enthusiasm while others remained querulous. Susan herself was ambivalent: "It was like – – like second-grade stuff, really. Not history at all. . . . But it was neat, though, it was fun because, like Mr. Thompson said, you found out whether you worked better in a group or not."

Students' reactions to the lesson also varied when grades for the 2-hour game were awarded. According to Susan, the teacher did not tell students how they would be graded; only at the game's end did he announce that "attitudes" during the play, not the group lists, were the basis. As a result, many students, particularly those who had found the examination "stupid," were very angry, whereas the compliant were quietly relieved. The unpredictable but "fun" routine prompted both reactions:

Betty, she was just like, "This is so dumb, this isn't history" and "Nyea, nyea, nyea," and "This isn't fair." She thought it was really dumb what we were doing. And so did some other kids. . . . And then he (Mr. Thompson) gave her a D and she was crying and all this stuff. And he said, "Well, Betty, I've been teaching for so many years and I'm not going to change. That's the way I grade." . . . I got a B. I don't know what I'd do if I'd gotten a D like Betty. My dad doesn't like me to be in these classes. I don't know what my dad would think about this test if I told him about it.

As described in Chapter 4, Mr. Ellison designs his lower-track course in English and history to appeal to students whom Southmoor teachers see as so academically disadvantaged and disdainful that instruction is virtually irrelevant. He uses personalized verbal games that entertain, such as crossword puzzles and acrostics, to "make it where it's almost fun to learn—and some of them even have trouble with that – – You might be able to convince them to work on a real assignment or a test if you gave them a lollipop or something." At the same time, usual classroom routines are suspended for fun and entertainment within the "little family" of the class. The tone is lightly ironical as teacher and students maintain a veneer of "joshing" harmony.

Ms. Campbell's 10th-grade English class bears some resemblance to a skeletal curriculum and also includes the emphasis on reading and writing skills that one would expect at Marshall, but it is distinguished by a psychosocial orientation. During the semester students read a novel (*Of Mice and Men*) and several short stories ("The Monkey's Paw," "Four Eyes"); they write one short theme; and the teacher instructs in an assortment of literary terms (characterization, metaphor), reading strategies (begin reading a chapter by previewing its title and headings), and a selection of grammar and spelling rules. However, identifying the "basic problem (of academically unsuccessful students) as poor parenting," Ms. Campbell selects and shapes the topics to instruct students in their "personal problems."

Ironically, these "relevant" lessons anger students as much as or more than they interest them. They confuse classroom participants' prerogatives and responsibilities and set in motion a cycle in which teachers' control grows increasingly arbitrary and calls forth student responses that are increasingly aggressively passive. For example, addressing students both as knowing adults and as subordinate, untutored children, Ms. Campbell attempted to make "relevant" the literary concept of characterization: "I want to show you an example of 'direct characterization.' Now! People your age are interested in relations with members of the opposite sex." At this, a sequence of "ooohs" and "ahhhs" went up around the class. Ms. Campbell smiled at the students' appreciation of her pertinent topic and continued: "You make a decision to get married – " A student interrupted, "And have babies!" But Ms. Campbell glided right on: " – Or you're going to break up. You're making a commitment or not. Sometimes adults make this commitment and, a few years down the road, they say – ." Again, a student interrupted, "Hit the road!" Still, Ms. Campbell continued: " – They aren't going to keep it."

Following this introduction, Ms. Campbell instructed students to "be ready to tell me which characterization techniques are used" in a short, teen-romance story about a couple's breakup. As Ms. Campbell read the story aloud, students rolled their eyes at her methodical, melodramatic intonation. A halting discussion followed. Finally, Ms. Campbell called for a "vote: How many of you think the first characterization technique is most important?" (for further discussion of curricular votes, see Chapter 3). Two students raised their hands for the first strategy, but for the second and third, no one raised a hand, as students simply ignored Ms. Campbell's efforts to get them to vote. Ms. Campbell concluded brightly, "Oh, so most of you don't know which technique is being used." She then proceeded to explain the strategies again. When she mispronounced a word during the explanation, she commented laughingly, again appealing to students as near-adults of a particular type, "I'm in bad shape after a 3-day weekend." A student added, "And lots of partying." At this, students turned away from the lesson and began discussing "partying" among themselves. To regain control, Ms. Campbell abruptly directed students to take out their work-sheets on a short story. Students complied slowly, aggressively passive in response to the teacher's confusing amalgamation of familiarity and control.

The "relevant" model multiplies such discordant encounters unnecessarily. Because Ms. Campbell solicits students' opinions and tries to relate to students "on their level," students feel free to give unsolicited opinions on *her* level. Thus, a student interrupted Ms. Campbell as she read over a worksheet: "Why are we going over the worksheet *before* we see the film?" Ms. Campbell responded sharply: "Wait a minute! Who's the teacher here (pointing to herself)?" The student retreated: "I was just making a suggestion." Ms. Campbell concluded firmly: "*I'll* do the suggesting." Such "trouble" reflects students' confused role and their sense of betrayal when teachers reassert unequal, traditional rules.

When teachers ask for but disagree with students' opinions on "personal" topics, even greater acrimony erupts. For instance, Ms. Campbell read aloud to the class the short story, "Four Eyes," about an Italian family's relationship with a schoolteacher who is unintentionally shown up by the family's very smart son, Joey. Following the reading, Ms. Campbell asked a series of "personal" questions, assuming that the story corresponded to her students' situations and that they would welcome discussion. Instead, each question provoked an increasingly inchoate buzz of comments. Ms. Campbell began: "Have any of you ever had a teacher out to get you?" Students looked at each other quizzically but remained silent, deciding perhaps that, in the classroom context, the question was hardly neutral. The teacher persisted: "Do any of you have parents like Joey's mother who think the teacher is always right?" Students muttered perversely but perhaps truthfully that their parents think teachers are "never right." "Do any of you have parents with a bad temper, like Joey's father, who take the strap to you?" At this, a student spoke up about his parents' "whupping" him. Ms. Campbell responded earnestly, but many students razzed the student as he talked, suggesting that he was "dragging that old stuff out again" and "putting on" for the teacher. Finally, the teacher brought up Joey's decision not to cry when his father spanked him. She asked: "What's going on between Joey and his father?" After initial quips from students ("World War III," "kid willpower"), which, however, Ms. Campbell did not acknowledge, she answered her own question: "It's a matter of pride . . . Joey is thinking, 'I'm not going to let him see me cry.'" A student then rejoined, in sharp disagreement: "Naw. The father's a prick – – (turning to face the class) I'd *laugh* if I were Joey." Students joined their classmate in raucous laughter.

The contrast between the teacher's sentimental interpretation of Joey's passive resistance and the student's interpretation, which portrays a child as able to infuriate as well as to resist an adult, mirrors fundamental differences in students' and the teacher's perceptions of "relevance." With any class of diverse individuals, it is unlikely one topic will be "relevant" to everyone or in the same way. Furthermore, "relevance" may not inhere in particular topics but may develop only as individuals think about relationships between the abstractions of school and their experiences. Finally, if "life skills" are necessarily moral, schools may not be the appropriate institution for their inculcation nor teachers the best agents for teaching them.

In sum, in the "relevant" pattern, students receive credit in English or history, but they study *Time* magazine, crossword puzzles, and clinical "problems." As one teacher remarked: "This course is a catchall for anybody. We'll give you any social studies credit that you want." Teachers also give students the subject matter that they presumably want. However, because "relevant" lessons often produce the antagonistic, uninterested "attitudes" that teachers design differentiated lessons to prevent, this model, like the other two, raises questions about whether children's interests and needs are a sufficient basis for the lower-track curriculum.

Some Principles of Differentiated Curriculum Content

Although manifold quirks and personalities make every school lesson unique, the subject matter in the eight Additional Needs classes in Maplehurst also exhibits several distinctive patterns. Teachers differentiate lower-track from regular-track knowledge according to a number of curricular and cultural principles.

First, there is not *one* lower-track curriculum in Maplehurst. Despite official transcripts that designate high-, average-, and lower-track classes as though each category were of a piece, lower-track content assumes three distinctive guises, which I have called skeletal, skills, and "relevant" patterns. The three represent a reduction, redefinition, or rejection of regular courses of study and suggest the fundamental complexity and confusion that Maplehurst's schools and students experience about who should study what and what school is for. For example, do Ms. Campbell's lower-track students study English or Life Problems—or some curious combination of the two? Might not Mr. Bauer's lower-track course, American History, be more aptly titled, Basic Reading Skills? In short, differentiated subject matter throws in question the purposes for which students and teachers come together: What uncertainties about self, other, school, and knowledge result when students and teachers expect world history but execute *Time* magazine?

Following from the first point, curricular decisions do not adhere nicely to global predictions, such as the notion that lower-track classes receive "less-powerful" or "lower-status" knowledge than regular-track classes. Nor, however, are they purely idiosyncratic or based in a distinctive remedial ideology. Instead, curricular decisions reflect a patterned ambiguity: As locally sensible and historically resonant translations of regular education, lower-track curricula vary with context. Thus, ideas about the value of school lessons for individuals and society, rather than reaching some permanent accommodation, will wax and wane, not only because various interest groups will succeed in attaining power over their stipulation but as well because the curricular struggle is definitive of the mores orienting a paradoxical culture. Particular patterns will arise in complex interactions between internal school differences associated with tracking and external differences across schools associated with school cultures and school communities. Thus, the entanglements of curriculum and culture will give rise to disconcerting paradoxes rather than certain platitudes: For example, do Mr. Robinson's *lower-track* history students get "higher-status knowledge," at least in terms of its academic substance, than some of Marshall's *regular-track* history students?

Judgments about the significance of lower-track knowledge are further complicated and confused because in all three modes of content differentiation, teachers devote surprisingly little explicit attention to school knowledge itself. The distribution of knowledge occurs almost axiomatically, while students stand at the center of teachers' attention.

Two corollaries follow. On the one hand, Maplehurst's teachers do not see lower-track students as all the same, despite "homogeneous grouping." Instead, while they distinguish lower-track from regular-track students in their unpredictability, they also differentiate among lower-track students: "Slow" delinquents, for example, are of quite a different ilk than "slow" students with "good going-to-school skills." Depending on such characterizations, teachers supply different subject content: The worse the students' "attitudes" and "behaviors," the more narrowly moralistic and the less seriously intellectual the lesson. Thus, "relevant" therapy predominates with troublesome students (who, however, may be driven further beyond the pale by it), whereas the quasi-academic, skeletal pattern is reserved for "good" lower-track students (who, however, may be lulled into thinking they are indeed receiving a regular-track education).

On the other hand, because the distribution of knowledge occurs almost by default, the import of school knowledge and of judgments about it are muddied. The meaning or consequences of such phrases as "the necessity of being relevant," "higher-order thinking skills," "not going into depth," or "lessons that are just the same as my other classes," receive little sustained reflection. Yet because talk about curriculum remains commonsensical, teachers may unwittingly use knowledge in ways that contradict their and the school's educative purposes. Mounting lessons that "work" and get them through the day, they are genuinely surprised—and deeply discouraged—when students resist the controlling "adaptations." Both teachers and students come away from failed encounters with suspicions that things are not quite right but with little suspicion that curriculum may be at the core of the problem.

Illustrating these principles, then, lower-track teachers in Maplehurst who use the *skeletal* pattern, and who are particularly in evidence at classical Southmoor, borrow the language of the academy. Valuing traditional, liberal arts knowledge, but also uncertain of its appropriateness for all students, they offer "slow" but purportedly well-behaved students "the same" topics they provide in academic, regular-track English and history classes, albeit with "less detail" and "fewer connections." Taking a different tack, teachers in the *skills* pattern, particularly strong at "nothing-out-of-the-ordinary" Marshall, echo the social-efficiency interest group in its assumptions that school knowledge should be "disciplined" and "practical." Although teachers harbor doubts that education consists of time and training, they nevertheless transform history into "basic skills" and offer students who purportedly disdain academics a "concrete," "no-nonsense" regimen. Lastly, teachers who adhere to the pattern of *"relevance"* mirror the developmentalist's concern for the needs and interests of the child. Teachers "reach out to" near-adult, "street-wise" adolescents with "last-ditch" lessons in which "bookish" content is replaced with or skewed toward presumably more appealing "life skills," or less appealing "survival skills." Although teachers hope such a curriculum will moderate students' hostility and promote the right "attitude," "relevance" may also insult students and prompt them to question teachers' authority to pronounce on issues of life styles and values and, eventually, on school knowledge itself.

In sum, the traditional rationale for the curriculum as a means of preserving and passing on the culture's accumulated wisdom endures in Maplehurst's regular classes. Although its effects are not easily predicted, it infiltrates the various constructions of remedial curricula as well (Krug, 1960; Westbury, 1988b). At the same time, as alternative curricular rationales have developed during the 20th century, they have not only presented new genres of school knowledge but have bent traditionally academic subjects to new, chiefly instrumental, purposes (Kliebard, 1988). Thus, English is sometimes replaced with Personal Communication or, if English is retained, it may be reconstructed to justify its worth in meeting communication needs or job skills. Thus, neither distinctive in their own integrity nor simply "the same" as the regular curriculum, lower-track lessons are its ambiguous refractions.

A COMMON CURRICULAR FORM

The ambiguities among and within the three patterns of content differentiation—academic but watered-down knowledge; skills-based but routinized units; and "relevant" but invasive, potentially insulting topics—leave Additional Needs students and teachers uncertain about their purposes. Adding to their confusion is the *form* of the lower-track curriculum. That form—how teachers present knowledge and how students are allowed to engage with it—is just as much a part of the knowledge students experience as is a lesson's substantive content. Unlike the varied content patterns, in Maplehurst's eight classes the curricular form is uniform: Teachers present simplified, "structured" activities, breaking knowledge into discrete, manageable bits that students retrieve under the teachers' watchful guardianship.

The rationalized form secures the control that distinguishes regular- and lower-track lessons in Maplehurst. However, because control is achieved technically (Apple, 1979; 1983) for the most part, through its incorporation in the format of daily lessons, its presence and effects are not readily apparent to participants. For instance, individualized worksheets provide for silent industriousness without teachers having to belabor discipline. Technical control also embodies contradictions that may mitigate its effects (McNeil, 1986) as, for example, when teachers sabotage the "structure" they have worked hard to create because they know that learning situations must also have elements of "spontaneity." Finally, even though curricular control is not heavy-handed, it is extremely powerful: Precisely because teachers and students do not discern it, they fail to develop resistance strategies.

Thus, as I describe in this section, the form of Maplehurst's lower-track lessons bewilders students. It trivializes and reduces their and teachers' engagement with school knowledge even though, paradoxically, simplifying and standardizing are undertaken to ensure students' access to knowledge by breaking it into feasible units, limiting objectives to the "realistic," and being sure criteria have been mastered. Bewilderment deepens even further because with rationalized, technical forms of control, lower-track lessons often appear to be under *no one's* control: Luck, the appearance of "trying," or the vagaries of individual teachers seem to account for school success in Maplehurst as much as talent, knowing, or students' serious engagement.

Knowledge: Bits and Pieces

Maplehurst teachers convey lower-track English and history as circumscribed arrays of discrete, noncontroversial, informational tidbits. In the textbooks they choose and the course sequences they design, they render lower-track knowledge simplistic.

Simple Texts. Teachers use radically simplified texts in Additional Needs courses. They choose texts with the very best intentions: "to accommodate students' poor reading skills," to avoid "frustrating" students uninterested in "abstract" ideas, and to allow individuals to "work at their own pace," without being held back by "very limited" or belligerent classmates or by the need for teacher assistance. Teachers expect that students will engage with materials because they are "at their level."

The following is a representative paragraph from a three-page, large-print chapter about the American Revolution (Schwartz & O'Conner, 1974):

> By 1750 there were thirteen English colonies in the New World. Most of the people lived between the Atlantic Coast and a line of mountains called the Appalachians. This stretch of land is called the Atlantic Coastal Plain. It is narrow in the northern part and wider in the southern. The thirteen English colonies may be divided into four sections: New England, the Middle Colonies, the Southern Colonies, and the border strip, or frontier.

Other paragraphs in the chapter continue the detached, moderate tone. All are easily decoded, with unadorned syntax, simple vocabulary, and objective information.

However, for some of the ninth graders, the chapter's very simplicity may be disconcerting because their reading levels on standardized tests average between the 25th and 50th percentiles and range from the 2nd to the 98th percentile. The text also disconcerts because, however simple, it is cryptic. First, the plain report is of doubtful import: Because its facts are unconnected to each other, to other events and contexts, or to a theory of American development, they "do not add up." Failing to provide a framework, the eviscerated text renders the "basic information that any educated person should know"—the number of colonies, the shape of the Atlantic Coastal Plain—difficult rather than easy to understand or remember. Second, the bits-and-pieces form portrays school knowledge as inconsequential as well as unconnected. If students are not quite sure what all the fuss is about with the American Revolution, the inert text will hardly spur inquiry.

Curricular Sequencing. The form teachers give to the lower-track courses—how they sequence topics, units, and activities—also defines school knowledge as one clear-cut item followed by but unrelated to another equally plain one. Such disconnectedness makes courses banal. Haphazardness might not be surprising in "flexible" classes, where frequent changes in direction are instituted to maintain students' interest. However, regimented classes also suffer the bits-and-pieces effects, even though students who "like a routine . . . can come in, get down to work, and know what's what." As a student in Mr. Thompson's class explained, when faced with "those little questions" about *Time* magazine, she and her classmates only go through the motions:

> Some articles, people don't even read. You, you take a percentage out of how many people sit there and actually read the articles, and you won't get very much. Because most of the time, you know, all you have to do is just skim through all those little questions.

In short, like the texts that are so simplified that their meaning is difficult to understand even though they are easy to decode, courses designed to put knowledge within reach may also, paradoxically, suggest the lack of significance of such readily accessible knowledge. Whole disciplines, as well as courses, historical chronicles, and impassioned novels, appear as little more than strings, or lists (McNeil, 1986), of noncontroversial, unimportant, leaden facts. A student voiced his uncertain reaction, while also tacitly acknowledging the control:

> I don't feel like I'm learning anything particularly. Every day, it's the same work. But it doesn't add up – – – It's just, – like English: You don't have to know how to do grammar sentences to live in the world – – I'm just trying to get through this school. So I do it.

Students: Passive Retrievers of Knowledge

The most common format in which Maplehurst's lower-track students confront knowledge is the daily worksheet. Like the texts they "reinforce," worksheets contribute to a definition of knowledge as minimally informative tidbits. In addition, they delineate a passive rather than a powerful relationship to knowledge for students: On worksheets, Additional Needs students engage with knowledge principally by retrieving, memorizing, or guessing at information. However, as with other aspects of lower-track lessons, the nature of the role is not blatantly or unequivocally controlling or alienating.

Usually "geared" to a two- or three-page reading assignment, worksheets are composed mostly of simple, short-answer, unambiguous questions that guide students' reading and foreshadow the questions they will encounter on tests. Students copy definitions of words (many easy-to-read texts have simplified glossaries so students do not have to consult confusing dictionaries), match persons and events that are easily retrieved from the text (George Washington: First President of the United States), decide whether statements are true or false, or choose one of three or four answers as the best completion of a sentence. Usually, all students in a lower-track class follow the same worksheet, but they work on them individually. As with remedial texts, teachers explain that the simple, "individualized" worksheets allow students to work "independently" and successfully, despite poor skills, truancy, or disturbing peers. This is a representative worksheet question:

> Farming was not easy in New England because the
>   a. cost of land was too high.
>   b. land was not well-suited to farming.
>   c. farmer could not get his crops to market.

As an exact replica of a sentence in the text, the answer is incontrovertible. Less certain fill-in-the-blank questions are rare, short-answer definitions even rarer, and essay questions virtually nonexistent. When essays are required, as in skeletal classes, teachers certify answers that students then copy, memorize, and reiterate verbatim.

By contrast, although regular-track students also encounter worksheets (Apple, 1983; McNeil, 1986; Sedlak et al., 1986), teachers use them differently in the regular-track context so that the student's relationship to knowledge is active and intellectually consequential. For example, in an English class at Southmoor, small groups of sophomores followed a worksheet according to which they were to outline the plot of a short story by Richard Wright, decide whether the treatment of blacks in the story could happen in Maplehurst, and compare Wright's story to one by Langston Hughes that they had read previously. Students spent their time and energy in discussion. One student in each group served as secretary, recording on the worksheet a summary of the group's ideas. The teacher circulated during the discussions and led the whole-class recitation in which the conclusions of the small groups were shared, compared, and debated.

Although worksheets present lower-track students with a circumscribed role, students react to them ambivalently. On the one hand, students question the passive role, particularly when contradictions between educative and controlling purposes emerge. For example, one of Mr. Thompson's students noted the ambiguity generated by the "easy" routine of 20 questions:

At first, I thought, "Well, this is going to be easy to get a grade in here." But then, I thought, "It's kinda dumb," because *every* time you go in, you just hear people say, "Oh, god, we have to go through this *Time* magazine thing again." You feel kinda bummed out because you know what you're going to get into before you even start.

Even when worksheets are replaced with creative activities, teachers restructure the latter with arbitrary role restraints against which students chafe. For example, Ms. Campbell's students balked at writing "a theme about your favorite character in *Of Mice and Men*" because the teacher, adhering to notions borrowed from composition research about brain-storming, insisted that all students begin with an identical "structuring" paragraph that the class would compose together. Several students pro-tested that the introduction "won't have nothing to do with *my* paper on Crooks." Finally, Ms. Campbell acknowledged students' restiveness: "Hey. I know some of you, like Rita, are thinking, 'I want to write this myself.' Believe me, I'm going to let you have that chance." When Rita responded under her breath, "I'll bet," Ms. Campbell reprimanded her: "I don't like that kind of remark." Rita persisted: "Well, gee, we did all this in middle school and could write things ourselves." The teacher retorted heatedly that Rita could "go to the Writing Lab immediately and work by yourself or stay here and quit making those remarks"! Faced with a compliant role or no role at all, Rita fell into stony silence.

On the other hand, much of the time students accept and adhere to the routinized work and the passive role even when they do not face ultima-tums like Ms. Campbell's. After all, lower-track worksheets look educa-tional and are both touted and widely recognized as such. They are "easy," requiring only that students retrieve self-evident information instead of manipulating or evaluating texts. If students run into a problem with one item, they are not "frustrated" because they can simply "go on to" another of the 10 to 20 unrelated items. Furthermore, failure with one question does not affect grades too adversely, since there are so many tidbits to add up. Students are also relaxed about worksheets: Because they complete them privately and noncommittally, students face neither personal stress nor potential ridicule by peers or teacher (see Metz, 1978).

Teachers: Guardians of The Right Answer

The form of the lower-track curriculum also presents Maplehurst teachers as guardians of The Right Answer. All direct talk—whether recitations, minilectures, or "open-ended" discussions—so that it too, like worksheets, conveys oversimplified knowledge and passive student participation. Accordingly, knowledge is univocal: It is indisputable and unambiguous and it is what one person—the teacher—has in mind. Because knowledge is indeterminate until teachers certify it, they use it to control students. Therefore, to succeed in lower-track recitations, students must seek certainty by focusing on the teacher's thinking rather than on their own, their peers', or other authorities. Teachers justify this approach by saying that lower-track students demand The Right Answer: "They don't want to do the work of figuring it out themselves." According to teachers, students are also unable to tolerate ambiguity: "They don't want to know that things are complex; they want it right or wrong, black or white."

Hence, teachers pose recitation questions whose very form implies single, limited answers. Whether directly interrogative—"How many colonies were there in Revolutionary America?"—or (as on worksheets) true-false, multiple choice, or matching, the form of the questions does not suggest the option of extended, complex discourse. Students' choices are limited to T *or* F, without considering the possibility that T *and* F may be right, depending on the situation, or that alternative answers from other frameworks are feasible.

Teachers also restrict recitations to consideration of noncontroversial facts to maintain guardianship. Should a controversy nevertheless arise, they reformulate it as a factual matter whose meaning is patently obvious. For instance, in Ms. Campbell's 10th-grade English class, students saw the film *The Learning Tree*, which portrays the lives of several black families living in a largely white community in Kansas. After spending three class periods viewing the film and completing a worksheet on each reel, the class discussed the film, during which Ms. Campbell solicited the movie's theme. Arthur, a black student, volunteered: "It's about the different values of two boys growing up - - Marcus will have different values from Newt because he's from a broken home, so he'll be raised differently, and have different ideas about things." Instead of praising Arthur's articulate response, Ms. Campbell frowned slightly and reiterated her question: "But what's the *main* theme?" Arthur then shrugged and relinquished his topic. Savvily guessing that the teacher had in mind the Marshall formula designating four literary themes for all literature (i.e., man vs. man, man vs. society, man vs. nature, and man vs. self), he spat out the "right answer," succinctly reduced to a single word: "It's about the conflict between two races in a small town. Prejudice." Satisfied, Ms. Campbell smiled, noted that "prejudice" is one variation of the "man versus man theme," and went on with her own thoughts about "prejudice." Although a student like Arthur might have "personal" knowledge about growing up black, the "relevant" topic is treated univocally.

Given such a controlling format, one might imagine that Maplehurst's lower-track classrooms are very orderly places, with teachers clearly in charge of knowledge and subordinate students. Or one might imagine an embattled setting with students resisting teachers' control and an alienating role. However, neither scenario captures the ambiguity of lower-track roles and relationships in Maplehurst. Paradoxically, the notion that knowledge is the equivalent of what the teacher has in mind both mitigates and maintains the teacher's control.

For example, lower-track success requires that students divine what is in the mind of another. However, success at such an endeavor is highly unlikely. In addition, lessons that are limited to one person's facts may not intrigue others. Thus, the teacher's strict guardianship of The Right Answer promotes students' withdrawal from rather than their engagement with school knowledge because success is rare and motivation low. However, student withdrawal worsens classroom dynamics. It makes teaching more difficult and increases unpredictability. Facing this dilemma, Maplehurst's lower-track teachers often shift the form of their control to maintain it. However, instead of sharing control with students or clamping down with a vengeance, they direct lessons in which neither they nor anyone appears to be in control.

The ambiguous dynamic—control without control—operates in the way teachers treat "thinking processes." On the one hand, teachers enjoin students to "Think"! They prize "exact" thinking and they reward The Right Answer. To further such goals, teachers instruct in "thinking skills." For example, one teacher admonished students, "Be sure you match persons and persons. Don't make a stupid mistake and match a person to a nonperson." Another urged students to "eliminate the obvious (wrong answer) when doing matching. . . . Time-words, like *century* or *decade*, can't be presidents or places."

On the other hand, teachers rarely ask about—and thereby designate unimportant—what lower-track students have on *their* minds. Indeed, the use to which students put "thinking strategies" suggests how inconsequential these strategies are. Confronted with a question about the number of Senate seats up for reelection during the year, for instance, many students used the correct "strategy" (look for a number if the question is numerical) but recorded incorrect answers of 435 and 100. However, their errors were not the result of poor reading skills or "stupid mistakes." Rather, students did not read at all: Using the "strategy," they "skimmed" the article looking for a number and any number would do. In other words, the "strategy" made sense as a stratagem: Students using it to cope with the daily stream of trivial questions by-passed the "effort" of comprehending current events altogether.

Similarly inconsequential is giving a wrong answer in a recitation. Teachers do not ask for an explanation of how a student arrives at an answer or for a reasoned defense of the student's choice. Instead, they simply provide The Right Answer themselves, often using a matter-of-fact tone that suggests the answer's self-evidence. Or they go right on to another student, calling on that person to "take a different shot at the question." They keep students guessing by providing suggestive "prompts" that hint at the words and ideas they have in mind. They reiterate particular themes until they function almost magically, as answers that have such a high probability of being credited that classes of students can chorus them.

By making little of wrong answers, whether by giving the correct response themselves or by priming student guessing, teachers encourage students' continued participation in recitations. At the same time, however, their practices also suggest that school knowledge is insignificant and that knowing is not an effort over which either teachers or students have control. In this ambiguity, the lower-track curriculum assumes the form of a game of chance. As in the lotteries that so many Americans play, knowing in school is only a game. Although the game has consequences for winners and losers, success at it is a matter of a lucky guess, not of talent, "hard work," or control by a gamemaster.

Converting the acquisition of knowledge into a matter of luck serves the interests of both teachers and students in Maplehurst's lower-track classrooms. For students, it removes some of the onus of being a lower-track student. If they are not in control of school success, they do not have to upbraid themselves for not being smarter or not working harder. At the same time, the noncontroversial, disconnected form of school knowledge suggests its triviality and makes concern about Right Answers ridiculous. Thus, chancy lessons play on lower-track students' ambivalence about schooling: Knowing that schooling is important and that they are not very good at it, they can assuage their anxiety because school knowledge is simplistic and beyond their control. They can relax, play the school game lackadaisically, and hope for luck in "hitting on" the Right Answer. For teachers, school success through luck encourages students' relaxed participation in lessons, masks and thereby maintains the centralized control that teachers wield, and protects teachers from blame when "easily frustrated" students inevitably fail at the task of guessing what they have in mind.

Thus, the single pattern that distinguishes the form of the lower-track curriculum generates ambiguity as much as its differentiated content does. If lower-track lessons have a highly controlling form in which knowledge is univocal bits, students are passive retrievers, and teachers are guardians of The Right Answer, that form also undercuts itself: The easy, straightforward format enables and engages students yet, paradoxically, oversimplified knowledge also prompts ambivalence and distance. Equally paradoxically, teachers with centralized control find themselves unable to actually teach.

In the next chapter, I detail the convoluted twists and turns of lower-track knowledge and control that I have described in general in this chapter. By again looking closely at a single lesson, I specify the processes and contexts that influence the emergence, evolution, and meaning of the ambiguous dynamic in Maplehurst. The analysis documents that school knowledge is subtle and strong in its impact. Even though teachers and students may not recall or remark them, mundane curricular negotiations are a source of the differences schools make. They are the medium through which youth encounter their relationships to the knowledge and ways of knowing that society deems most worthy.

CHAPTER 9

How Students
Interpret School Knowledge

In Chapter 8, when discussing the teacher's definition of the differentiated content and form of the lower-track curriculum in Maplehurst, I argued its fundamental ambiguity and the power of that ambiguity. I explore this thesis further in this chapter by specifying the processes and contexts that shape particular emergence and evolution of this ambiguity. Neither foreordained nor uniform, lower-track lessons result from people's choices, which vary according to their circumstances. By examining how Mr. Robinson's ninth-grade American history lesson about European immigrants unfolds, I trace how school participants compose ambiguity, and I mark the central part that knowledge and knowing play in lower-track classes, even though they are not always so intended or apprehended by participants.

I add to the previous analysis an account of the student's perspective on the lower-track curriculum as well. Rather than assuming that the teacher's definition is omnipotent or that the student's view is self-evident—for example, that lower-track students do not care about school lessons because they are inherently uninterested or unskilled in them—I posit the student's perspective as a structural feature of classrooms. Visible in the classroom's informal underlife (Goffman, 1963), it is an evaluative, sub-rosa commentary on the teacher's lesson. Investigating it clarifies connections among the curriculum control and the "trouble" that distinguishes lower-track classes.

In what follows, I trace how the principles that inform the lower-track curriculum come alive in one well-respected teacher's intriguing yet ill-fated lesson about "cycles of prejudice." In the first section, Mr. Robinson's formal lesson plan, his intentions, and his teaching illustrate the general skeletal pattern I outlined in the last chapter. In the second section, I shift the focus from the teacher's perspective to the students', to consider how and with what intended and unintended effects students respond and react to Mr. Robinson's lesson. As I describe, in the lesson's brief history, incidents of "trouble," although ephemeral, accumulate so that by the lesson's end, the ninth graders eschew the teacher and the lesson completely and turn instead to each other and to "messing around." To examine this shift further, in the last section I move beyond the single lesson to explore the ambivalence with which students understand the intricate play between curriculum, "trouble," and control. The analysis suggests the decided impact that schools have on students as much as on teachers and knowledge.

THE TEACHER'S PERSPECTIVE
ON THE LOWER-TRACK CURRICULUM

Mr. Robinson's ninth-grade American history lesson about immigration enacts not only his unique vision of historical studies but also his understanding, as a Southmoor faculty member, of the school's lower-track students and teachers and therefore of the complex combination of classically academic and remedial knowledge that "the community wants" and students "need." Examining the lesson plan, the teacher's stated intentions and his teaching, and then, in the next section, classroom interactions, exposes the main organizing principle of the lower-track curriculum: oscillations between educative and instrumental purposes. It also discloses how, at Southmoor, teachers respond to the oscillations by emphasizing order.

Curriculum as Lesson Plan

Considered in its formal outline, Mr. Robinson's lesson appears to be virtually "the same" as in his regular history classes. Part of a larger, 3-week unit about immigration, it uses two class periods. In the first, Mr. Robinson plans for students to view a sophisticated documentary film about southern and eastern European immigrants to the United States, *Storm of Strangers*. The following day, they will engage in a whole-group recitation to review details of the film and to "figure out its central message." They will also compose an "essay" summarizing their conclusions. Echoing features of Southmoor's regular lessons, Mr. Robinson's lower-track plan designates a significant topic in American history, emphasizes student activities that require "higher order thinking" (e.g., "figuring out"), and instructs in verbal skills of writing and public discourse that are often neglected even in regular-track classes in many American high schools (Boyer, 1983; Goodlad, 1984; Sizer, 1985). In short, as a measure of the lower-track curriculum, the lesson plan appears to be neither trivial, routinized, nor alienating.

Curriculum as Teacher Statement

However, interviews and informal conversations with Mr. Robinson deepen and shift the perspective gained from perusing the lesson plan. On the one hand, Mr. Robinson's explanations of his purposes corroborate the plan. For instance, Mr. Robinson proclaims that academically unsuccessful students will succeed at Southmoor "only if they are provided an adaptive curriculum." Therefore, he modifies the regular curriculum while retaining aspects of its academic focus: "The lower-track course follows the same course outline as my other (regular) classes but differs in difficulty and total scope." Moreover, the skeletal version rejects the usual remedial emphasis on "trivial content" and "mechanical" seatwork on worksheets and substitutes "oral communication . . . (which) motivates (lower-track) students and they are good at it."

On the other hand, other statements by the teacher suggest that curricular "adaptations" may be more than minor tinkering with the regular curriculum. Lower-track students, seen as the "twits" of the social order and the "dregs" of the academic hierarchy, not only cannot "go into the depth" that regular students achieve, but they are "unpredictable and negative . . . they're immature and hyper and never keep their mouths shut." Coupling social understandings about age with scholastic considerations about ability, Mr. Robinson justifies a curriculum that is differentiated from regular history not only in its "difficulty and total scope" but in its emphasis on control of students' "immaturity."

To secure behavioral control, Mr. Robinson circumscribes curricular knowledge. "The same course outline" is differentiated after all, as is apparent in the textbooks Mr. Robinson assigns. Regular ninth graders have two books, a dense standard chronology and a collection of case studies designed to encourage students "to develop their own points of view using skills of critical thinking and analysis." Mr. Robinson describes the regular student's independent relationship to knowledge: He wants students to "make inferences from conflicting facts," to describe events of the past "in their own words," to "bring (the events of the past) to Southmoor today and see history as relevant," and to "think critically but without simply being skeptical." By contrast, Mr. Robinson provides lower-track students with a thin, "easy-to-read," large-print text that, for example, covers the Civil War in two pages of bland generalizations interspersed with a smattering of proper names and large blocks of pictures. Like some other lower-track teachers in Maplehurst, he does not allow students to take books from the classroom "because the books may never come back." Instead, students read the short chapters aloud, paragraph by paragraph in a style reminiscent of elementary school, and write answers to the multiple-choice questions at the end of chapters. Mr. Robinson explains that to ask "slow" students to read the dense chronology or to adhere to the "pace" or "critical thinking" in regular classes would be "criminal" and would only lead to "frustration."

Curriculum as Teacher Performance

Adding observations of Mr. Robinson's classroom behavior to his lesson plan and his statements of intent delineates further twists and turns in the oscillating play between education and social control. Coding his teaching according to preformulated observational schemes (e.g., Amidon & Hunter, 1966) would confirm its broadly educative, "authentic" "open-endedness." It is "the same" as his direction of regular-track recitations, punctuated with lively exchanges about turn-of-the-century immigration, and different from the silence and ritual exchange in many skills-based and "relevant" lessons. For example, Mr. Robinson begins the review of the film on the second day with an "easy," inviting, unstructured question: "What was the film about?" He "gets the lesson moving" by evaluating positively all student responses, no matter how tentative or brief: "a fire"; "immigrants"; working conditions that were "bad." He encourages participation with comments that affirm students' abilities: "See, you can do it." He generates a sense of lively involvement with his brisk, up-beat enthusiasm.

In particular, Mr. Robinson's lower-track recitations are characterized by opportunistic turn-taking (a variant on both the principle of one-upmanship discussed in Chapter 4 and of luck discussed in Chapter 8): He broadcasts a question to the class at large, students call out answers as they come to mind, and the teacher eventually selects an answer toward which he will direct the next question. The practice encourages lower-track students' participation in public recitations by presenting them little risk of embarrassment. Under the structure, individuals are not "put in the glare of the spotlight," many responses are never evaluated at all, and the fast-paced, overlapping responses make it difficult to identify the contributor of any particular answer. The practice also contributes to the lower-track lesson's resemblance to the regular lesson in creating an aura of energy and "spontaneity."

The content in Mr. Robinson's lesson appears as "open" to student contributions as its form. For example, after securing students' participation with an encouraging beginning, Mr. Robinson asks the class to "think and figure out" the real "story" of immigration presented in *Storm of Strangers*, cautioning them that it is not the familiar melting-pot story of immigration, or what Mr. Robinson characterizes as the "rags to riches story":

The immigrants come over, they work hard, they accomplish. Kids, the next generation, they move out (of the ghetto). But that *still* isn't the point of the story - - - That's the rags to riches, isn't it? You come here with NOTHING and after a couple of generations, you're rich. (Speaking softly, dramatically, and leaning toward the class) But - that's - not - what - the - story's - about. What *is* the story about? What do you think it is?

For the next 10 minutes, almost all students take up Mr. Robinson's grammatically open-ended question. Continuing with fast-paced, opportunistic turn-taking, students work to "figure out" the irony that, usual myths notwithstanding, not only was prejudice rather than wealth awaiting immigrants in the New World, but that, in addition, the prejudice came largely from earlier immigrants. Mr. Robinson summarizes this counterintuitive idea that immigration is "cycles of prejudice":

Immigrants came over with nothing, but through hard work, education, and getting rich, the next generation of immigrants succeed in getting out of the ghetto and into part of the middle class. They become American Pie . . . (They) become part of the power structure . . . and now THEY have this hatred, this prejudice, toward - - the new - - - immigrants that come in.

Mr. Robinson concludes this recitative portion of the lesson, like a good Southmoor teacher, by pointing to the value of historical studies and the continuing validity of the idea of prejudice as "cycles": "And we still have these feelings (of prejudice) today . . . about people coming from Asia, we had the Cubans (of 1980)."

Curriculum as Sociocultural Construction

If the curriculum is conceptualized as a series of discrete teaching acts, Mr. Robinson's behavior suggests that he expects lower-track students, like his regular students, to "discover" rather than simply memorize and regurgitate the notion that prejudice is cyclical. However, the "discoveries" take on a less "spontaneous" cast if Mr. Robinson's performance is put in context, so that its significance is gauged not against precoded teaching rules but in relation to students' responses and reactions in the emergent stream of the lesson. That is, Mr. Robinson's lesson is less clearly educative if the curriculum is seen as an unfolding social construction rather than as a teacher production. For example, although opportunistic turn-taking "works"—it promotes students' willingness to participate actively with topics the teacher judges appropriate—the practice also limits the student's role to guessing, codifies knowledge as univocal, shouted out bits and pieces, and confirms the teacher as guardian of the "right answer." Furthermore, because opportunistic turn-taking can confuse the topic under discussion by allowing many ideas to be shouted out, as well as prompting overlapping talk and interruptions and raising the general hubbub, the practice generates the "unpredictability" that can call forth and justify teacher control.

Hence, Mr. Robinson rarely asks students to explain how they arrive at answers. Instead, he reacts to one student's wrong answer by ignoring it or simply going on to another student for "a different shot at it." His loose, rapid-fire direction of recitations, as well as the simplicity of his questions, provides for only brief, unelaborated responses. As a result, students are distanced from knowledge, even as the format encourages their limited participation. Because the way students get answers is not examined, one guess appears as good as another. Because the answer is in the teacher's mind, guessing is as satisfactory—and as potentially successful—a means of apprehension as more rigorous or logical methods. Because students "focus on the teacher" rather than on themselves or the material as the source of the right answer, they need rely less on their own reasoning. In short, in Mr. Robinson's lesson, the student's engagement with curricular knowledge and with knowing are secondary to the teacher's central control of them. A student corrected my understanding of "the key to getting a good grade" in lower-track classes. I summarized a long discussion of the student's role by saying: "So you sit, listen, and do your work?" "Yeah," he agreed, but then translated, "just focus on the teacher, yeah."

That increasing control is the "default option" (Cazden, 1988) to which Mr. Robinson reverts when faced with the ambiguities and unpredictability engendered by opportunistic turn-taking is further illustrated in disagreements, those windows on the particular balances that teachers and students establish between learning and order (see Chapter 3). This disagreement arose at the end of the 10-minute recitation about the "real story" of immigration, in which students tried, and repeatedly failed, to guess the thesis the teacher had in mind. Voiced by Dave, it is neither silly, mindless, nor a game of "get the teacher," as some lower-track arguments are characterized (Cusick, 1983), but concerns the lesson's content and form. Teacher and student argue both about whether prejudice is a mechanical "cycle" and about who, in the classroom, has the right to pronounce authoritatively on knowledge:

> T: And, we still have these feelings [of prejudice] today . . . about people coming from Asia, we had the Cubans.

DAVE: Yeah, but with the Cubans, we had a right to feel that
      way⌈–
  T: ⌊Well, okay, okay⌈–
DAVE: ⌊– cause they were criminals.
    T: We've got to be very careful, we've gotta be very careful in our
actions. They were, they was certain, there were some criminals and so forth, but we also gotta keep into the idea of just
other people coming in. Now listen, we're gonna put this
together, okay? Gonna put it down in a paragraph that helps us
understand what this film is and this paragraph will be on the
test.

    Here, a lower-track student engages appropriately with the substance
of a history lesson. Rather than having no interest in "abstract" knowledge
about immigration, Dave logically extends Mr. Robinson's topic regarding
the persistence of prejudice. Even though the teacher cuts him off, he
squeezes in additional data: The Cubans "were criminals." Moreover, Dave
offers an alternative hypothesis that grows directly out of his comprehension of Mr. Robinson's analysis: Prejudice may not be a "cycle" but a
matter of particular circumstances, such as whether immigrants have
"criminal" pasts. Moreover, in disagreeing with the teacher, Dave is not out
of line but is responding to Mr. Robinson's explicit injunctions in this
lesson and Southmoor's implicit norms supporting students' ability to
"figure out" lessons. His objection is neither hostile nor "off-the-wall" but
is politely qualified and voiced at an appropriate juncture in the discourse:
"Yeah, but" says Dave, acknowledging if also rejecting Mr. Robinson's
position.

    By contrast, Mr. Robinson dismisses rather than welcomes Dave's
idea, thereby illustrating lower-track teachers' confused expectations. His
reaction also exemplifies in miniature the general process that he and
other Southmoor faculty members use to manage the confusion their
ambiguous lessons produce: Teachers restrict knowledge to control "trouble." In the face of student questions about the information the teacher has
provided, The Right Answer and the teacher's guardianship of it are
reasserted.

    First, Mr. Robinson simply interrupts Dave in mid-sentence, giving him
no chance to explain why prejudice might not be a "cycle." Then, when Dave
persists in explaining that the Cubans "were criminals," the teacher, after a
number of false starts, suggests that Dave's analysis is not "careful," it does
not "keep into" the main point, and it is preventing the class from moving on
to important upcoming activities (preparing for an exam). Finally, although
Mr. Robinson admits that there were "some criminals," he simply reiterates

his position on prejudice in response to Dave's alternative hypothesis: "We also gotta *keep into the idea* of just other people coming in" (my emphasis). The teacher then closes the disagreement, not by having resolved it with evidence, definitions, or rational argumentation, but by shifting from the recitation about the film to a different activity, group paragraph writing.

Mr. Robinson's negotiating position reflects expectations furnished by tracking as it is meaningful within Southmoor's culture: Additional Needs students' objections to a lesson's content cannot represent either valuable information or civil argumentation because "you can't get the depth and things just get out of hand so easily." Instead, one develops a curriculum restricted to a simple view of prejudice that will not "frustrate" intellectually "slow" students. Equally important, limiting students' participation to responses rather than evaluative reactions ensures good order among developmentally "immature" students who "just don't know how to carry on a reasonable argument."

At the same time, a restricted curriculum also manifests teachers' culturally sensible resolution of the Southmoor teacher's ambivalence regarding lower-track students (see Chapter 5). Lower-track teachers distance themselves from the lower-track role because, as Mr. Robinson put it, "Additional Needs classes are pretty low on the priority list at Southmoor." Control of troublesome students, on the other hand, contributes to the institution's ability to proceed in its main operation. Another lower-track faculty member commented:

> I try to be selective in what I teach. I mean, I'm not going into the past perfect tense with these kids. But, you know, nobody asks me what I'm doing in class. I mean, I put worksheets in the principals' or counselors' mailboxes, but they never ask me about it. As long as I *take care of* the classes, that's about it. (My emphasis)

PATTERNS IN NEGOTIATIONS OF KNOWLEDGE ACROSS A LOWER-TRACK LESSON

If circumscribing knowledge to control the "troublesome" behavior represented in a student's disagreement is sensible from Southmoor teachers' perspective and, however ambiguously, allows them to "take care of" lower-track students, the chaos that develops in lower-track lessons nevertheless suggests its inefficacy. Teachers, including Mr. Robinson, hypothesize the inevitability of such "trouble," pointing to low-skilled students' "frustration," their lack of interest in anything but "socializing with their friends," and their childishly short attention spans. However, examining the dynamic of classroom interactions as it evolves across the course of lower-track lessons uncovers a more complicated picture of how and why "trouble" emerges.

As I have discussed earlier, the seemingly inevitable disorder in lower-track lessons reflects students' confused responses to the ambiguity of the lower-track curriculum as they wonder whether they should think creatively to compose an "important" paragraph or simply "keep into (the teacher's) ideas." In addition, lessons present students with the marginality of their role in the organization. Students know what lower-track means because they *experience* the difference between passive subordination and independent engagement in lessons that combine elements of the regular and remedial curricula. If students refuse a subordinate role, they upset the classroom order that teachers must then reestablish. If students persist in an independent stance toward school knowledge, they can be judged insubordinate.

Thus, following Dave's disruptive remarks about Cuban immigrants, Mr. Robinson quickly recaptures the attention of the class by shifting to a new activity, which students readily acknowledge as "important": preparing for an exam. First, Mr. Robinson tells students that they will work as a group to "put . . . together" their discussion of the film, adding that "writing a whoole paragraph is difficult, maybe the biggest thing we've done." Then, he instructs students to copy the paragraph into their notebooks and memorize it so that they can reproduce it in response to an upcoming "essay test question." Yet despite the inviting, serious frame, the initial interchanges in the writing activity display increasingly restricted knowledge and an increasingly restricted role for students as knowers:

> T: Are you ready? How are we going to start this thing (the paragraph) out?
> TIM: One word.
> T: That's right. So wha - , we'll start with what word?
> JOHN: Immigrants.
> T: All right.
> S: (deprecatingly) Reeeal hard.
> T: So, what else we gonna say? "Immigrants" what?
> JOHN: Im - migrants, immigrants came from⌈-"
> T: ⌊"*Came.*"
> JOHN: "Came *from.*"
> T: Well, let's just say "came - - what?"
> DAN: "To America."
> T: "Into," all right? We'll just say, "into this country." Why did they come?

The noticeable feature of this short piece of talk is the contrast between the teacher's successful elicitation of student participation and the degree and arbitrariness with which he then limits it. The teacher provides no specifications for the composition of the paragraph other than that "we will put this (recitation about the film) together." Moreover, his broad opening question—"How are we going to start this thing out?"—suggests that students' ideas will be important to the final product (and students' behavior suggests this as their interpretation). Nevertheless, the teacher corrects all responses but the first one: "Came from" becomes "came," "to America" becomes "into this country." Mr. Robinson furnishes neither substantive nor stylistic reasons for his rejections and modifications of students' contributions.

Given the task of guessing the teacher's plan for the paragraph (and, sometimes, even his "exact" words), the error rate climbs even higher during the subsequent 15 minutes of composition. For instance, students call out more than 20 short responses before they "hit upon" the answer to Mr. Robinson's leading question, "Why did they (the immigrants) come?" Amid exclamations about "jobs," "*better* jobs," "God," "freedom," "adventure," and "education," one student interjects his tacit recognition of the singular focus: "I know *the word*, but I just can't think of it" (my emphasis). Gradually, the six-sentence paragraph is composed, but it validates fewer than one third of the students' "words"; it contains no hint of Dave's earlier objections about the processes of prejudice.

As their role narrows and becomes increasingly humiliating because their incorrect guesses accumulate, students disassociate themselves from it by turning to the alternative, antiphonal underlife (Goffman, 1963). Defined by students acting in response to each other, the underlife is an illicit realm of students' concerns in which students exchange notes, avoid evaluation, modify work tasks, eat, and engage in other activities not countenanced by the formal organization. It is also an arena through which students, especially at the secondary school level, offer ironic commentary on the teacher's competence, school lessons, and differences in their identity from the role the organization provides for them. Because the underlife challenges the teacher's definition of the classroom situation—the student's role, the climate and teacher's role, and the content and form of the curriculum—teachers find it difficult to ignore.

In Mr. Robinson's lesson the underlife manifests itself only sporadically during the opening recitations when students are attentive to the subject matter and the teacher. But it appears emphatically and at length in the paragraph writing as students suffer repeated, public failure. At first, the underlife takes the mild form of joking around. Joining together, students underscore and relieve some of their tension by appropriating the opportunistic turn-taking structure to produce strings of one-liners, instead of one-word answers. For instance, students respond with sarcasm rather than seriousness to composing the second sentence of the paragraph. To Mr. Robinson's prompt, "What did immigrants find when they came here?" they reply "*ev-er-y-thing* they wanted," "the best alley in town," and "income taxes." Although Mr. Robinson interprets this discourse as unruly shenanigans, it is tied intimately to the lesson. With jokes, students protect themselves from negative evaluations by indicating that they may not really be trying to answer the question. The jokes furnish a group solidarity that contests the teacher's power (see Willis, 1977, for a discussion of the importance of "having a laff"). The quips are also congruent with the premium Southmoor puts on verbal repartee, and they exhibit students' attentiveness to the material of the lesson. "The best alley in town" captures well Mr. Robinson's theme about the disjunction between the ideals immigrants sought and the discouraging reality they found.

However, Mr. Robinson sanctions the quips, and by continuing to insist that student contributions match his ideas, exacerbates the issues of his power and student subordination. The joking changes to dissonance. Jokes increase in frequency, more students shout them out, they are more highly charged, and they diverge increasingly from the topic under discussion. In short, students produce the interruptive, "off-the-wall" non sequiturs that make lower-track classes a "circus." For instance, when contributions for the paragraph's conclusion suffer the repeated rejections of earlier efforts, students break into a string of bizarre one-liners about "what . . . the old immigrants did to the new immigrants":

> JUAN: They took over the world.
> DAVE: They started World War III⌈–
>   TIM: ⌊And everyone died.
> JOHN: The earth exploded⌈–
>   DAN: ·   ⌊And now we're here on Venus!

In the concluding portion of Mr. Robinson's lesson, conflict between teacher and students deepens beyond jokes, even bizarre jokes, and the underlife moves from a "contained" form, providing students a means for fitting into the lesson, to a "disruptive" form in which students abandon it completely (Goffman, 1963). Although briefly, students experience the feeling that they have nothing to lose by discounting schooling. They mock the lesson by confirming with a vengeance the role Southmoor allots lower-track students: The relatively advantaged and committed students become "troublemakers."

The bitter struggle centers on curricular knowledge and knowing, as can be illustrated by comparing the earlier Cuban disagreement with a later one that coincides with the conclusion of the acrimonious writing activity to show how serious "trouble" grows over the short course of one lesson. In both, Mr. Robinson and Dave are the principals, and the topic of disagreement is whether prejudice is an automatic occurrence. In contrast to the politeness of the earlier exchange, the later disagreement is hostile and extensive.

The disagreement begins when Dave reintroduces his lingering "confusion" about how prejudice operates. Wondering whether prejudice in America is increasing because immigration continues or whether the amount of prejudice is constant, with discrimination against a new group simply redirecting old prejudice from earlier immigrant groups, Dave asks: "Are they (Americans) still prejudiced . . . against the Irish?"

301	DAVE:	Wait. I'm, I'm confused now. Okay, if the Americans,
302		they were prejudiced against the Irish, right? And
303		also, the Irish became the new middle class. Are they
304		still prejudiced of them?
305		(5.0)
306	TIM:	I don't see where the Irish took off. The Eng-, er,
307		Americans are prejudiced of the Jews now.
308		(3.0) (giggle)
309	T:	Let's just finish this (paragraph) off and then we'll
310		answer your kee-wes-chuns.
311	Ss:	(undecipherable)
312	T:	(reading the last sentence from the blackboard) "And now
313		the new middle class treated them (the newly arrived
314		immigrants) with hate and prejudice, just like they had
315		been treated." Now, we ready arrived at that, we
316		have this whole thing settled.
317	DAVE:	Now answer my question.
318	T:	Yessss. Be sure you get it down. "And now the new
319		middle class treated them with hate and prejudice - -
320		just as they had been treated." Okay?
321	DAVE:	You gonna answer my question?
322	T:	Now, do I have to, shall we finish that "just as they had
323		been treated" or can you - does this make sense to you?
324	Ss:	(chatter)
325	T:	"The other immigrants came over - - -
326	Ss:	(chatter)
327	T:	"And now the new middle class treated them with hate and

```
328          prejudice." Okay?
329    Ss: (chatter)
330  JOHN: Is this paragraph done now?
331     T: Yes.
332  JOHN: Guudd.
```

This second disagreement between Mr. Robinson and Dave is very volatile. The teacher's response to Dave's opening question (in which Tim joins in lines 306–307) is notably more grudging than in the Cuban interchange. Twice he offers only long silences (lines 305; 308). He follows with mockery, demeaning the students' questions as "key-wes-chuns" (line 310). Then he stalls, suggesting that the paragraph on which the class has been working may not be quite complete (line 309) and reading aloud parts of the last sentence four times (lines 312–314, 318–320, 322–323, 327–328). He also insinuates that the issue of the "cycles of prejudice" is uncontroversial. For example, he asserts that "we have this whole thing settled" (lines 315–316), and he appeals to the class to say that the paragraph "makes sense to you" (lines 322–323), if not to Dave and Tim. In short, Mr. Robinson does all he can to forestall reopening the question of prejudice, even though it is the centerpiece of his lesson.

Students react to the teacher's maneuvers with considerably less patience and acquiescence than in the Cuban interchange. That earlier event and the punishing paragraph writing leave their legacy. Coalescing in opposition to the teacher, students second each other's demands that Mr. Robinson take their substantive questions seriously. Thus, Dave is joined by Tim in "confusion" about the lesson's main idea. Still more students side with the two boys as Mr. Robinson stalls: The noise level rises and side conversations and under-the-breath comments multiply (lines 324, 326, 329). In contrast to earlier cooperativeness, students withhold agreement with the teacher's suggestion that the paragraph "makes sense" or "is settled." Civility declines further as Dave taunts, openly demanding that his "key-wes-chun" be answered (lines 317; 321). Finally, a student—not the teacher—determines that the paragraph is indeed "done" (line 330), sarcastically evaluates its completion (line 332), and thus puts an end to Mr. Robinson's delaying tactics.

The struggle between students and teacher over the meaning of prejudice escalates even further when Mr. Robinson turns to the students' questions:

```
333     T: Okay. Now, let's go back to the couple of questions.
334         What was it that you said?
335  DAVE: Why, awright, the 'mericans were
```

336   prejud⌈iced
337   T: ⌊No. It's not, it's ⌈not
338   DAVE: ⌊Naw, naw, naw,
339   T: Well, no, but now lookit, but now lookit. You're
340   starting off with the Americans. What are the
341   Americans?
342   DAVE: Awright, awright, awright. But
343   we, th⌈ey,
344   T: ⌊But wait, ⌈wait,
345   DAVE: ⌊Th⌈ey
346   T: ⌊WAIT! Who - - were - - the - -
347   Americans?
348   DAVE: Wait, ⌈uh –
349   JOHN: ⌊The Indians.
350   T: The *Indians* were the Americans.
351   DAVE: Awright. But just listen to me.
352   T: Okay.
353   DAVE: We came over, right? Let's say, Scandinavians,
354   Germans⌈,
355   T: ⌊That was after.
356   DAVE: Awright, the Irish came, right?
357   T: In the 1840s, '50s, '60s.
358   DAVE: Well, who was prejudiced against them?
359   T: The people that were already here.
360   TIM: Awright. Now, all of a sudden, the people that were
361   already here, that were prejudiced against them, the
362   Irish – Are they still prejudiced against the Irish?

In this explosive series of disagreements, conflict centers on subject matter and intellectual prerogatives. Before Dave can fully reiterate his query about what happens to prejudice, Mr. Robinson interrupts him (line 337). In full conflict, the two exchange interruptions (lines 338, 344, 345, 346) and heated imprecations to "wait" (lines 344, 346, 348).

Getting the last word (line 350), Mr. Robinson insults Dave. He implies that Dave is indeed "confused," but not about the analysis of prejudice. He simply does not know the meaning of *Americans*, a term that is familiar even to elementary school children. He also implies that Dave's question is not germane to the discussion. However, Mr. Robinson, not Dave, is off-base. Although *Americans* appears to be a readily accessible concept, its meaning is not commonsensical but specialized. Students need to know the technical use Mr. Robinson is making of *Americans* if they are to understand who non-American immigrants are and, therefore, how prejudice works in "cycles." Yet Mr. Robinson provides no definition. Indeed, his clarification that Americans are "the Indians" (line 350) only muddies the connection between becoming Americanized and becoming prejudiced.

The disagreement goes on for another 7 minutes until the dismissal bell releases Mr. Robinson and the ninth graders. During the time, students barrage Mr. Robinson's explanation with counterevidence. Asserting that "the Indians were not prejudiced against the first white men," they raise the question of how the original "Americans" avoided participating in the "cycle." They also suggest that the historical topic is more complex than "the idea of just other people coming in." When Mr. Robinson declares that "prejudice against the Irish *disappeared* . . . and now, they're fully accepted . . . as evidenced by John Kennedy's election to the Presidency," students counter that *they* do not necessarily like the Kennedys. Moreover, they note that prejudice against Jews and blacks has not disappeared even though subsequent immigrant groups furnish replacement targets. Overall, students' counterarguments point toward a more complex, historical interpretation of prejudice than Mr. Robinson's. It distinguishes immigrant groups rather than assuming that all are the same (for anthropological discussion on this point, see Jacob & Jordan, 1987, and Ogbu, 1978).

Yet Mr. Robinson dismisses all such evidence out of hand and treats argumentation as insubordinate. He closes the conflict regarding the "cycle of prejudice" by relying on power, not rational argumentation, clear definitions, or exposition of opinions. When John asks again *why* earlier immigrants, when they became Americans, treated later immigrants badly, Mr. Robinson states flatly and irrevocably, "I've already EXPLAINED that." His lesson confronts students with a no-win situation: They can adhere to a subordinate role that offers them few opportunities to demonstrate the intellectual interest or ability that Southmoor values or, if they engage seriously, this regular-track behavior is deemed "trouble making."

Students often choose to reject school knowledge, civil discourse, and the teacher, turning instead to peers and the underlife. Blatantly "out-of-control," students chat, wander the room, joke, scoot noisily in their desks, talk out, share gum, and pack up their book bags. Previously effective invitations from the teacher to "figure out" an issue or "warnings" that "one page on the test will deal with this" now fail to recapture attention. The student underlife, intimately intertwined with the formal lesson, overwhelms the lesson as students devalue and reject the teacher's definition of the classroom. Over the brief course of Mr. Robinson's lesson, "trouble" and marginality are socially constructed in a complex interaction of a manifest curriculum (immigrants finding their places in 20th-century

America), a hidden curriculum (lower-track students finding their places in 20th-century Southmoor), and a student-directed evaluative underlife that is shaped by and shapes both curricula.

Throughout, students orient increasingly to each other rather than to the teacher; they challenge ideas with growing unruliness; and they refuse to go on with the lesson until Mr. Robinson recognizes their concerns. However, their snide behavior is not inherently hostile, ignorant, or uninterested. Instead, acting obstreperously reciprocates and negatively assesses Mr. Robinson's refusal to "go back to the couple of questions" (line 333), to teach, and, therefore, to respect students' ability to contribute to knowledge.

Other lower-track classes at Southmoor, when they attempt group recitations, adhere to the pattern evidenced in Mr. Robinson's lesson. Escalating conflict also occurs at Marshall, although there the student underlife takes a culturally congruent form of distant silence rather than chaos. At both schools, incidents of curriculum conflict accumulate within and across lessons, developing a history and significance that their individual occurrences belie. As teachers meet student disagreements with greater control, they spark student efforts to preserve an identity. Such efforts, signaled lightly at first, can, if discounted, escalate into an even greater struggle. Thus, the significance of "trouble" grows exponentially as curricular negotiations explode. In less than an hour, a process of schismogenesis (Bateson, 1972, cited by Erickson, 1984), or accelerating differentiation, can occur in which teacher and students become differentiated antagonists.

If students have the final word on whether teachers can teach, their victory is nevertheless pyrrhic. When they choose to dismiss school lessons as demeaning, they are also turning away from knowledge. Moreover, the implications of such "disruption"—teachers unable to teach, schools with too many dropouts, students who look away from knowledge—cast in a different light the ambiguities of the lower-track curriculum, including success by luck, remote-control teaching, and mechanical routines.

THE STUDENTS' PERSPECTIVE

Mr. Robinson's American history lesson raises a number of questions about lower-track students. From the teacher's perspective, and from passing observations, students do appear silly, obstreperous, and sometimes belligerent. But do students understand their participation in this way? Are their backgrounds such that they are unwilling or uninterested in "trying," as teachers lament? Are they so lacking in social skills that they cannot pass courses by lying low, protectively withholding their disagreements with the teacher, as many regular-track adolescents in other schools often do (McNeil, 1986; Sedlak et al., 1986)? Why are Southmoor's Additional Needs students openly combative, whereas Marshall's exhibit a more contained, aggressive passivity? In short, what do Maplehurst's lower-track students say about their role, the teacher's, and the curriculum?

I explore the student perspective by supplementing the data from lessons with materials from interviews in which students explained further their interpretations of classroom events. These data suggest that to the well-established ideas and dispositions that academically unsuccessful students bring to school, the school adds its influence as well. Like their teachers, students also mediate institutional cultures.

In interviews, lower-track students convey their intense ambivalence regarding school (see also Metz, 1986). Whereas casual conversations with academically successful adolescents invariably converge on the topic of what they want to be when they grow up, academically unsuccessful adolescents call attention to the precariousness of their present situations by using metaphors of unsettledness and imbalance. Repeatedly, they mention the need to "get my act together," "get set in my life," or "get completely scheduled." In addition to implying that they are in some way remiss, the phrases simultaneously convey a sense of students' responsibility and good intentions (or, at least, an understanding that students should speak to an adult as though they have such intentions [Leacock, 1969; Varenne, 1982]). Moreover, "getting (one's) act together" suggests that individuals should control their situations. Even though students know that they are not academically talented, they say that if they "try," the school situation can be successfully "set."

Thus, rather than resisting or lacking concern about school, lower-track students know and accept the social importance of the institution, particularly of the respected schools they attend. But they also know that they are unsatisfactory performers. Adding to their discomfiture is their in-between status as adolescents. Still further, Maplehurst students aspire to and often come from social positions for which education is increasingly the requisite ticket. In short, age, institution, and class foster student insecurities, making them markedly vulnerable to the ambiguities of the lower-track curriculum and the uncertain student role it implies. As Mr. Robinson's ninth graders experienced, a subordinate role contravenes norms of adolescence, family, and the school itself, but an assertive role will be deemed insubordinate.

Lower-track students are particularly anxious about establishing themselves in school because they understand that their place there symbolizes their progress through the cultural stages of life, from younger to older—and better—levels. As one put it, "School pulls you up into life."

Therefore, students are sensitive to the school's embodiments of the prerogatives of age (see also Hargreaves, 1967). In the important adolescent task of "growing up," freshmen positively disdain middle school and long to be sophomores who are excused from study halls and "have their freedom." By contrast, students who misbehave are seen as callow "babies; you'd have to *stoop* to be at their level." Criticisms of lower-track high school lessons as "babyish—we did that in *elementary* school" are as common as the refrain "borrring." "Babyish" lessons insult adolescent pride.

In a fundamental sense, being "held back" in school is as emotionally wrenching as being "held back" in life:

> I stayed back in seventh grade because of the (private) school and I guess it is 86% of the people just stay back and they, like, keep a kid back a year to let them, to see how they progress and everything and give them a lot better experience. . . . But I didn't like the idea of being held back and I *swore*, I PROMISED myself, that when I got outta that school, I'd just go up, like I did when I came here this year.

Thus, high school students also discover that progress through the stages of school and culture is not an automatic function like aging. Instead, "school gets tougher as you go along."

Hence, the general doubts that characterize the adolescent stage of life in the United States (Sizer, 1985) are magnified by placement in lower-track classes. One reason is that the lower-track curriculum provides mixed messages about succeeding in school. On the one hand, school tells students that, like children or like near-adults close to leaving school, they should dutifully complete an array of worksheets and passively acquiesce in the teachers' control and their versions of The Right Answer. On the other hand, passivity violates norms of adolescent independence, and, taken to an extreme, can be judged a scholastic deficiency. Yet active engagement with knowledge can be deemed mutinous, as Mr. Robinson's ninth graders discovered. As a result, students find it nearly impossible to win recognition of their considerable skills, information, or values. A student voiced her sense of vulnerability in the face of the teacher's univocal definition of the curriculum by invoking standards, her deficiencies, and a kind of stubborn pride:

> "English I have to take. It isn't one of the classes I get into. . . . I mean, like adverbs, nouns, pronouns, all that. It's just that's something I'm *never* going to get. NEVER. That's bad."

Thus, school both exacerbates and assuages students' sense that they are on-the-fence. Students in lower-track classes know that if they do poorly, whatever that may mean, only stigmatizing special education classes or too difficult regular classes stand between them and dropping out. Yet lessons that play between unquestioning docility and critical engagement make it hard for students to assess their situations: "Adapted" for students' benefit, they nevertheless keep students anxiously involved and legitimately distant.

Yet despite their borderline position in Maplehurst schools, lower-track students express pro-school sentiments. Their positive dispositions reflect their social status and many parents' absolute demands for school success:

> My dad said, "If you don't start getting good grades, we're going to get rid of your cat." Or, "You're grounded." Stuff like that. So I tried hard because, you know (quaveringly), my cat is my pride and joy. . . . I used to be scared of my parents, but it's not right to be scared of your parents.

Pro-school sentiments, for example, that no high school is better than the one they attend, also reflect students' participation in the self-assured cultures of both schools. Students also comment repeatedly on a diploma's importance for the jobs to which they aspire (such as nurse, owner-manager of a grocery, computer repairman, teacher, secretary, mechanic, artist, or professional athlete with a major in physical education). Even when lower-track students admit that they are "sometimes tired of school," they add, "but I still try." All scoff at transferring, some mention college, and none acknowledge the option of dropping out.

Because Southmoor's and Marshall's students "drink from (a school's) cultural stream" (Waller, 1932, p. 106), their perspectives differ significantly, particularly concerning their stance toward teachers. In contrast to Marshall's lower-track students who adamantly maintain that they cannot name a good teacher because they "have never had one," Southmoor students hold teachers in high regard. Mediating a school culture in which teachers are highly valued, powerful members, students easily identify favorite, "good" teachers. Although all can talk about teachers they have not liked, they more often describe teachers who "help and explain when I don't get it." Lower-track students at Southmoor expect that teachers, as knowledgeable adults, will be helpful to them as they make their way through school and the stages of youth.

In particular, Southmoor students see teachers as persons, not as the faceless "enemy" that Marshall students disparage. They also expect teachers to see them as persons, whereas Marshall students keep already remote teachers at an even longer arm's length. When a Marshall teacher tries to introduce "relevant" topics or expects students to invest in lessons, students reaa the behavior as invasive and domineering. Yet the worst thing a Southmoor teacher can do is ignore students:

> I could probably tell if a teacher is going to be mean, like by how he talks to you. . . . A teacher can be strict, then you know it's going to be hard. But like being mean is like totally, it's like ignoring you. It's just like saying, well, personally saying to you, "I don't think *you've* been doing this right." Strict is to the whole class. Mean is personally, to you. Like looking away and ignoring you when you're trying to raise your hand and not hearing your question.

Thus, Mr. Robinson's stalling in regard to students' "key-wes-chuns" is especially emotionally loaded in the Southmoor context.

Southmoor students also see teachers as powerful. They are the center of the classroom:

> I've kinda got cured of the smarting off I used to do in middle school. . . . You're supposed to go in the classroom and sit and just stare at your teacher. You're just supposed to sit there, and you should always just sort of, you know, look at your teacher, don't even think about anything around you. But, you know, it's weird, because sometimes I just go up there and it's like my whole mind goes to the teacher.

Given such assumptions about teachers' personableness and power, Southmoor students treat teachers with considerable deference. By contrast, Marshall students regard teachers as irrelevant hindrances or "bossy" meddlers and treat them with wary disdain. For example, a Southmoor student took a teacher's "feelings" into account when she protested that she could never tell him that his class was "boring" because "it would be *rude*. I mean, imagine how he would *feel!*" Southmoor students also defer to teachers' academic expertise, even when they can articulate a reasoned objection to the way a class is taught: "I may disagree (with the lack of any historical content in a class that is formally titled history), but I'm sure the *teacher* knows what he is doing, even if *I* don't." Similarly, another student excused a teacher by seeing her as an eccentric scholar: "I guess she's just totally into her subject. I mean, it's very *weird* that someone could like English so much." Indeed, from Southmoor students' perspectives, only "troublemakers" openly criticize a teacher or a lesson. Distinguishing them-selves from such ingrates, students dismiss them as "immature, but they think they're so big . . . they hassle teachers." Thus, Mr. Robinson's ninth graders did not understand their participation as "hassling." Rather, their disagreements about prejudice signal a respect for intellectual inquiry that they learn partly from Southmoor's culture.

A boy's explanation of his placement in an Additional Needs history class captures particularly well the combination of personableness, author-ity, and power that Southmoor teachers represent for students, which contrasts sharply with Marshall students' understanding that teachers are aloof, peremptory, rather useless pedants. In the student's words, the Southmoor teacher is "honest," cares about what is "good for (me)," and is also willing to "give (me) a break." He and the teacher strike a bargain, with rewards for both. The teacher gets the student to leave his faster-paced regular class; the student gets a higher grade for making the choice voluntarily:

> I like a teacher who's honest with me, you know, saying, "You're having a problem here." You know, "Here's a way to solve it." Like my (regular) history teacher told me, "Why don't you talk to the counselor and I'll tell her that you want an appointment with her and tell her that you'd like to - - you know - - know something about this Additional Needs history class, because I think it would do a lot of good for you, and I know the counselor would." He goes, you know, "Actually, your writing is terrible." And I go, "I know" (laughs self-consciously). And, uh, he gave me a break, you know. I told him, "I've never had any previous essay writing before. We did it in eighth grade and I wasn't there for that." And, um, he gave me a break. I should've gotten like a D (for the quarter grade) and he gave me a C, and so, you know, that's extra credit for trying hard, you know.

By contrast, Marshall students understand themselves as making their own "breaks." Not only are teachers unhelpful, but students know how to "con" counselors and "drop down a course" to "beat the system." Such an option makes sense in a school in which relations between adolescents and adults are stringently differentiated and where lower-track placement is a "good deal."

At both schools, whether given a "break" or making their own, all lower-track students with whom I spoke state a desire to survive high school and a tacit agreement to do what survival necessitates. If they are hardly "civilized" or angels, they nevertheless voice little of the ingrained antagonism to school of Willis's (1977) lads. Instead, they understand schooling's instrumental and symbolic importance, as well as their own precarious positions. As John Meyer (1986) has suggested, being in school may be preferable to being out:

> Students may seem, from a narrow *organizational* perspective to be trapped in a status in which they have surprisingly little power or real participation. But, institutionally, they are at the very center of things. This situation, cultural or religious rather than strictly organizational in character, may explain why they immerse themselves with such conformity and satisfaction in the system. In becoming a student, in contrast to simply being a child, they gain a great deal by way of direct access to central cultural meaning and status. (p. 357)

Thus, Southmoor students, participating on the margins of a traditionally academic culture, see themselves as "trying" hard, they see teachers as adults to be taken seriously, and they see academic lessons as what schools teach. Marshall students, participating in a disciplined ethos, also "try," seeing themselves as complying but not "bending" to the "no-nonsense" demands of taskmasterly teachers in an endeavor that will eventuate in a useful credential. Such tractable dispositions make lower-track students' "fights with the teacher" even more ironic.

Looking at one lower-track lesson provides a different orientation to the "circus" that is consistently documented as characteristic of many lower-track classrooms and that is understood as their necessary feature. It clarifies the crucial importance of school knowledge, even—or especially—in classes for the "slow." As Mr. Robinson's lesson indicates, the curriculum is not simply the topics and activities transmitted by a teacher, just as the underlife is not simply an illicit domain in which students concentrate on socializing with peers or "hassling the teacher." Nor is it an automatic "cycle of prejudice" generated by differences teachers and students bring to school, which schools cannot affect. Instead, as students indicate in interviews, they, like their teachers, acknowledge many of the precepts of each school's culture, although both groups also translate them to their own particular purposes. Unwittingly, teachers who oversimplify lessons to make knowledge accessible to "slow" students may insult their adolescence, just as students who persist with a serious topic may seem to assault the teacher's authority. Hence, lessons and the underlife are intricately intertwined constructions. In them, sociocultural differences—age, academic ability, role, and so forth—are *made* important within the school. Both are situated productions in which teachers use curricular knowledge to accomplish institutionally acknowledged but ambiguous norms of control and education, whereas students, also drawing on the culture, use knowledge to counter control so that they can make the requisite scholastic "effort." The institutionally generated pattern of conflict in which a process of differentiation begins, builds, and rends social relations within a class period is a profound irony, carrying consequences for students' present and future educational careers and for their understanding of how adult members of the culture treat initiates.

Part V
CONCLUSION

CHAPTER 10

Reconsidering Curriculum Differentiation: Patterned Ambiguity

Educational institutions center on, yet are decentered by, paradox. American schools in particular, because they translate a contrapuntal culture preoccupied since its beginnings with membership, differentiation, and the social order, encounter and enact enduring dilemmas. Striving to provide equal educational opportunities by offering standardized courses for all students, U.S. schools are impelled simultaneously to provide differentiated coursework that recognizes each child's unique abilities, interests, and aspirations. The process twists ironically because as schools differentiate, they also integrate, and student groups that are distinguished from others are also defined as themselves. In short, like the American polity, American schools exist within an uneasy tension between equally revered but contradictory precepts of community and individualism. In some circumstances the tension paralyzes, in others it is generative.

These stories from two conventional high schools illustrate the abiding pattern of play in culture and curriculum by telling of its particular evolution in tracked classes in the midwestern, middle-class city of Maplehurst. Furthermore, as recollected here, Maplehurst's stories reframe the issue of curriculum differentiation. Rather than a generalized answer to whether schools should track or whether tracking "works" or is fair, they disclose a series of questions: What does tracking mean to specific individuals who encounter it? *How* does tracking "work" and with what unforeseen as well as purposed consequences? How do curricular and cultural differentiation intertwine to affect private and public experiences of knowledge, self, and other? Such questions pose curriculum planning as an enduring human activity that entails sustained deliberation.

233

THE PREVALENCE, PATTERN,
AND POWER OF CURRICULAR AMBIGUITY

Closely and contextually considered, curricular policies and practices are characterized by ambiguity, not resoluteness. Oscillations in curriculum policy occur because school districts must promote both differentiated and integrated coursework to maintain legitimacy. In Maplehurst, for example, in the 1960s, the school board abolished ability grouping in one stroke and, in the next, initiated Additional Needs classes. Furthermore—and not unlike many other American high schools since Sputnik and *Brown v. the Board of Education*—Maplehurst's schools have expanded specialized tracks to "meet the needs of" gifted, bilingual, pregnant, Advanced Placement, dropout, and handicapped students. However, these differentiated programs coincide with tightened standardization, reinstated "basics," demands for excellence, and a required core curriculum that every educated person should have studied.

Curricular ambiguity is manifested in classroom practice as well as in general guidelines. Thus, in Maplehurst's lower track, lessons both accentuate and assuage teachers' and students' ambivalence about educational encounters. Described ambiguously as "the same" as regular lessons but "easier," more "practical," or "relevant," the lessons draw students in with promises of academic success, but education is often eschewed to maximize order; they require students to respect academic traditions but also anticipate students' indifference; and although teachers sometimes encourage boldness in students' appropriations of subject matter, in the "heavenly" and "disciplined" cultures of Southmoor and Marshall, they are also predisposed to halt even a hint of lower-track "trouble." As a result of these catch-22 conditions, requirements for active engagement, subordination, and insubordination are blurred, and Maplehurst's reasonably skilled and committed Additional Needs students respond to the lower-track curriculum with the confusion and, sometimes, with the hostility or disdain exhibited by disadvantaged students in imperiled schools. Sometimes it makes sense for students to relinquish their own knowledge for the teachers': Then they are "good" and they gain access to unfamiliar disciplines. But they are also occasionally required to use personal knowledge: Then they must work to reinterpret it if it is to connect to abstract school knowledge.

Although characteristic of curriculum differentiation, ambiguity receives little practical or theoretical attention. Mixed data are dismissed or are attributed to inadequate research procedures. Sometimes they are used to avoid contemplation when issues are deemed inveterately complicated. People often resort to the commonsensical dichotomization furnished by the paradoxical culture: They pose curriculum differentiation as a straightforward procedure whose fairness and efficacy (or inequity and inefficacy) can be objectively proven once and for all.

The research presented here offers a third approach: It acknowledges the prevalence of ambiguity but reconceives it to illumine its pattern and its power. Curricular ambiguity is understandable as a manifestation of the broader culture's paradoxical imperatives to differentiate and integrate each and all. Although the imperatives are contradictory and, commonsensically, suggest a choice between opposites, because both are valued they present unremitting dilemmas instead. Therefore, curriculum differentiation manifests a pattern of continuing oscillation.

Moreover, such patterned ambiguity is a source of the power of curriculum differentiation. Ambiguous experiences can be as influential as clearly good (or bad) ones precisely because they resist confident interpretation. Although the notion may appear counterintuitive, people may persist in practices whose effects they do not intend because the effects are equivocal and do not galvanize action. Tracking persists because differentiation and discrimination in schools are subtly, not certainly, associated, and because the practice's mixed normative referents, permutations, and effects confound judgments about its import. The school setting magnifies uncertainty because tasks and roles are not structured to support careful, sustained reflection. As in Maplehurst's lower track, simply surviving high school and getting through the day are often more self-evidently imperative than teaching, curriculum, or education.

In short, conceived as a straightforward choice, curriculum differentiation is misconstrued. As the comparison of tracking at Southmoor and Marshall documents, tracking alone is not the problem. Many variables interact with grouping to affect its meaning and processes. Nor is tracking uniform, even in two high schools that share many objective characteristics. Not all of Maplehurst's regular classes present "high-status knowledge" and not all of its lower-track classes are stigmatizing. Instead, the meaning of tracking depends on how and with what knowledge teachers and students in particular contexts engage. Because curriculum contexts are an intricate nexus of face-to-face interactions, organizational cultures, and sociocultural structures, their impact is not easy to predict.

Accordingly, as the Maplehurst stories illustrate, lower-track classes can be different from regular classes, but they can also be different from each other. Some lower-track classes are chaotic but others are regimented. Some students (more often those at Marshall) find lower-track placement a "good deal"; others (particularly in the conditions that prevail at Southmoor) find it stigmatizing. Similarly, some teachers, particularly those who work in the "no-nonsense" milieu of Marshall, are relieved rather than oppressed by not having to meet the demands of precocious high achievers. But others, particularly in the rarified ethos of Southmoor, are often as estranged as their lower-track students. Evidence from other schools verifies that the meaning of tracking varies with context: Lower-track classes can be caring (Valli, 1990); the lower-track curriculum can be rigorous (Wehlage, et al., 1980); regular-track classes can be as mindlessly controlling as those in the lower track (McNeil, 1986); even placement in "high-status," talented and gifted classes can signify alienation rather than anointment (Metz, 1986).

Thus, tracking is easily a red herring. When oversimplified, it diverts attention from the ubiquity and variety of curriculum differentiation in American schools, from its patterned alternation with integrative processes, and from the perplexing choices and conflict that necessarily surround the allocation of school knowledge. Most importantly, polarized debate precludes the development of what Edelman (1977) calls a "self-consciously tentative" comprehension of the unremitting complexity of the cultural and political imperatives that undergird public institutions. In the long run, polemical discourse demoralizes school participants because it holds out the promise of an easy solution to difficult problems but cannot deliver. Each reform effort—whether to abolish tracking or to refine it—succumbs to defeat, only to be followed by a new but equally simple-to-fix crisis so that, over time, school participants disengage because they have heard it all before. In the process, they lose sight of the common ground that they in fact share and of their efficacy and responsibility as agents with resources that can be used to contribute to the building of humane worlds. Even though the cultural values underlying canonical and individualized curricula are contradictory, Americans cherish both, so that choice of one rather than the other is impossible. When this pattern of irresoluble dilemma is acknowledged, reconsiderations of curriculum theory, practice, and policy follow.

RECONSIDERING THEORY

One of the most frequently posed questions about tracking is whether lower-track classes are different from or similar to regular classes. The question is usually analyzed statistically. For example, various studies set regular- and lower-track classes side by side to measure achievement outcomes, the amount of curriculum covered, time-on-task, or the competence or expectations of teachers. Qualitative studies may also orient to this question and manipulate data in terms of frequency and quantity.

However, statistical analysis that assumes clear-cut differences be-tween regular- and lower-track classes and that necessarily discounts or averages out large chunks of incongruent data miscasts curriculum differen-tiation. As this cultural and curricular analysis elaborates, lower- and regular-track classes are not only different, they are also remarkably sim-ilar; if this were not the case, lower-track classes would not be recognizable as classrooms. Accordingly, the meaning of tracking resides not in empiri-cally demonstrable thresholds of difference or similarity but in the fluctuat-ing play between differences and similarities.

Put another way, interpretive analysis shifts one word in the question about whether tracked classes are different *or* similar to refocus considera-tion on how tracked classes are simultaneously, paradoxically, different *and* similar. This theoretical shift is necessary to do justice to the variability, stability, and subtle power of human meaning-making. Not measurement of discrete, concrete entities but interpretation of relationships between them is the target. The orientation also points to the contingent, multiple effects of tracking. Because schoolroom practices evoke wider institutional and social contexts, some factors set limits on others so that the impact of any one is not readily isolated or predictable.

Hence, lower-track classes can be reconceived very generally as *versions* of a particular school's regular classes, rather than as readily distinguishable phenomena. For example, the three patterns of lower-track curriculum content described in Chapter 8 are versions of long-standing historical patterns characteristic of regular-track curriculum: The skeletal pattern echoes regular-track syllabi that are designed in accord with aca-demic tradition; the skills-based pattern echoes the selection of regular-track knowledge according to principles of efficiency and social control; and the "relevant" content echoes the rationale that undergirds lessons based on principles of child development.

Furthermore, general patterns are locally specified. Because patterns are seldom tidily distributed between high schools so that correlations can be drawn between a particular school culture and a particular curriculum, the patterned variations in curricular allocations are better conveyed meta-phorically. Metaphors establish comparisons that point to meanings that arise in the play, or translation, between regular- and lower-track situa-tions.

Therefore, I conceptualize lower-track classes at Southmoor as *caricatures* of the college-preparatory high school's regular educational encounters, whereas lower-track classes at Marshall are *hyperbolic* versions of the disciplined high school's practical competence. Both metaphors specify a distinctive relationship between a school's regular- and lower-track classes and indicate which version of the many versions that are possible is constructed. Both capture how a school culture can be shared without being uniform, as, for instance, when norms of "professionalism" are evoked by Southmoor teachers but are refracted very differently in the regular and lower tracks.

And both metaphors call attention to the very small or infrequent differences that can nevertheless shift crucially the meaning of what is otherwise a common school structure. Thus, when Mr. Ellison asks what the Japanese named their empire during World War II, his question represents the modal pattern of teacher talk. At first, Additional Needs students acknowledge the teacher's right to ask questions by attempting to answer. However, as Mr. Ellison repeats one question over and over, it ceases to represent legitimate teacher questioning and becomes its parody. Continued further, the questioning eventually insults students who respond by dismissing the teacher and school knowledge as utterly inconsequential. As a caricature of teacher questions, Mr. Ellison's does not have more or less of some feature. Rather, the caricature rearranges, accents, or obscures specific aspects of its referent (legitimate teacher questions) to generate a qualitatively different gestalt. Within that gestalt, the meaning of school knowledge, roles, and academic and social relationships undergo change. Although generated only momentarily or over the brief space of a single class period, such differentiation may establish conditions that promote its recurrence and subsequent magnification. Over time, it may undercut the legitimacy of academic encounters altogether.

That relationships between regular- and lower-track classes are intangible (by definition relations are *between* entities, not measures of the entities themselves) in no way contradicts the powerful or divergent meanings that track placement can have. As Gilbert Ryle suggests (cited by Geertz, 1973, p. 6), the same slight movement of an eyelid may signal a twitch, a wink, a rehearsal of a twitch (or wink), or a parody of either. But, even though all of the meanings correlate with one objective event of eye movement, the differences in meaning are vast—and crucially important if one is trying to respond appropriately. Similarly, curriculum differentiation is heightened because its meaning is multivocal: Students and teachers orient to the irony produced by slight discrepancies between actual and anticipated events, but they are perplexed by their significance because the discrepancies are fleeting and contradictory.

An interpretive analysis also contextualizes curriculum differentiation by moving beyond classroom events to consider their links to the larger organization of the school. One linking medium is classroom talk. Across individual lower-track classes, discourse is patterned without being formulaic. The patterns reflect the structure of tracking as it is shaped by the precepts of membership and differentiation that are acknowledged by members of a school organization.

For example, although amorphous, classroom climate is visible concretely in the mundane details of everyday talk. Teachers in Southmoor's Additional Needs classes direct shifting, ambiguous participation structures, replete with opportunistic turn-taking, unfulfilled disagreements, entertaining games, and one-upmanship. However, the resulting chaos is not a function of disorganized or uninformed teachers who do not know how to direct discussion; nor is it caused by disorderly, unskilled students who do not care to speak properly. Rather, chaotic interchanges are skewed, locally sensible translations of the intellectual "spontaneity," enthusiastic teacher showmanship, and easy camaraderie between teachers and students that are so prized in Southmoor's regular classes. Moreover, by comparison, talk in Marshall's lower-track classrooms echoes different institutionally acknowledged definitions of teacher, student, and knowledge. That is why lower-track teachers there direct participation structures that are invariant, routinized versions of the school's "no-nonsense," "practical," regular-track classes.

Finally, an interpretive analysis traces curriculum beyond classroom and school contexts to communities. The question of the relationship between schools and society dominates much educational research, especially since Coleman's (1966) survey of the importance of differences between schools for cognitive outcomes. Many studies confirm his conclusion that their impact on achievement is slight compared with that of family background. Other scholars refine the question of the difference that schools make by arguing that within-school differentiation through tracking is the crucial determinant of achievement differentials (Alexander & McDill, 1976; Jencks & Brown, 1975; Rosenbaum, 1976). A third group of studies addresses the *interaction* of differences between and within schools (Grant, 1988; Jackson, 1981; Lightfoot, 1983; Metz, 1978, 1986; Swidler, 1979; Wehlage, Stone, & Kliebard, 1980).* Many who pursue this third line of research suggest that academic achievement is not the only, or necessarily the most important, effect that schools have and that schools are sites whose essence is only very inadequately captured in the one-time, averaged snapshots of test scores, library size, career checks, transcript counts, or attitude surveys. Rather, schools provide political and sociocultural as well as scholastic experiences whose import unfolds historically.

---

*Goodlad (1984) and Oakes (1985), among others, also examine the interaction of differences between and within schools, but the characterization of tracking and school differences is statistical, not cultural.

Extending studies in the third group, this account of Maplehurst's schools specifies that the meaning of differentiation arises in a complex interaction between differentiation within a school (through tracking) and differences between schools (through school cultures). Thus, it describes Southmoor's and Marshall's distinctive cultures—"heavenly" at Southmoor and "ordinary" at Marshall. Locating culture in a school's definitions of its students and its faculty, it analyzes the cultures to indicate mechanisms that link them reciprocally with both classrooms and communities.

Thus, first, the culture of a high school reflects (and re-creates) an acknowledged definition of regular students. Broader than academic ability or achievement, faculty *perceptions* include projections of sociocultural characteristics of students and their future social positions, as well as many other characteristics. However, faculty definitions are selective. As Marshall's survey of parents' occupations indicates (Chapter 7), institutional definitions are not necessarily replicative of objectively described facts. Rather, they interpret and thereby determine the facts. Moreover, although "merely" definitional, shared perceptions assume lives of their own: Teachers act on them when they provide the lessons they deem appropriate for regular students whom they perceive to be "upper middle class" and headed for graduate studies and professional careers or students who are "blue collar" and headed for technical school and working class jobs.

At the same time, a school culture is also grounded in a professional or bureaucratic mode of operation (Chapters 5 and 7). Faculty members develop characteristic operating procedures in response to the specific histories and politics of institutions that transcend classroom exigencies. For example, the remote control teaching in Marshall's lower track is understandable, not simply as a negative response to lower-track, lower-class, and, therefore, lower-status clients. Rather, as described in Chapter 7, remote control teaching is a protective response to changes in the organization and the community that increasingly devalue the academic expertise of teachers. Although the teachers say that Marshall's community does not care about education, it may be instead that the community's notion of worthy curriculum differs from that of the academic teachers.

In sum, stories from Maplehurst provide a basis for reconsidering theories of curriculum differentiation. They throw in question the prevailing rationalistic theory that posits tracking as a neutral technique for measuring and matching children's skills and school tasks to promote gains in achievement test scores. At the same time, they do not support the competing revisionist theory that the school order automatically replicates the social order, for instance, by distributing high-status knowledge to high-status students. Instead, as Maplehurst illumines, school knowledge is not neutral; it *is* distributed by social class (and by other sociocultural variables such as age, gender, race, appearance, or academic ability). However, the school distribution does not correspond perfectly or mechanically to the social order: It is mediated in a highly unpredictable fashion by human perceptions of what sociocultural variables mean. Hence, schools *translate* the social order. People in schools enact curriculum differentiation by rendering selected features of the wider social text as they also modify the text creatively to fit particular classroom, school, and community contexts. Because people in the diverse school communities of a pluralistic, paradoxical culture have multifaceted resources on which to draw, they re-create (and are re-created in) highly diverse amalgamations of individualism and community.

RECONSIDERING PRACTICE

When tracking is viewed as a sociocultural and political as well as a scholastic process, one which is constructed as teachers and students in particular institutional contexts negotiate definitions of roles and school knowledge, three issues recur for participants' considered reflection. The issues are normative and local—what Schwab (1969) called practical. They cannot be resolved by direct reference to research, although research may provide illuminating data and helpful concepts. Instead, they require sustained deliberation that includes the people who are most directly involved. Deliberation itself then becomes a fourth issue of concern in regard to curriculum differentiation.

The first issue is the basis for grouping students. In Maplehurst's schools, the formal rationale for track placement is individual academic achievement. However, as we have seen, achievement often seems to operate informally as a proxy for race (Chapter 5), gender (Chapter 3), behavior (Chapter 9), or social class (Chapter 7), raising the specter of discriminatory and unequal rather than individualized educational opportunity. However, even if strictly individualized, placement decisions remain difficult. For instance, using the least biased testing procedures, we would still lack information about how particular children will perform in particular classrooms, about their willingness to engage, or about their compensating but untested abilities. For these reasons, placement decisions are unending: They require continual review.

Queries about the actual processes and effects of tracking follow questions about placement and are equally deserving of on-going consideration. Because we have few naturalistic descriptions of the curriculum-in-use in classrooms, the most fundamental processes remain opaque. How *are* achievement or other, possibly more important, outcomes produced?

What unanticipated or unintended as well as planned outcomes occur? *Which* circumstances influence particular outcomes?

In the absence of such practical curricular knowledge, many unexamined presuppositions about lower-track teaching and curriculum persist, as the stories from Maplehurst illustrate. For example, Maplehurst teachers often speak with assurance about providing "relevant" lower-track lessons or lessons "at the student's level"; they deem such curricula "fair" as well as "necessary." However, the teachers seldom consider calling themselves to account for what "relevance" means or the consequences of "relevant" lessons. Yet, as we have seen, these may include negative, self-fulfilling prophecies if lessons embody influential adults' disparaging assessments of students' present life-styles and future destinations. Even though "relevant" lessons may be taught with positive intentions, if teachers aim at "where the students are at," they risk simply reiterating what students already know rather than enhancing their knowledge. Furthermore, if given a therapeutic cast, "relevant" lessons may invade students' privacy: Like a black hole, they absorb and bring into the public realm of the schoolroom all knowledge domains, even matters that are fundamentally the concern of private individuals. Additional Needs students in Maplehurst often sense the ambiguity, with the ironic result that precisely because the lessons are "personalized," students turn away from engagement with academics.

Other seldom examined but potentially influential processes include the impact of tracking on *teachers* (Chapters 4 and 6). In Maplehurst, for example, teachers' work reciprocates students' about as much as it shapes it (see also Metz, 1978). Because teachers gain some of their status from the students they teach, Maplehurst teachers who work quite competently in regular classes resort to inconsistent or highly routinized methods with their lower-track classes. Similarly, the central importance of school knowledge for classroom dynamics is seldom charted (Chapters 8 and 9). Maplehurst teachers (like many scholars and policymakers) identify grouping, not curriculum and pedagogy, as the key to success with academically unsuccessful students. As a result, they give little explicit attention to the content and form of "adaptive" lessons, with the result that they rarely see the contradictions that arise between educative and controlling purposes.

Finally, the third problem brought to the fore by an interpretive perspective is the relationship between curricular and cultural differentiation. As discussed in the previous section, precepts of individualism and egalitarianism lead us to ask whether particular groups of students are advantaged or disadvantaged by tracking. As Maplehurst's stories suggest, the relationship is more ambiguous and indeterminate than traditional and revisionist curricular theories suggest. Schools mediate between individuals and the wider society, but the mediation is translative, rather than strictly transformative or transmissive.

Intrinsic to the enduring issues of placement, process, and circumstance is a fourth whose importance conventional studies typically overlook: the ways people talk about curriculum differentiation. As this cultural and curricular analysis documents, curriculum differentiation is not only reflected in a vernacular of education; in a fundamental sense, it is constituted in it. Thus, although talk is often deemed an impractical, solipsistic luxury that diverts attention from necessary action, this analysis argues that talk *is* action. What people say to each other in classrooms, schools, and communities both echoes and structures their scholastic and sociocultural relations. Whether talk is explicit or obscure; whether it is undertaken in lessons, faculty lounges, national reports, or research documents; whether people say what they in fact believe or lie; even whether people's words match purported facts: People *use* words to talk into existence relations of difference and membership in scholastic and social orders. The words available to them and the choices that appear sensible signal and reconstitute the webs of culture by which people are simultaneously supported and constrained.

Maplehurst's stories, like stories from other schools, convey facets of the vernacular of education. Some of its metaphors are striking; some are specific to local histories; some constitute a dialect or argot of teaching. But all, for the most part, function axiomatically.

Nevertheless, as Clifford Geertz (1975) argues in a now classic essay, people's utterances, especially their most mundane utterances, deserve systematic analysis. Everyday talk makes up a cultural system of commonsense whose potency is at least as great as traditional manifestations of cultural meaning such as art, religion, totems, or ritual. For example, Maplehurst teachers act on but rarely examine such maxims as "Don't smile 'til Christmas," "Good schools have strong leaders," or "Slow students need structure." Such capsule explanations of complex phenomena justify their truth value by appeals to direct experience or consensus, but, as Geertz explains, they are as arbitrary, ordered, and interpretive as any other cultural form. To explicate the realm of commonsense, Geertz specifies that analyses must seek to explain the "tonalities," style, and marks of attitude that give it its "maddening air of simple wisdom" (pp. 17-18).

Geertz's essay about commonsense resonates with Seymour Sarason's (1971) description of the culture of the school. In schools, according to Sarason, discussions of the most central issues are silenced. Teachers seldom inquire into what is taught, how knowledge is distributed, or how schooling is evaluated because such issues are taken at face value: "Everyone knows" (except fools or unsocialized children and outsiders) that "math is more basic than art" or that "children from good homes have the right attitudes." To question the aphorisms is to contravene the norms of the school. In short, the school institutionalizes a meaning system of common sense and thereby renders its chief principles and activities unmentionable.

However, if voiced, inscribed, and explicated, the vernacular of education can provide important practical information about curriculum differentiation. Teachers can begin to develop portraits of the idiosyncratic cultures within which they work. As the Maplehurst stories exemplify, understanding organizational contexts is a key to making sense of variations in the meaning and classroom enactments of curricular and cultural differentiation. Furthermore, if given the time and freedom to study how they and others talk about schooling, teachers will better understand their own practice. Because everyday school language is the bedrock of school structures, it encodes the pedagogical lore that informs and is intrinsic to teaching and curriculum. Therefore, exposing the lore unveils many unspoken but powerful assumptions, ideologies, values, and purposes.

Maplehurst's stories allow us to imagine some of the curricular information that teachers there might uncover if they could attend seriously to school language. For example, some words of the vernacular jump out and beg for attention. Thus, when a teacher characterized Marshall as a "nothing-out-of-the-ordinary" school, I was struck by the metaphor's evocations. It prompted me to heed other teachers' different phrases, which nevertheless conveyed a similar figure. Taken together, the phrases connoted a constellation of loosely associated domains of the high school: run-of-the-mill students, remote control teaching, "practical" knowledge, and the real-world, "concrete" purposes of the school. In other words, the metaphor was like a thread, or a theory (Kliebard, 1982), that made divergent notions and domains of the organization coherent without homogenizing them.

Furthermore, I began to see that teachers enact the metaphors. They brought pedestrianism to life and made it consequential when they taught perfunctorily, emphasized "a tradition of discipline," and denied impractical "belief" in the possibility of academic excellence with "your typical blue-collar kids." Students often imbibed the metaphor, discrediting intellectual or idealistic activities because they were not "businesslike" or "worth the cost"; they responded most comfortably to school knowledge comprised of self-evidently "basic" skills and facts, which, like currency, were valuable primarily as they could be exchanged in the marketplace. The metaphor also grounded some faculty members' succinct explanation of Marshall's low-key relationship to its community: The school gave the "blue-collar" community the "no-nonsense" education it wanted, even when members did not value basic skills.

Metaphors also call attention to connections between educational institutions and other human activities. In this regard, they provide a means of exploring the wider cultural landscape in which schools serve distinctive, limited functions. For example, Marshall's pedestrianism conjoins mental and manual processes. Thinking is no more mysterious than body-building, classrooms are gymnasiums, and students work out with "exercises" at the end of the chapter to strengthen their minds just as they might work out to build up their muscles. The metaphor also resonates with economics: Marshall participants speak of the "practical" lessons in time and training which will "pay off" in the world of work; the school organizes a "consumer economy" in which students can choose any track of courses they want. Connections spill over further into psychosociological domains when teachers present lower-track students a "relevant" rather than a uselessly "abstract" curriculum: like therapy, the lessons will efficiently "adjust" students to the "middle-class Marshall classroom."

In short, teachers can study the vernacular of education to divine the distinctive meaning systems, or cultures, of individual schools. Defining metaphors indicate their idiosyncratic, quasi-bounded arena and their congruent although not necessarily uniform practices and symbols. Defining metaphors also furnish a means of comparing schools and to better comprehend the value of their diversity. For example, Marshall's pedestrianism contrasts sharply with the "perfect" education that teachers mention in describing Southmoor. Finally, defining metaphors allow exploration of what schools are for. By sketching their relationship to other realms of human activity such as the marketplace, teachers can more adequately assess the limits and possibility of schooling.

The vernacular of education is also comprised of less spectacular metaphors than "nothing-out-of-the-ordinary" or "heavenly." For example, banal words such as *ability, effort, individualized, practical,* or *bookish* are nevertheless remarkable by virtue of the regularity with which they punctuate school participants' talk. Although taken for granted and, indeed, not even seen as metaphorical, such words bear examination as much as more startling figures of speech.

For example, when teachers use the terms *ability* and *effort,* they set up a pedagogically and culturally salient structure of opposition between the intellectual and the social, or between the academic and the behavioral. Teachers who speak of "ability" often refer to students' inherent talent. "Ability" is synonymous with IQ or native intelligence. By contrast, teachers regard "effort" as a volitional, attitudinal phenomenon: students' willingness to "try." In U.S. schools, students with little "ability" may nevertheless succeed in school if they "try."

However, the structure implied in the opposition between "ability" and "effort" is multidimensional rather than bivalent because both of the key terms connote different meanings in different contexts. Thus, at Southmoor, students demonstrate "effort" when they participate in opportunistic turn-taking in chaotic recitations, but, at Marshall, "effort" often involves working silently, compliantly, and individually on routinized worksheets.

Furthermore, teachers mean more than one thing by each of the terms. They may confound "ability" and achievement so that the "ability" to read indicates the performance of reading, not the capacity or the potential to learn to read. Particularly for Southmoor teachers, low "ability" may signal students' fundamental unteachability. Compared with regular students, Additional Needs students are so much the "basic bottom" that they cannot be taught.

"Effort" is as multivocal as "ability." Thus, at Marshall, "trying" is as crucial a determinant of school success as "ability" is at Southmoor. Teachers exhort students to "try" because all, regardless of "ability," can "try" if they only will. However, "trying" at the "disciplined" high school can also function as a slogan for compliance and social control. Moreover, making an "effort" is not limited to students: The school also "tries," chiefly by providing the differentiated, "low-low" courses that correspond to students' levels of "ability."

Other terms, as common as *ability* and *effort*, also recur with varying connotations and denotations. For example, many school participants justify curriculum differentiation as a means of providing for "individualized" instruction. However, the curriculum that results often resembles markedly the traditional school curriculum; lower-track worksheets are referred to as "individualized," but all members of a class work through the same batch. Thus, "individualized" programs may be much less differentiated than the vernacular of education implies. Because "individualization" is used commonsensically, it glosses a variety of practices, only some of which are positively enacted.

"Practical" and "bookish" knowledge embody similar ambiguity. At Southmoor, classically academic knowledge is considered "high status." Traditional topics, "spontaneous" assignments, and a "heavenly" atmosphere characterize Advanced Placement, gifted, and regular-track classes. Academics are valued to such an extent that they infuse lower-track lessons as well, particularly in the skeletal pattern of content differentiation. By contrast, at Marshall, worthy knowledge is instrumental and regular- and high-track classes are less prestigious than Southmoor's. Indeed, in many respects, Marshall's regular-track curriculum resembles that which other schools offer to working class, lower-track students: Regular students memorize facts; learn basic academic skills; apply formulae for writing essays, interpreting literary themes, or developing "thinking strategies"; use an abundance of individualized worksheets; and follow rules and routines. By contrast, Southmoor's lower-track classes sometimes offer students elements of a more abstract, elitist, "high status" curriculum as, for example, when Mr. Robinson asks students to interpret the "real" message of a sophisticated film about immigration. Such examples suggest the intricacy and imprecision of talk about curriculum differentiation. They challenge more easily remembered but misleading formulae such as the assumption that lower-track classes correspond necessarily to "lower status knowledge," lower teacher expectations, or lower-class students.

In sum, the vernacular of education is not privileged. Attention to it is not warranted because of its truth value (although teacher knowledge is certainly a languishing resource in most studies of curriculum, development projects, and policy mandates). Nor is it warranted so that teachers can be dealt with "on their level" (although "communicating with teachers" is often reduced to speaking the commonsensical argot). Rather, the vernacular of education deserves recording because words are ephemeral cultural artifacts that people use to accomplish a number of tasks but whose significance can only be clarified if they are written down. However, the vernacular can not only be voiced and inscribed; it must also be held up for reflection, criticism, and interpretation. Acknowledging differentiating practices and discussing them seriously, rather than denying, oversimplifying, or rendering them commonsensical, are crucial: By tracing the twists and turns of everyday discourse, teachers can think about the complex subtleties of their work and about the power of language to shape as well as to reflect curricular practice. Indeed, if this analysis is correct, the most practical tracking reform might be one in which teachers systematically collect and analyze the talk in classrooms and corridors.

RECONSIDERING POLICY

The chief policy question in regard to curriculum differentiation is not simply what shall policy be, but who shall make it. The preponderant answer in regard to agency is: those farthest from the classrooms and schools. (Although restructuring promises to increase teacher and parent prerogatives, it does not necessarily extend them to issues of curriculum differentiation.) This response shapes the substance of policy so that of late, curriculum policy assumes a grand scale. Pronouncements abound about *the* lower track, *the* Western canon, and *the* American high school. Such pronouncements suggest both that tracks, valued knowledge, and high schools are the same and, politically, that issues of equity and excellence demand that they should be.

The stories from Maplehurst may seem to corroborate the policy conclusion that tracking should be ended in U.S. high schools. After all, at both Marshall and Southmoor, lower-track classes exhibit processes that subvert the potential of veteran teachers, reasonably committed students, and thoughtfully planned, "adaptive" school lessons.

However, to draw such a conclusion from these stories is a misinterpretation. First, the data are not statistically generalizable; evidence from two schools, not chosen randomly, cannot be extrapolated to other settings as proof that tracking is bad in general. Even to add them together with other interpretive studies in a sort of metaanalysis is methodologically unsound. Second, the value of these detailed, contextualized accounts is that they illustrate how people make tracking, rather than how tracking makes them. Therefore, Maplehurst's translations remind that the global profundities of school policy—Equality, Secondary Education, Tracking, Curriculum—occur only in concrete instances. To think about and act meaningfully in regard to curriculum differentiation requires consideration of its local, variable enactments. As Joseph Schwab (1969) described the matter:

> The curriculum [is] brought to bear not in some archetypical classroom but in a particular locus in time and space with smells, shadows, seats, and conditions outside its walls which may have much to do with what is achieved inside. Generalities [about curriculum, students, teachers, schooling] may be true. But they attain this status in virtue of what they leave out, and the omissions affect what remains. A Guernsey cow is not only something more than a cow, having specific features omitted from description of the genus; it is also cowy in ways differing from the cowiness of a Texas longhorn. The specific not only adds to the generic; it also modulates it. (p. 33)

Thus, although U.S. classrooms and schools are remarkably similar in many respects, their equally remarkable idiosyncrasies are not simply quaintly human details that flesh out the stable, determinative structures of schooling; they "modulate" them so that formally similar roles, statuses, and processes take on different meaning in different circumstances. Adequate policies must take such diversity into account. The unit of analysis for policymakers intent on curriculum differentiation should be the local school and its classrooms, and the unit of action should be the promotion of serious, sustained deliberation within school-communities.

For example, Additional Needs students at Marshall and Southmoor encounter and bring to school many similar ideas, skills, and advantages. Moreover, lower-track classes at both high schools leave a great deal to be desired. Nevertheless, to be a lower-track student at Southmoor is a very different reality from being a lower-track student at Marshall. Southmoor students suffer considerable stigma and drop out at a much higher than expected rate (although some also feel a decidedly personal attachment to teachers and many participate vigorously in lessons which offer considerable intellectual substance). By contrast, Marshall students see lower-track placement as a smart "con" of the "system" and engage in lessons with aggressive passivity (although some also acquire satisfaction in the daily regimen of worksheets and appreciate the protection from public failure that such a curriculum sponsors). Such different realities for students (along with reciprocal differences for teachers, curricula, and the purposes of the schools) matter for adequate curriculum policy.

Accordingly, present, large-scale, curriculum struggles are misguided, whether they seek to expand tracking in ever more specialized refinements or to abolish it and mainstream lower-track students in cooperative or mastery learning classrooms. On the one hand, because they simplify curricular processes, such policies overestimate the effects curriculum can produce. As Keddie (1971) put it, regardless of whether A-stream (high-track) classes are "high status" or not, abolishing tracking in schools will not abolish social differentiation:

> It seems likely that the hierarchical categories of ability and knowledge may well persist in unstreamed classrooms and lead to the differentiation of undifferentiated curricula, because teachers differentiate in selection of content and in pedagogy between pupils perceived as high and low ability. The origins of these categories are likely to lie outside the school and within the structure of the society itself in its wider distribution of power. (p. 156)

On the other hand, and even more seriously, simplistic, polarized debate about tracking diverts attention from the critical institutional determinants of scholastic experiences in all tracks: curriculum and pedagogy. When the debate fosters policy mandates that limit the professional prerogatives of educators, they result in unintended consequences that strike at the heart of schooling. Imagine the possible effects at Southmoor of a directive from the district office or the State Department of Public Instruction to end tracking: Experienced, scholarly experts might feel deprofessionalized, they might teach with increased detachment, and that in turn might distance less able students further from schooling. At Marshall, detracking might well raise the dropout rate and undermine the legitimacy of the school. These comments are not intended as an apology for tracking in general or at either Maplehurst high school. Rather, they reiterate Seymour Sarason's conclusions about school change: If we want to do something about school practice, we have to first understand what it is; then we must deliberate together to ascertain correctly what we want.

A fundamental error in broad policy mandates is their failure to acknowledge the simultaneity of differentiation and integration processes, particularly in a paradoxical culture. Instead, the prevailing assumption is that difference necessarily signals inequality and that asymmetry is synonymous with hierarchy. However, individual differences are a fundamental value in American culture. Differences bear respect because they enrich us and are central to our beliefs about what it is to be human. Respect for differences forms the rationale, not only for ability grouping and tracking, but for other forms of curriculum differentiation, including Advanced Placement, gifted, bilingual, and special education, as well as black history, gender studies, or cultural studies. Critics of tracking rarely argue for doing away with these levels of differentiation. But what makes these manifestations of curriculum differentiation justifiable if tracking is not?

Finally, policymakers reduce curriculum issues even further by their reliance on standardized, quantified outcomes—invariably the testing of student achievement—as the key measure of excellence and equity in schools. Classroom and school processes receive little consideration in evaluations. Yet, as this cultural and curricular analysis documents, processes *are* products: Students' and teachers' daily experiences with each other and with knowledge, although they are so mundane as to be overlooked (and certainly costly to study), are outcomes at least as meaningful for participants and the polity as test scores. They are also more valid indicators of *education* than student learning. In Maplehurst, students at Southmoor and Marshall score quite similarly on achievement tests but their experiences of schooling, self, adults, peers, and place diverge markedly. Even in the brief space of a single class period, processes of differentiation can occur; these may accumulate in abject alienation, fiery resistance, or, most often in Maplehurst's schools, in an ambivalence that allows schooling to continue but with little serious engagement among the participants.

If not broad mandates designed to ensure high and equitable standards, what more modest (and potentially more humane) curriculum policies might policymakers consider? First, as Dell Hymes (1980) has proposed, policymakers might provide structured support for an archive of case studies of schools, on a scale similar to that for the collection of statistical data which is a commonplace of policy today (although when

William Torrey Harris suggested it around the turn of the century, the idea was radical). Such a project hinges on taking seriously the significance of the idiosyncrasies of individual school contexts as necessary to untangling the unremitting contradictions in standard studies of student achievement, effective teaching, curriculum patterns, and school effects. Moreover, detailed ethnographies would provide the data and concepts with which to begin a comparative ethnology of education, in which different types of schools might be identified and the functions of schools in relation to other educative agencies might be clarified. Such fundamental understanding is crucial when so much is expected of public education, but a crisis in support is recurrent and growing. Defining metaphors—the specific words that people use to capture the gestalt of a school and its relationship to the wider community—may provide a fluid classificatory system for such a typology.

Second, policymakers might support the practical design of curriculum. In some cases, the paradoxes of U.S. culture are creatively resolved, at least momentarily, as teachers respond imaginatively to both student differences and their curricular implications: They "restore (academic) knowledge which appears at first to be so remote and obscure back to its origins in human experience" (Kliebard, 1977a, discussing Dewey's curriculum theory). For example, Heath (1982) worked with first-grade teachers who were puzzled by the disproportionate failure of black children in their classes: Students seemed unable to answer even the simplest recall questions, although they were clearly not mentally handicapped. First, Heath used her expertise as an anthropologist to study and compare the types of questions black children were asked at home and in school. Then, with the teachers, she designed curriculum materials that were culturally congruent, that is, materials that took into account the questions the black children competently fielded at home and the topics they knew about from their home environments. Gradually, as the black children became successful and comfortable in the classroom, teachers used home questions and topics to bridge to school questions and topics. At the same time, white children could use the black curriculum materials to expand their own repertoires of question asking. In short, Heath and the teachers acknowledged differences between students. However, instead of interpreting them as problems that required remediation to a univocal school standard or, alternatively, as evidence that black children can only succeed with and deserve a separate, black curriculum, they interpreted differences as enrichments. The culturally congruent curriculum was not reserved for the "special" or "different": It enriched the language and lives of all classroom participants.

Finally, if determination of the knowledge worth teaching is an enduring human responsibility rather than an easily solved, technical puzzle

(Kliebard, 1977b), then policy should sustain rather than prematurely close serious curricular deliberations. Rather than calls for consensus, discussion is important because, as the Maplehurst stories illustrate, curriculum differentiation is constituted in talk. Moreover, where discourse is circumscribed by commonsensical platitudes or by peremptory regulation so that diverse perspectives and negotiation are unacknowledged, unintended consequences result. Thus, insistence on universal standards, no matter how noble the intentions of the standard bearers, will ignore different estimates of worthy knowledge. Then, schools cease to be public institutions (Greene, 1985): Silent schools fail to center the distinctive, civil speech and hearing of individuals through which all may come in touch with a rich, common humanity and, thereby, each with his and her own uniqueness. Even though, in a large, complex, efficiency-driven society, sustained deliberation in which we talk and listen to each other is difficult and expensive, it is crucial to both understanding and practicing humane education.

Tracking is a cultural lightning rod. The persistent oscillations in the research literature, the polemical rhetoric of policy, and the pervasive, ambivalent, and too frequently negative versions of curriculum indicate that the issue grounds serious, complicated struggles over who we are and how we will live together. Our responses to it must be correspondingly serious. Therefore, to ask whether schools should (or should not) differentiate curriculum is the wrong question and to look to research results for unassailable direction is a misguided expectation. To argue universal policies and standards is to disregard multivocal humanity, the mediating influence of schools, and our prerogatives and responsibilities as persons who make meaningful choices. Instead, curriculum differentiation, as a scholastic, sociocultural, and political process, deserves serious, sustained, "self-consciously tentative" deliberation. Through discourse together, we may comprehend the spectacular diversity of American culture, critique the conditions that all too frequently constrain its manifestations in schools (for all students and teachers, but all too often particularly for those who are lower track or lower status), and act to value it as an affirmation of the distinctive humanity of each and all of us.

References

Agar, M. (1986). *Speaking of ethnography*. Beverly Hills, CA: Sage.

Alexander, K. L., & McDill, E. L. (1976). Selection and allocation within schools: Some causes and consequences of curriculum placement. *American Sociological Review, 41*, 963–980.

Amidon, E., & Hunter, E. (1966). *Improving teaching: The analysis of classroom verbal interaction*. New York: Holt, Rinehart and Winston.

Apple, M. (1979). *Ideology and curriculum*. London: Routledge and Kegan Paul.

Apple, M. (1983). Curriculum reform and the logic of technical control. In M. Apple and L. Weis (Eds.), *Ideology and Practice in Schooling* (pp. 143–166). Philadelphia: Temple University Press.

Au, K. (1980). Participation structures in a reading lesson with Hawaiian children: Analysis of a culturally appropriate instructional event. *Anthropology and Education Quarterly, 11*, 91–115.

Ball, S. J. (1981). *Beachside comprehensive: A case-study of secondary schooling*. Cambridge, England: Cambridge University Press.

Barr, R., & Dreeben, R. (1983). *How schools work*. Chicago: University of Chicago Press.

Bateson, G. (1972). *Steps to an ecology of mind*. New York: Ballantine.

Battistoni, R. (1985). *Public schooling and the education of democratic citizens*. Jackson: University of Mississippi Press.

Bellack, A. (1978). *Competing ideologies in research on teaching*. Uppsala, Sweden: Department of Education, Uppsala University.

Bellack, A., Kliebard, H., Hyman, R., & Smith, F., Jr. (1966). *The language of the classroom*. New York: Teachers College Press.

Bellah, R., Madsen, R., Sullivan, W., Swidler, A., & Tipton, S. (1985). *Habits of the heart: Individualism and commitment in American life*. New York: Harper & Row.

Benjamin, W. (1969). The task of the translator (H. Zohn, Trans.). In H. Arendt (Ed.), *Illuminations* (pp. 69–82). New York: Schocken Books. (Original work published 1923)

Bernstein, R. (1983). *Beyond objectivism and relativism: Science, hermeneutics, and praxis*. Philadelphia: University of Philadelphia Press.

Bloom, B. (1981). *All our children learning*. New York: McGraw-Hill.

Bloom, B., Hastings, J., & Madaus, G. (1971). *Handbook on formative and summative evaluation of student learning*. New York: McGraw-Hill.

Bowles, S., & Gintis, H. (1976). *Schooling in capitalist America: Educational reform and the contradictions of economic life.* New York: Basic Books.

Boyer, E. L. (1983). *High school: A report on secondary education.* New York: Harper & Row.

Brann, E. (1979). *Paradoxes of education in a republic.* Chicago: The University of Chicago Press.

Bruner, J. (1977). *The process of education* (2nd ed.). Cambridge, MA: Harvard University Press.

Cazden, C. (1986). Classroom discourse. In M. C. Wittrock (Ed.), *Handbook of research on teaching* (3rd ed., pp. 432–463). New York: Macmillan.

Cazden, C. (1988). *Classroom discourse: The language of teaching and learning.* Portsmouth, NH: Heinemann Educational Books.

Chomsky, N. (1965). *Aspects of the theory of syntax.* Cambridge: Massachusetts Institute of Technology Press.

Clark, B. (1972). The organizational saga in higher education. *Administrative Science Quarterly, 17,* 178–184.

Clement, D., Eisenhart, M., & Harding, J. (1979). The veneer of harmony: Social-race relations in a southern desegregated school. In R. Rist (Ed.), *Desegregated schools: Appraisals of an American experiment* (pp. 15–64). New York: Academic Press.

Clifford, J., & Marcus, G. (1986). *Writing culture: The poetics and politics of ethnography.* Berkeley, CA: University of California Press.

Cohen, D. (1985). Origins. In A. Powell, E. Farrar, & D. Cohen, *The shopping mall high school: Winners and losers in the educational marketplace* (pp. 233–308). Boston: Houghton Mifflin.

Coleman, J. (1961). *The adolescent society: The social life of the teenager and its impact on education.* New York: Free Press.

Coleman, J. (1966). *Equality of educational opportunity.* Washington, DC: U.S. Department of Health, Education, and Welfare.

Cusick, P. (1973). *Inside high school: The student's world.* New York: Holt, Rinehart and Winston.

Cusick, P. (1983). *The egalitarian ideal and the American high school: Studies of three schools.* New York: Longman.

Dewey, J. (1929). Individuality, equality, and superiority. In J. Ratner (Ed.), *Characters and events* (Vol. 2, pp. 486–492). New York: Holt and Co. (Reprinted from *The New Republic,* Dec. 13, 1922)

Dillon, J. (1988). *Questioning and teaching: A manual of practice.* New York: Teachers College Press.

Douglas, M., & Wildavsky, A. (1982). *Risk and culture.* Berkeley: University of California Press.

Edelman, M. (1977). *Political language: Words that succeed and policies that fail.* New York: Academic Press.

Edwards, A. D. (1978). The "language of history" and the communication of historical knowledge. In A. K. Dickinson & P. J. Lee (Eds.), *History teaching and historical understanding* (pp. 54–71). London: Heinemann Educational Books.

Edwards, A. D., & Furlong, V. (1978). *The language of teaching*. London: Heinemann Educational Books.

Erickson, F. (1982). Classroom discourse as improvisation: Relations between academic task structures and social participation structures in lessons. In L. C. Wilkinson (Ed.), *Communication in the classroom* (pp. 153-181). New York: Academic Press.

Erickson, F. (1984). School literacy, reasoning, and civility: An anthropologist's perspective. *Review of Educational Research, 54*, 525-546.

Erickson, F. (1986). Qualitative methods in research on teaching. In M. Wittrock (Ed.), *Handbook of research on teaching* (3rd ed., pp. 119-161). New York: Macmillan.

Erickson, F., & Schultz, J. (1982). *The counselor as gatekeeper: Social interaction in interviews*. New York: Academic Press.

Feldman, M., & Seifman, E. (Eds.). (1969). *The social studies: Structure, models, and strategies*. Englewood Cliffs, NJ: Prentice Hall.

Finley, M. (1984). Teachers and tracking in a comprehensive high school. *Sociology of Education, 57*, 233-243.

Finn, C. (1989). National standards: A plan for consensus. *Teachers College Record, 90*, 3-9.

Fish, S. (1980). *Is there a text in this class? The authority of interpretive communities*. Cambridge, MA: Harvard University Press.

Frankel, R. M. (1982). From sentence to sequences: Understanding the medical encounter through micro-interactional analysis. *Discourse Processes, 6*, 36-72.

Furlong, V. (1977). Anancy goes to school: A case study of pupils' knowledge of their teachers. In P. Woods & M. Hammersley (Eds.), *School experience: Explorations in the sociology of education* (pp. 162-185). London: Croom Helm.

Gamoran, A. (1989). Measuring curriculum differentiation. *American Journal of Education, 97*, 129-143.

Gamoran, A., & Berends, M. (1987). The effects of stratification in secondary schools: Synthesis of survey and ethnographic research. *Review of Educational Research, 57*, 415-435.

Garfinkel, H. (1967). *Studies in Ethnomethodology*. Englewood Cliffs, NJ: Prentice Hall.

Geertz, C. (1973). *The interpretation of cultures: Selected essays*. New York: Basic Books.

Geertz, C. (1983). Common sense as a cultural system. In C. Geertz, *Local knowledge: Further essays in interpretive anthropology* (pp. 73-93). New York: Basic Books.

Geertz, C. (1986). *Works and lives: The anthropologist as author*. Stanford, CA: Stanford University Press.

Goffman, E. (1961). *Encounters: Two studies in the sociology of interaction*. Indianapolis: Bobbs-Merrill.

Goldberg, M., Passow, A. H., & Justman, J. (1966). *The effects of ability grouping*. New York: Teachers College Press.

Goldstein, B. (1990). Refugee students' perceptions of curriculum differentiation. In R. Page & L. Valli (Eds.), *Curriculum differentiation: Interpretive studies in U.S. secondary schools* (pp. 137-158). Albany: State University of New York Press.

Goodlad, J. (1984). *A place called school: Prospects for the future.* New York: McGraw-Hill.

Grant, G. (1986). *The world we created at Hamilton High.* Cambridge, MA: Harvard University Press.

Greene, M. (1985). Public education and the public space. *The Kettering Review,* pp. 55-60.

Hargreaves, D. (1967). *Social relations in a secondary school.* London: Routledge and Kegan Paul.

Hargreaves, D., Hester, D., & Mellor, F. (1975). *Deviance in classrooms.* London: Routledge and Kegan Paul.

Heath, S. (1982). Questioning at home and at school: A comparative study. In G. Spindler (Ed.), *Doing the ethnography of schooling: Educational anthropology in action* (pp. 103-127). New York: Holt, Rinehart & Winston.

Heath, S., & Branscombe, A. (1985). Intelligent writing in an audience community: Teacher, students and researcher. In S. Freedman (Ed.), *The acquisition of written language: Response and revision* (pp. 3-32). Norwood, NJ: Ablex.

Henry, J. (1963). *Culture against man.* New York: Random House.

Hirsch, E. D. (1987). *Cultural literacy: What every American needs to know.* Boston: Houghton Mifflin.

Hymes, D. (1980). Educational ethnology. In D. Hymes, *Language in Education* (pp. 119-125). Washington, DC: Center for Applied Linguistics.

Hymes, D. (1982). What is ethnography? In P. Gilmore & A. Glatthorn (Eds.), *Children in and out of school: Ethnography and education* (pp. 21-32). Washington, DC: Center for Applied Linguistics.

Jackson, P. (1968). *Life in classrooms.* New York: Holt, Rinehart & Winston.

Jackson, P. (1981). Comprehending a well-run comprehensive: A report on a visit to a large suburban high school. *Daedalus, 110,* 81-96.

Jacob, E., & Jordan, C. (Eds.). (1987). Explaining the school performance of minority students [Special issue]. *Anthropology and Education Quarterly, 18.*

Jelinek, M., Smircich, L., & Hirsch, P. (Eds.). (1983). Organizational culture [Special issue]. *Administrative Science Quarterly, 28.*

Jencks, C., with Smith, M., Acland, H., Bane, M., Cohen, D., Gintis, H., Heyns, B., & Michelson, S. (1973). *Inequality: A reassessment of the effects of family and schooling in America.* New York: Harper & Row.

Jencks, C., & Brown, M. (1975). The effects of high schools on their students. *Harvard Educational Review, 45,* 273-324.

Joffe, C. (1977). *Friendly intruders: Childcare professionals and family life.* Berkeley: University of California Press.

Kammen, M. (1974). *People of paradox: An inquiry concerning the origins of American civilization.* New York: A. Knopf.

Keddie, N. (1971). Classroom knowledge. In M. F. D. Young (Ed.), *Knowledge and control: New directions for the sociology of education* (pp. 133-150). London: Collier-Macmillan.

Kett, J. (1977). *Rites of passage: Adolescence in America, 1790 to the present.* New York: Basic Books.

Kliebard, H. (1977a). Bureaucracy and curriculum theory. In A. Bellack & H. Kliebard (Eds.), *Curriculum and evaluation* (pp. 608-626). Berkeley, CA: McCutchan.

Kliebard, H. (1977b). Curriculum theory: Give me a "for instance." *Curriculum Inquiry, 6,* 257-276.

Kliebard, H. (1982). Curriculum theory as metaphor. *Theory into Practice, 21,* 11-17.

Kliebard, H. (1986). *The struggle for the American curriculum: 1893-1958.* London: Routledge and Kegan Paul.

Kliebard, H. (1988). The liberal arts curriculum and its enemies: The effort to redefine general education. In I. Westbury & A. Purves (Eds.), *The eighty-seventh yearbook of the national society for the study of education: Part II. Cultural literacy and the idea of general education* (pp. 29-51). Chicago: University of Chicago Press.

Krug, E. A. (1960). *The secondary school curriculum.* New York: Harper & Brothers.

Kulik, C., & Kulik, J. (1982). Effects of ability grouping on secondary school students: A meta-analysis of evaluation findings. *American Educational Research Journal, 19,* 415-428.

Labaree, D. (1987). Politics, markets, and the compromised curriculum. *Harvard Educational Review, 57,* 483-494.

Labov, W. (1970). *The study of nonstandard English.* Champaign, IL: National Council of Teachers of English.

Lacey, C. (1970). *Hightown grammar: The school as a social system.* Manchester, England: Manchester University Press.

Leacock, E. (1969). *Teaching and learning in city schools: A comparative study.* New York: Basic Books.

Lesko, N. (1990). Curriculum differentiation as social redemption: The case of school-aged mothers. In R. Page and L. Valli (Eds.), *Curriculum differentiation: Interpretive studies in U.S. secondary schools* (pp. 113-136). Albany: State University of New York Press.

Lightfoot, S. (1983). *The good high school: Portraits of character and culture.* New York: Basic Books.

McClosky, R. (1971). The American ideology. In M. Kammen (Ed.), *The contrapuntal civilization: Essays toward a new understanding of the American experience* (pp. 36-57). New York: Crowell.

McDermott, R., & Aron, J. (1978). Pirandello in the classroom: On the possibility of equal educational opportunity in American culture. In M. Reynolds (Ed.), *Futures of education for exceptional children: Emerging structures* (pp. 41-64). Minneapolis: National Support Systems Project.

McNeil, L. (1986). *Contradictions of control: School structure and school knowledge.* London: Routledge and Kegan Paul.

Mehan, H. (1979). *Learning lessons: Social organization in the classroom.* Cambridge, MA: Harvard University Press.

Merelman, R. (1984). *Making something of ourselves: On culture and politics in the United States.* Berkeley: University of California Press.

Metz, M. (1978). *Classrooms and corridors: The crisis of authority in desegregated secondary schools.* Berkeley: University of California Press.

Metz, M. (1986). *Different by design: The context and character of three magnet schools.* London: Routledge and Kegan Paul.

Meyer, J. (1986). Types of explanation in the sociology of education. In J. Richardson (Ed.), *Handbook of theory and research for the sociology of education,* pp. 341-359. New York: Greenwood Press.

Meyer, J., & Rowan, B. (1978). The structure of educational organizations. In M. Meyer (Ed.), *Environments and organizations* (pp. 233-263). San Francisco: Jossey-Bass.

Miller, J. H. (1979). The function of rhetorical study at the present time. *Bulletin of the Association of Departments of English, 62,* 10-18.

National Commission on Excellence in Education. (1983). *A nation at risk: The imperative for educational reform.* Washington, DC: Government Printing Office.

Oakes, J. (1985). *Keeping track: How schools structure inequality.* New Haven, CT: Yale University Press.

Oakes, J. (1990). *Multiplying inequalities: The effects of race, social class, and tracking on opportunities to learn math and science.* Santa Monica, CA: The RAND Corporation.

Oakes, J., Gamoran, A., & Page, R. (in press). Curriculum differentiation: Opportunities, outcomes, and meanings. In P. Jackson (Ed.), *Handbook of research on curriculum.* New York: Macmillan.

Ogbu, J. (1978). *Minority education and caste: The American system in cross-cultural perspective.* New York: Academic Press.

Page, R., & Valli, L. (Eds.). (1990). *Curriculum differentiation: Interpretive studies in U.S. secondary schools.* Albany: State University of New York Press.

Passow, A. H. (1988). Issues of access to knowledge: Grouping and tracking. In L. Tanner (Ed.), *The eighty-seventh yearbook of the national society for the study of education: Part I. Critical issues in curriculum* (pp. 205-225). Chicago: University of Chicago Press.

Perin, C. (1977). *Everything in its place: Social order and land use in America.* Princeton, NJ: Princeton University Press.

Philips, S. (1983). *The invisible culture: Communication in classroom and community on the Warm Springs Indian Reservation.* New York: Longman.

Pomerantz, A. (1978). Compliment responses: Notes on the cooperation of multiple restraints. In J. Schenkein (Ed.), *Studies in the organization of conversational interaction* (pp. 79-112). New York: Academic Press.

Powell, A., Farrar, E., & Cohen, D. (1985). *The shopping mall high school: Winners and losers in the education market place.* Boston: Houghton Mifflin.

Riesman, D., with Glazer, N., & Denney, R. (1950). *The lonely crowd: A study of the changing American character.* New Haven, CT: Yale University Press.

Rist, R. (1973). *The urban school: A factory for failure.* Cambridge: Massachusetts Institute of Technology Press.

Rist, R. (1977). On understanding the processes of schooling: The contributions of labeling theory. In J. Karabel and A. H. Halsey (Eds.), *Power and ideology in education* (pp. 292-305). New York: Oxford University Press.

Rist, R. (Ed.). (1979). *Desegregated schools: Appraisals of an American experience.* New York: Academic Press.

Rosenbaum, J. (1976). *Making inequality: The hidden curriculum of high school tracking.* New York: John Wiley.

Rosenthal, R., & Jacobsen, L. (1968). *Pygmalion in the classroom: Teacher expectation and pupils' intellectual development.* New York: Holt, Rinehart & Winston.

Ryan, K. (Ed.). (1970). *Don't smile until Christmas: Accounts of the first year of teaching.* Chicago: University of Chicago Press.

Ryle, G. (1949). *The concept of mind.* London: Hutchinson.

Sacks, H. (1972). An investigation of the usability of conversational data for doing sociology. In D. Sudnow (Ed.), *Studies in social interaction* (pp. 31-74). New York: Free Press.

Sarason, S. (1971). *The culture of the school and the problem of change.* Boston: Allyn & Bacon.

Schegloff, E., Jefferson, G., & Sacks, H. (1977). A preference for self-correction in the organization of repair in conversation. *Language, 53,* 361-382.

Schlechty, P. (1976). *Teaching and social behavior: Towards an organizational theory of instruction.* Boston: Allyn & Bacon.

Schneider, D. (1968). *American kinship: A cultural account.* Englewood Cliffs, NJ: Prentice-Hall.

Schön, D. (1983). *The reflective practitioner: How professionals think in action.* New York: Basic Books.

Schutz, A. (1962). *Collected Papers* (Vol. 1). M. Natanson (Ed.). The Hague: Martinus Nijhoff.

Schwab, J. (1969). The practical: A language for curriculum. *School Review, 78,* 1-23.

Schwartz, F. (1981). Supporting or subverting learning: Peer group patterns in four tracked schools. *Anthropology and Education Quarterly, 12,* 99-121.

Schwartz, M., & O'Conner, J. (1974). *The new exploring American history.* New York: Globe.

Sedlak, M., Wheeler, C., Pullin, D., & Cusick, P. (1986). *Selling students short: Classroom bargains and academic reform in the American high school.* New York: Teachers College Press.

Sharp, R., & Green, A. (1975). *Education and social control: A study in progressive primary education.* London: Routledge and Kegan Paul.

Shaver, J., & Berlak, H. (Eds.). (1968). *Democracy, pluralism, and the social studies: Readings and commentary.* Boston: Houghton Mifflin.

Sizer, T. (1985). *Horace's compromise: The dilemma of the American high school.* Boston: Houghton Mifflin.

Slavin, R. (1987). Ability grouping and student achievement in elementary schools: A best evidence synthesis. *Review of Educational Research, 57,* 292–336.

Slavin, R. (Ed.). (1989). *Ability grouping in secondary schools: A best evidence synthesis.* Unpublished manuscript, University of Wisconsin, National Center on Effective Secondary Schools, Madison.

Spindler, G. (Ed.). (1982). *Doing the ethnography of schooling: Educational anthropology in action.* New York: Holt, Rinehart & Winston.

Spindler, L., & Spindler, G. (1982). Roger Harker and Schonhausen: From familiar to strange and back again. In G. Spindler (Ed.), *Doing the ethnography of schooling: Educational anthropology in action* (pp. 20–46). New York: Holt, Rinehart & Winston.

Stinchcombe, A. (1964). *Rebellion in a high school.* Chicago: Quadrangle Books.

Swindler, A. (1979). *Organization without authority: Dilemmas of social control in the schools.* Cambridge, MA: University of Harvard Press.

Turner, R. (1960). Modes of social ascent through education: Sponsored and contest mobility. *American Sociological Review, 25,* 855–867.

Tye, B. (1985). *Multiple realities: A study of 13 American high schools.* Lanham, MD: University Press of America.

Tyler, R. (1949). *Basic principles of curriculum and instruction.* Chicago: University of Chicago Press.

Valli, L. (1986). *Becoming clerical workers.* London: Routledge and Kegan Paul.

Valli, L. (1990). A curriculum of effort: Tracking students in a Catholic high school. In R. Page & L. Valli (Eds.), *Curriculum differentiation: Interpretive studies in U.S. secondary schools* (pp. 45–66). Albany: State University of New York Press.

Varenne, H. (1974). From grading and freedom of choice to ranking and segregation in an American high school. *Anthropology and Education Quarterly, 5,* 9–15.

Varenne, H. (1977). *Americans together: Structured diversity in a midwestern town.* New York: Teachers College Press.

Varenne, H. (1981). Symbolizing American culture in schools. *Character, 2,* 1–9.

Varenne, H. (1982). Jocks and freaks: Social interaction among American senior high students. In G. Spindler (Ed.), *Doing the ethnography of schooling* (pp. 210–235). New York: Holt, Rinehart and Winston.

Varenne, H. (1983). *American school language: Culturally patterned conflicts in a suburban high school.* New York: Irvington.

Varenne, H. (1986). *Symbolizing America.* Lincoln: University of Nebraska Press.

Waller, W. (1932). *The sociology of teaching.* New York: Wiley & Sons.

Wehlage, G. (1981). The purposes of generalization in field-study research. In T. Popkewitz, R. Tabachnick, & G. Wehlage (Eds.), *The study of schooling: Field-based methodologies in educational research and evaluation* (pp. 211–226). New York: Praeger.

Wehlage, G., Stone, C., & Kliebard, H. (1980). *Dropouts and schools: Case studies of the dilemmas educators face.* Madison: Wisconsin Governor's Employment and Training Office.

Weick, K. (1978). Educational organizations as loosely coupled systems. *Administrative Science Quarterly, 23,* 541-552.

Werthman, C. (1963). Delinquents in schools: A test for the legitimacy of authority. *Berkeley Journal of Sociology, 8,* 39-60.

Westbury, I. (1988a). Who can be taught what? General education in the secondary school. In I. Westbury & A. Purves (Eds.), *The eighty-seventh yearbook of the National Society for the Study of Education: Part II. Cultural literacy and the idea of general education* (pp. 171-197). Chicago: University of Chicago Press.

Westbury, I. (1988b). How should we be judging the American high school? *Journal of Curriculum Studies, 20,* 291-315.

White, R., & Lippett, R. (1960). *Autocracy and democracy: An experimental inquiry.* New York: Harper.

Willis, P. (1977). *Learning to labor: How working class kids get working class jobs.* Westmead, England: Saxon House.

Wolcott, H. (1974). The teacher as an enemy. In G. Spindler (Ed.), *Education and cultural process: Toward an anthropology of education* (pp. 411-425). New York: Holt, Rinehart and Winston.

Index

Ability groups. *See* Lower track; Regular track; Tracking
Academic ability, as a factor in curriculum differentiation, 33–34, 40–44, 82–83, 86–88, 106–108, 151–153, 181–182, 186–187, 190, 241, 244–245
Additional Needs classes. *See also* Lower track; Lower-track curriculum; Lower-track students; Lower-track teachers
  design, 22
  dropout rate in, 92
  funding, 28–29, 119–120, 160
  history, 113–126, 160–165
  size, 85, 114, 160
  variations among, 22, 105, 148–149
Administrators. *See* Principal
Age, as a factor in curriculum differentiation, 91, 94, 99–100, 102, 110, 111–112, 135–136, 155, 185–188, 190, 224–225
Alexander, K., 9, 239
Ambiguity. *See also* Ambivalence; Control; Culture; Lower-track curriculum; Lower-track students, role of; Lower-track teachers, role of; Marginalization; Role conflict
  in American culture, 14–16, 233–236
  in the functions of the American high school, 16–19, 233
  in the lower-track curriculum, 179–182, 205–207, 233–236
  in the perspective of lower-track students, 223–226
  in the role of the lower-track student, 75–78, 143–144, 148–149
  in the perspective of lower-track teachers, 33–36
  in the role of the lower-track teacher, 108–113

power of, 233–236
production of, in lessons, 3–7, 37–53, 94–102, 208–209
Ambivalence. *See also* Ambiguity; Control; Culture; Lower-track curriculum; Lower-track students, role of; Lower-track teachers, role of; Marginalization; Role conflict
  in American polity, 13–16
  of lower-track students, 3–7, 223–230
  of lower-track teachers, 3–7, 33–36, 108–110, 149–150, 157–158
Amidon, E., 211
Apple, M., xii, 137, 199, 202
Aron, J., 131
Assignments. *See* English; History; Lower-track lessons
Au, K., 19
Autonomy. *See* Teacher autonomy

Ball, S., 10
Barr, R., 10, 81
Bateson, G., 223
Battistoni, R., 50
Bellack, A., 9, 19, 26, 50, 63, 93, 101, 143
Bellah, R., 14
Benjamin, W., xi
Berends, M., 9
Berlak, H., 185
Bernstein, R., 25
Bloom, B., 137, 187
Bowles, S., 20, 34, 50
Boyer, E., 17, 209
Brann, E., 14
Branscombe, A., 10
Brookhart, V., xii
Brown, M., 9, 239
Bruner, J., 5, 189

Weick, K., 113
Westbury, I., 182, 198
Wheeler, C., 51
White, R., 81
Wildavsky, A., 15–16
Willis, P., 20, 34, 131, 157, 218, 229

Wolcott, H., 157
Worksheets. *See also* Lower-track curriculum
  in lower-track lessons, 94–104,
      131–135, 139–147, 186–190,
      191–192
  in regular-track lessons, 202–203

About the Author

Reba Page teaches about and studies curriculum theory, interpretive research methods, and sociocultural foundations of education, interests which developed during her doctoral studies in Curriculum and Instruction at the University of Wisconsin, Madison. She is author of several articles about curriculum differentiation and school culture, is U.S. editor of the *Journal of Curriculum Studies*, and, with Linda Valli, is co-editor of *Curriculum Differentiation: Interpretive Studies in U.S. Secondary Schools* (Albany: SUNY Press). Prior to her university work, she taught high school English, history, and special education classes for 10 years.

DATE DUE

DE 8 '97			
OC 28 '02			
NO 25 '02			